BUNDESTAGSWAHL '98:
End of an Era?

Editors

STEPHEN PADGETT
THOMAS SAALFELD

FRANK CASS
LONDON • PORTLAND, OR

First published in 2000 in Great Britain by
FRANK CASS AND COMPANY LIMITED
Newbury House,
900 Eastern Avenue,
London IG2 7HH, England

and in the United States of America by
FRANK CASS
c/o ISBS
5804 N.E. Hassalo Street,
Portland, Oregon 97213-3644

Copyright © 2000 Frank Cass & Co. Ltd

Website: *www.frankcass.com*

British Library Cataloguing in Publication Data

Bundestagswahl '98 : end of an era?
  1. Germany (Federal Republic). Bundestag 2. Elections –
  Germany 3. Germany – Politics and government – 1990-
  I. Padgett, Stephen, 1951– II. Saalfeld, Thomas, 1960-
  324.9'43

ISBN 0 7146 5019 6 (hb)
ISBN 0 7146 8076 1 (pb)

Library of Congress Cataloging-in-Publication Data

Bundestagswahl '98 : end of an era? / editors, Stephen Padgett, Thomas
Saalfeld.
    p. cm.
  Includes index.
  ISBN 0-7146-5019-6. – ISBN 0-7146-8076-1 (pbk.)
  1. Germany. Bundestag–Elections, 1998. 2. Political parties-
Germany. I. Padgett, Stephen, 1951–   II. Saalfeld, Thomas,
1960–
JN3971.A95B86   1999
324.943'0876–dc21   99-36580
                                                                         CIP

This group of studies first appeared in a Special Issue of *German Politics*,
Vol.8, No.2 (August 1999) ISSN 0964-4008 [*Bundestagswahl* '98: End of an Era?].

Printed in Great Britain by Anthony Rowe Ltd., Chippenham, Wilts.

Contents

Introduction

STEPHEN PADGETT AND THOMAS SAALFELD

Elections can be defining moments in politics, but their significance is not always immediately clear. Whilst there is little doubt that the Bundestag election of September 1998 represents a watershed in German politics, its full implications have yet to be digested. The election was remarkable in a number of ways. It brought to a close 16 years of Christian-Liberal government under Helmut Kohl, the longest serving Chancellor in the history of the Federal Republic. Defeat resulted in Kohl's resignation as CDU leader, with Theodor Waigel standing down as leader of the CSU. For the first time in the electoral history of the Federal Republic, a change in government resulted directly from the incumbent's defeat at the polls rather than changes in the parties' coalition choices. For only the second time in the Federal Republic (after 1972), the Social Democratic Party (SPD) became the strongest party in the Bundestag. The magnitude of the SPD's lead over the Christian Democrats is unprecedented, polling 5.8 per cent more than the CDU/CSU. After relatively speedy negotiations, a coalition between the SPD and the Greens was formed for the first time at national level. For the first time since 1969, the FDP is not in government, having lost its pivotal role in the party system. Moreover, the outcome of the election shows that there are feasible coalition options without the FDP and short of a Grand Coalition. Changes in Germany's 'electoral geography' produced a majority of the left (SPD, Greens and PDS) for the first time in the Federal Republic's history. At the same time, the aggregate vote of the German People's Union (DVU), Republikaner and the National Democratic Party (NPD) at some 3.3 per cent, amounted to the highest share for the extreme right since 1969. Beyond these simple facts, however, lie many unanswered questions about political life after Kohl. What does the election tell us about changing electoral alignments? Does it point towards new orientations within the parties, or a reconfiguration of the party system? Can we expect it to signal significant changes in policy, or in the character and style of government and politics? These are the questions which we set out to address in this volume. We do so in two ways: by analysing

Stephen Padgett, University of Liverpool; Thomas Saalfeld, University of Kent at Canterbury retrospectively the developments which culminated in the 1998 election, and by interrogating the evidence of the election itself.

The first set of questions relate to the electorate and its social foundations. This was the first post-war German election in which a change of government was precipitated directly by an election, as opposed to changing coalition alignments amongst the parties. Does this suggest a structural realignment of the electorate which can be expected to establish the foundations of a red–green majority for the foreseeable future, or merely the situational response to circumstances uniquely favourable to the SPD and the Greens? Relating electoral behaviour to social change, Wolfgang Gibowski points towards the latter conclusion. The electorate reflects the fluidity of German society at the end of the 1990s. The erosion of social collectiveness and identities has weakened traditional ties between parties and voters. This decline in socially structured partisanship means that electoral choice rests very heavily upon perceptions about Chancellor candidates, and about the competence of the parties in dealing with key issues. Thus, the outcome of the 1998 election is seen in terms of Schröder's dynamism in contrast to the faded attractions of the incumbent, and the success of the SPD in projecting its readiness (*'Wir sind bereit'*) to tackle Germany's pressing economic problems. Situational rather than structural factors account for the shifting majority which brought the red–green coalition to power.

The conclusion is clear from Gibowski's analysis of the social foundations of electoral behaviour in 1998. Both the *Volksparteien* retained their *Stammwählerschaft* of traditional voters. Two-thirds of trade union members in the manual working class voted for the SPD, whilst almost three-quarters of practising Catholics voted for the CDU/CSU. The confinement of socially structured partisanship to these relatively small and declining social groups, however, leaves the electorate subject to shifts of allegiance on the part of unattached or weakly attached voters. In 1998, the decisive shifts were amongst the middle class, middle aged in the west, and amongst manual workers in the east. In both these social groups, the SPD decisively reversed the advantage their rivals had previously held. Neither of these trends can be taken to be indicative of structural realignment. Rather, they point towards 'situational' electoral change, as voters with weak partisan alignments changed their vote from previous elections on the basis of their perceptions about the relative merits of the leading candidates, and party competence. The performance of the red–green coalition will be of decisive importance for the ability of the SPD to retain this support.

The importance of perceptions in the electorate about the competence of the respective parties in handling key issues is the theme of Jürgen Maier and Hans Rattinger's article. Survey data points towards economic issues as the main battle-ground of electoral competition. In 1998, perceptions of the economic situation were markedly more negative than in the previous election. Surprisingly, perhaps, this downturn in economic assessments appears to have had little effect on perceptions about the economic competence of the government parties. The decisive factor seems to have been a sharp increase in the perceived competence of the SPD in handling the economy. Whilst the CDU/CSU retained a pronounced advantage in terms of its traditional policy areas of law and order and external security, the SPD was well ahead throughout 1998 in perceptions of general economic competence. Although the lead narrowed as the election approached, and was even reversed in the immediate run-up to polling day, the SPD retained a significant advantage in relation to the crucial issues of unemployment and pensions.[1] With unemployment overshadowing all other issues in public perceptions of 'issue salience', this might be seen as a decisive factor in the electoral outcome. As Cornelia Weins shows, the ascription to the SPD of problem-solving competence in relation to unemployment had a particularly strong impact on electoral behaviour in the east, underlining the conclusion that the impact of issues is greatest where social structured partisanship is weakest.

Survey data also allows us to assess the role of candidate preferences in electoral behaviour, and to identify the leadership qualities which carried Schröder to victory. On a range of qualities – credibility, responsibility, integrity and the representation of German interests – Kohl enjoyed a clear opinion lead. Schröder's advantage lay in a *sympathischer* image, charisma, and problem-solving competence, which gave him a huge lead (albeit one which narrowed as the election approached) over Kohl as preferred Chancellor. The role of candidates in the election is underlined by analysis of the media coverage of the campaign contained in the article by Holli Semetko and Klaus Schoenbach. Their first conclusion is that coverage was more intensive than in previous elections, due to the intense competitiveness of the election and, in contrast to previous contests, the uncertainty of the result. Some interesting differences of coverage were to be found between the public and private television channels. Private broadcasters devoted more coverage to the election, but in comparison to the public channels their focus was slanted towards the campaign and the candidates at the expense of substantive issues. The breakdown of coverage between Schröder and Kohl is particularly revealing. Whilst Kohl received more coverage than Schröder, the latter won a decisive victory in the battle for 'soundbites', a finding which goes some way towards explaining the public perceptions of the candidates' leadership qualities outlined above. The significance of the candidate effect on electoral behaviour combines with the increase in candidate-focused coverage in the private broadcasting sector to accentuate the 'presidential' character of election campaigning, and cannot but have an effect on the relationship between parties and their leaders.

Elmar Wiesendahl's article provides a theoretical perspective on the interrelated trends which have contributed to the emergence of a new type of party. In an increasingly amorphous and open electorate, and with the stabilising effects of socially structured partisanship in decline, he argues, modern parties are faced by a volatile and incalculable environment which defies rational strategic planning. In this new context, the social and ideological homogeneity of the 'milieu' party has given way to a more 'polymorphic' membership, with structural fragmentation between competing interests and tendencies. The resultant syndrome of 'organisational anarchy' undermines the capacity of the party for purposive rational action. Others have pointed similarly towards the 'Balkanisation' of internal party life into discreet policy domains dominated by *Nischenpolitiker* – policy experts, often associated with particular interests.[2] Organisational decomposition is paralleled by the increasing autonomy of the central party apparatus as the leadership strives to reassert its capacity to control the party machinery in the pursuit of rational vote-maximising and office-seeking strategies. One way of achieving this is through the selection of top party office holders and candidates by individual membership ballot, by-passing the traditional party apparatus and marginalising the intermediate-level functionary corps. These developments open up internal party life to the influence of the media, which serves as the main channel of communication between the party and its members. At the same time, the importance of the media in shaping opinion in an open and fluid electorate has greatly increased the influence of media management specialists at the heart of the central party apparatus. A pronounced orientation towards the media is thus the defining characteristic of the new party type.

The SPD's exploitation of political marketing technology in the 1998 election is indicative of these trends. Borrowing heavily from Labour's Millbank Tower operation of the previous year, the Social Democrats conducted the most modern and intensive campaign in German electoral history. 'Out-sourcing' their marketing infrastructure to eight commercial communications agencies, the SPD campaign was designed by professional specialists in opinion polling, advertising, media analysis and management, event marketing and speech-writing. In a thematic rather than policy-oriented campaign, the party crafted an image around five key themes; a blend of *innovation* and *order* in the economy, *justice* in the social state, advocacy on behalf of *families*, and an emphasis on *youth and the future*, interlaced with a strong appeal to the prevailing *Wechselstimmung* (mood of change). The focal point of the campaign, however, was the image of

Gerhard Schröder as the personification of competence and political will. Fine-tuning the themes via focus group analysis of the public response, and ensuring the party was 'on-message' through daily briefings, the operation combined technical sophistication with intra-party discipline, qualities previously lacking from SPD campaigns.

The first six months of the red–green coalition may also be indicative of a new-look SPD, initially (until July 1999) with Bodo Hombach as head of the Chancellor's Office managing government in a style not dissimilar to that of his previous role as Schröder's campaign manager. Whilst the politics of the *Neue Mitte* has yet to take shape, the marginalisation and subsequent resignation of the more orthodox Social Democrat Oskar Lafontaine as Finance Minister suggests Schröder's determination to harmonise government policy with public opinion.

If the 1998 election points towards the emergence of a new type of party, it is also indicative of a new systemic configuration of parties. As Stephen Padgett shows, the unpredictability of the election reflected the increasing complexity, fluidity and openness of a party system nearing the margins of stability. First, in an increasingly disaggregated five-party system (six including the extreme right), the capacity of the *Volksparteien* for playing their customary role as central pillars of party stability is significantly reduced. The effects of disaggregation can be seen in the reliance of recent governments on *Überhangmandate* to consolidate otherwise slender majorities. Further decline in the *Volkspartei* share of the vote will endanger the customary pattern of one-plus-one coalition formation. Second, an open and competitive electoral landscape, in which structural influences on voting behaviour are outweighed by situational factors, means there is a high potential for party system change. Third, on the ideological dimension, two countervailing tendencies can be seen: a widening of the ideological range of the party system, simultaneous with a convergence between the two main parties. Consequently the *Volksparteien* command less of the political territory than previously. Moreover, the parties are increasingly multivalent in their ideological profiles. Ideological multivalence was the key to the SPD's success in the 1998 election, but it may prove difficult to sustain in government. In a disaggregated party system, with the electoral landscape in flux and with parties exhibiting multivalent identities, inter-party relations become correspondingly multifaceted and complex. As we shall see, strategic positioning faces all the parties with difficult choices. Clearly, the logic of inter-party relations in the new systemic configuration no longer conforms to the old triangular model.[3] Although there are some signs of the emergence of a 'two block model', however, most of the evidence suggests a more fluid pattern of inter-party relations, and a party system with considerable potential for flux.

What are the implications of this fluid and open party landscape for political leadership in the post-Kohl era? Much has been made of the similarity between Schröder and the British Labour Prime Minister Tony Blair. Similar to Blair's rhetoric of the 'Third Way' and a 'stakeholder society',[4] Schröder speaks of the 'New Political Centre'. Like Blair, he claims to represent a 'modernised' as opposed to 'old-fashioned', class-based and welfarist social democracy. He also emphasises a co-operation between government and economic interests, stakeholding and consensus. Yet Schröder is a much more traditional Social Democrat than his British counterpart. As Perry Anderson rightly points out, Schröder 'comes from the debris of postwar German society' and obtained his secondary education at night school. In the late 1970s he was leader of the left-wing Young Socialists (Jusos) of the SPD. Unlike Blair, Schröder was not leader of his party when he was elected Federal Chancellor, sharing power with Oskar Lafontaine both in the party and in government. Schröder's position was strengthened only after Lafontaine's spectacular resignation as Finance Minister and SPD Chairman in March 1999. Schröder's subsequent election as party leader means that, like Willy Brandt and Helmut Kohl (but unlike his immediate Social Democratic predecessor Helmut Schmidt), he now leads both his party and the federal government. Nevertheless, the SPD remains a much more decentralised party than the British Labour Party, with much intra-party power wielded by the SPD's federal-state party elites and premiers. In addition, being Federal Chancellor of Germany's 'semisovereign'[5] or 'grand coalition state'[6] makes Blair-style leadership with its emphasis on hierarchical co-ordination difficult. Political leadership in Germany's Federal Republic is constrained by the realities of coalition politics and requires governing in networks with an emphasis on horizontal co-ordination.

Two articles in this volume deal with the need for the Federal Chancellor to be a co-ordinator and manager of a multitude of interests both within his party and the country rather than a leader at the apex of a hierarchy. Peter Pulzer analyses Helmut Kohl's career from his political apprenticeship in the state of Rhineland-Palatinate to the position of Federal Chancellor. He emphasises the fact that Kohl, unlike his Christian Democratic predecessors, became party leader before he was elected Chancellor. Throughout the 1970s he and other Christian Democratic modernisers built up the CDU organisation outside parliament. Kohl always understood that the CDU's long-term electoral success depended on command of a sound party structure and that his own success depended on his strong position within the CDU.

Thomas Saalfeld's article on Helmut Kohl's coalition management reinforces this point. He argues that the longevity of the CDU/CSU–FDP coalition was not inevitable given the policy differences between CDU, CSU and FDP on a number of issues from foreign policy to civil liberties and immigration. He argues that Kohl was remarkably successful in establishing a long-term working relationship between the coalition parties and generating the necessary consensus within the CDU for co-operation with the FDP, which was by no means always painless for the CDU/CSU. Through his credible commitment to a long-term coalition, the employment of a successful mix of flexible conflict management mechanisms and his ability to 'deliver' CDU/CSU compliance with coalition compromises, Kohl's leadership style seems to be a major factor in the stability of the CDU/CSU–FDP coalition.

The coalition was stable enough to withstand serious 'external shocks' such as the US Strategic Defense Initiative, economic problems or periods of disastrous results for the Bonn government parties in federal-state elections. In recent years, a number of important studies have analysed the destabilising influence of such 'exogenous shocks' on coalition stability.[7] Yet both Peter Pulzer and Thomas Saalfeld emphasise the fact that Kohl was repeatedly *helped* by such shocks. German unification, for example, arguably salvaged Kohl from electoral defeat and a palace revolt within the CDU. Kohl, as Peter Pulzer points out, combined good management with luck.

The first months of Schröder's chancellorship demonstrate that the new Chancellor operates under similar constraints, and that these institutional 'shackles' are more powerful and important than the superficial similarities with Blair. The Schröder government will have to adapt to the realities of German federalism. The 'bruises' the new government sustained in its first stand-offs with powerful SPD state governments (such as the state government of North Rhine-Westphalia under premier Wolfgang Clement) over its 'ecological tax reform' are a case in point. Following the 'red–green' coalition's defeat in the state elections of Hesse in February 1999, the government lost its overall majority in the Bundesrat and had to backtrack considerably on its plans to reform Germany's citizenship laws in order to reach a compromise with the FDP.

The new Schröder government's policy agenda initially attracted considerable criticism from business and journalists. The government proposed a more redistributive fiscal policy. A reduction in the social wage costs is to be financed by a new tax on energy consumption ('ecological tax'). The SPD and Schröder have made it clear before the election that job creation would be one of the government's priorities. As an institutional framework the government created an 'Alliance for Work', a neo-corporatist consultation body consisting of business, labour and government representatives. Being SPD leader at the time of cabinet formation, Oskar Lafontaine was in a position to pick his preferred position in the new

Schröder government. He decided to choose the Ministry of Finance with enhanced competencies in economic and European Union policy. Lafontaine was 'the first Western politician of aggressively Keynesian outlook in 25 years.[8] Within the first months of his tenure as Finance Minister his ministry attacked the powerful Federal Bank for its allegedly inflexible interest-rate regime. He antagonised the business community and was fiercely attacked by the latter. Yet he also antagonised important loyal party officials and party leaders even before the red–green coalition government was sworn in by attacking publicly the former SPD leader Rudolf Scharping and refusing to accept the latter's re-election as leader of the SPD parliamentary party in the Bundestag. Nevertheless, his premature resignation in March 1999 came as a surprise. The appointment of Hans Eichel, the former state premier of Hesse, as his successor was an important step to reassure the business community.

One of the more ambitious legal reforms both government parties set out in their election manifestos was the plan to reform the laws of citizenship to facilitate the naturalisation of the country's millions of immigrants, especially the children and grandchildren of 'guest workers' of the 1960s and 1970s. This reform had to be scaled down after a successful and often aggressive CDU/CSU campaign outside the Bundestag, which revealed a significant degree of public discontent with the measure, and after the loss of the federal-state elections in Hesse. This loss deprived the SPD–Green government of its majority in the Bundesrat and forced it to renegotiate the policy with the FDP.

The first few months of the coalition of the SPD and Greens were turbulent. Although the two parties have had experience with such coalitions at the federal-state level and, indeed, the new Green Environment Minister, Jürgen Trittin, had served under Schröder in the coalition cabinet of Lower Saxony, coalition management proved to be difficult in the initial phase of the coalition. Charles Lees analyses the first troubled months of the 'red–green' coalition of SPD and Greens/Alliance '90. Based on a detailed analysis of the experience of red–green coalitions on the federal-state level, he argues that the coalition's survival chances are better than often assumed. He reinforces the findings presented by Stephen Padgett and Thomas Saalfeld on the two parties' proximity in the ideological space, and the SPD's distance from possible alternative coalition partners on its right. He demonstrates that the SPD emphasised the post-materialist and libertarian dimension of its election programme when bargaining with the Greens. In analogy to the CDU/CSU–FDP coalition's selective emphasis on economic policy (see Thomas Saalfeld's contribution), the SPD and Greens are emphasising policy areas in which they share common ground. Lees also argues that the pattern of portfolio allocation negotiated between the two parties provides a good basis for stable co-operation with a disproportionate share of portfolios (including the Environment portfolio) for the Greens and all economically sensitive portfolios for the SPD. Both parties gained in a win–win situation. Although his findings are somewhat in contention with some of the formal spatial coalition theories based on the dimension-by-dimension median legislator,[9] evidence from the federal-state level seems to suggest that the pattern of portfolio allocation under Schröder is very much in line with similar successful patterns in the Länder.

The elections of 1998 ended the 'Kohl era'. They also marked the beginning of a new era, with government and parliament moving to Berlin and a generational change in German politics. Although Kohl has never seriously aspired to be remembered for an 'ism', an equivalent to 'Thatcherism' or 'Blairism', there were undoubtedly great achievements (especially the management of unification). There was also a so-called 'System Kohl' describing the Chancellor's style of governing, of managing political conflict and rapid change in flexible networks. The 'System Kohl', has been criticised for emphasis on the preservation of power and *status quo*, its tendency to govern in informal networks rather than constitutional bodies and its allegedly inadequate problem-solving capacity. Admirers, by contrast, have emphasised its ability to preserve political stability in times of very considerable political and socio-economic change and its ability to cope with the realities of party and coalition government in the 'semi-sovereign' German federal state. This volume does not purport to answer these questions. Rather, scholars from both sides of the Channel (or, from both sides of the Tunnel, as Peter Pulzer once remarked) attempt to map important longer term developments of voting behaviour, party organisation and coalition politics that contributed to the changes of 1998.

NOTES

1. Forschungsgruppe Wahlen Mannheim 1998, pp.64–70.
2. R. Meng, *Nach dem Ende der Parteien: Politik in der Mediengesellschaft* (Marburg: Schüren Presseverlag, 1997), pp.81–7.
3. See F.-U. Pappi, 'The West German Party System', in S. Bartonlini and P. Mair (eds.), *Party Politics in Contemporary Western Europe* (London: Frank Cass, 1984), pp.6–26.
4. P. Anderson, 'The German Question', *London Review of Books*, 7 Jan. 1999, p.11.
5. P.J. Katzenstein, *Policy and Politics in West Germany: The Growth of a Semisovereign State* (Philadelphia, PA: Temple University Press, 1987).
6. M.G. Schmidt, 'Germany: The Grand Coalition State', in J.M. Colomer (ed.), *Political Institutions in Europe* (London: Routledge, 1996).
7. Cf. M. Laver and K.A. Shepsle, *Making and Breaking Governments: Cabinets and Legislatures in Parliamentary Democracies* (Cambridge: Cambridge University Press, 1996); A. Lupia and K. Strøm, 'Coalition Termination and the Strategic Timing of Parliamentary Elections', *American Political Science Review*, 89 (1995), pp.648–65.
8. Anderson, 'The German Question', p.11.
9. Cf. Laver and Shepsle, *Making and Breaking Governments*.

Social Change and the Electorate:
An Analysis of the 1998 *Bundestagswahl*

WOLFGANG G. GIBOWSKI

The 1998 general election produced shifts in the percentage of votes received by the CDU/CSU and the SPD greater than in any previous country-wide election. After the 1994 election the Christian Democrats were ahead of the Social Democrats by five per cent. Now the situation is virtually reversed. The SPD overtook the CDU/CSU in both the western and eastern parts of Germany and replaced it as the governing party. For the first time in the history of German elections a change of federal government was brought about as a direct consequence of a general election. In the (west) German general elections held between 1969 and 1980 the SPD got better results than they have now. However, the CDU/CSU was always stronger (with the exception of 1972). Thus, the 40.9 per cent achieved by the SPD in 1998 is politically more significant than earlier higher percentages in the west German context.

The east–west comparison of 1998 corresponds to the pattern known to us from past general elections held in all of Germany. All western German parties (except for the DVU) do better in the western part of the country than they do in the east. The clearest east–west difference continues to be the results obtained by the PDS, who received more than 20 per cent of the vote in eastern Germany while they continued at around one per cent in the west. There are clear east–west differences with regard to the changes that have taken place in comparison with 1994. In the east the Christian Democrats lost a little more than twice as many votes as they did in the west. While the SPD was able to win nearly as many votes as the CDU/CSU lost in western Germany, in the eastern part of the country the SPD did not even come close to doing this. A large part of the CDU's landslide losses in the east went to the many smaller parties, which showed considerably stronger gains in the east than they did in the west. This applies in particular to the right-wing extremist DVU (2.8 per cent) which did not field any candidates in 1994.

In an article with the provocative title 'Germans Divided', Dalton noted a growing difference in voter behaviour in eastern and western Germany on

Wolfgang Gibowski, University of Stuttgart

TABLE 1

BUNDESTAG ELECTION RESULTS 1998 AND DIFFERENCES TO
THE RESULTS OF 1994

	Total		West		East		Seats	
SPD	40.9	+4.5	42.3	+4.8	35.1	+3.6	298	+46
Greens	6.7	-0.6	7.3	-0.6	4.1	-0.2	47	-2
CDU/CSU	35.1	-6.3	37.0	-5.1	27.3	-11.2	245	-49
FDP	6.2	-0.7	7.0	-0.7	3.3	-0.2	44	-3
PDS	5.1	+0.7	1.2	+0.2	21.6	+1.8	35	+5
REP	1.8	-0.1	1.9	-0.1	1.5	+0.2		
DVU	1.2	+1.2	0.8	+0.8	2.8	+2.8		
Others	2.9	+1.2	2.5	+0.6	4.3	+3.2		
Total	100%		100%		100%		669	-3
Percent Voting	82.2	+3.2	82.8	+2.3	80.0	+7.4		

Note: The SPD seats include 13 Überhangmandate

the basis of the results of the 1994 general election.[1] The results of the 1998 general election showed that, with the exception of the gains for the DVU, there was no further widening of differences between voting patterns in eastern and western Germany.[2] The well known four-party system in western Germany continues to stand in contrast to the three-party system in eastern Germany. The changes noted in both regions point in the same direction for both parties, although, as in the case of the CDU, they were stronger in the east than they were in the west. The fact that voter turnout showed a considerably stronger increase in the east (6.9 per cent) than in the west (2.2 per cent) helped to even out the very sizeable differences noted in the past. There have been no indications of a further deepening of differences in voting patterns between east and west or of any growth in factors separating the electorates. The SPD's co-operation with the PDS in Mecklenburg-Western Pomerania and Saxony-Anhalt, although questionable when viewed from a different political perspective, is a definite example to the contrary.[3]

THE POLITICAL CLIMATE BETWEEN ELECTIONS

The dramatic changes that occurred in the 1998 *Bundestagswahl* were by no means a 'bolt out of the blue'. Rather they can be explained in terms of the developments that took place in the political climate in the course of the past legislative term.

The incumbent CDU/CSU and FDP government won the election in 1994 largely on the back of a long-predicted period of economic recovery which set in early in the election year after a phase of economic stagnation.[4]

The importance of a favourable economic situation, and correspondingly positive public perceptions, for satisfaction with a government has been subject to intensive analysis over previous elections.[5] In 1994 Chancellor Helmut Kohl succeeded in linking public perceptions of economic recovery with his leadership and thus with the economic competence of his government. As a consequence, the German public linked the Kohl government with its expectations for at least a gradual improvement in the employment situation.

Unemployment has been the most urgent problem faced by people living in the east since reunification, with similar concerns speading to the west since 1993. Upward trends on the labour market in 1994 and 1995 went into decline again as of 1996, and it became increasingly clear to the public that, while a good economic situation might mitigate the unemployment problem to a certain degree, it was in no way able to resolve the problem on a long-term basis. It may seem contradictory and unjust to make a government solely responsible for the situation on the employment market. On the other hand, the legislative branch of government has responsibility for the timely correction of undesirable structural trends.

It is unlikely that voters would have attributed these structural problems to the incumbent government so decisively if the image of the SPD had remained as it was in the first year after the general election. In a subordinate opposition role and weakened by constant debates about the leadership qualities of party chairman Rudolf Scharping, the image of the SPD was desolate.

This situation is, of course, reflected in representative polls. As of mid-1995 the SPD was seen as playing an increasingly marginal opposition role, the CDU/CSU leading by a considerable margin in the approval ratings (see Figure 3). This changed only after what came to be called a 'historical' SPD party conference held in Mannheim in November 1995 at which the premier of Saarland, Oskar Lafontaine, surprised the country by winning the party chairmanship from Rudolf Scharping in a challenge vote. From then on the SPD's opposition work improved, facilitated by a weakening situation on the employment market. Whilst public perceptions of the economy were not entirely negative, people had learned by then that a good economic situation would not necessarily lead to an improvement in the employment situation.

The rest of the legislative term was characterised by debate on various reforms, the necessity of which had been largely accepted by the politically interested public but were nonetheless a subject of party-political controversy. Under Lafontaine's leadership the Social Democrats made systematic use of the red–green majority in the Bundesrat to block or amend government bills. This applied in particular to a tax reform strongly called for by the experts, for which the Kohl government was dependent on a

FIGURE 1

MOST IMPORTANT PROBLEMS IN GERMANY

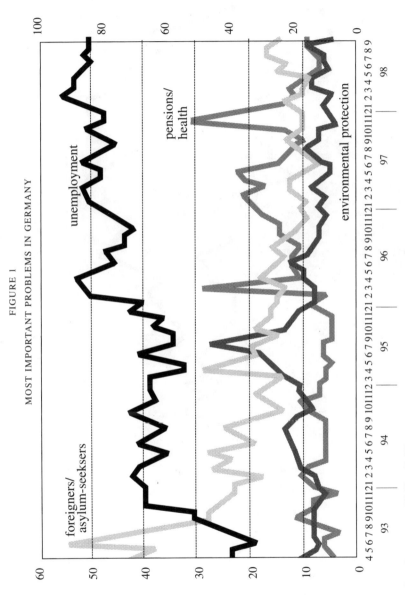

Source: Forschungsgruppe Wahlen: Politbarometer

FIGURE 2

SATISFIED WITH GOVERNMENT AND OPPOSITION (SPD) (means of scale values +5 to –5)

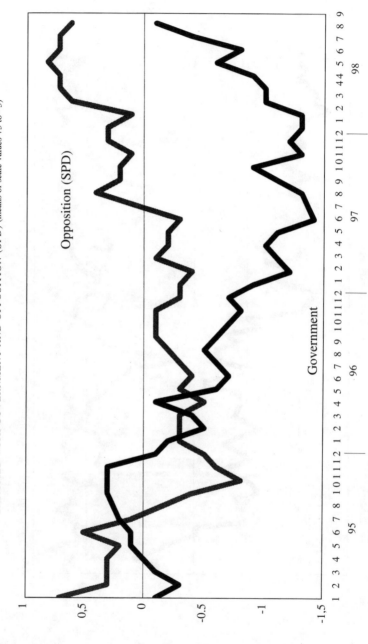

Source: Forschungsgruppe Wahlen: Politbarometer

FIGURE 3

POLITICAL MOOD IN GERMANY

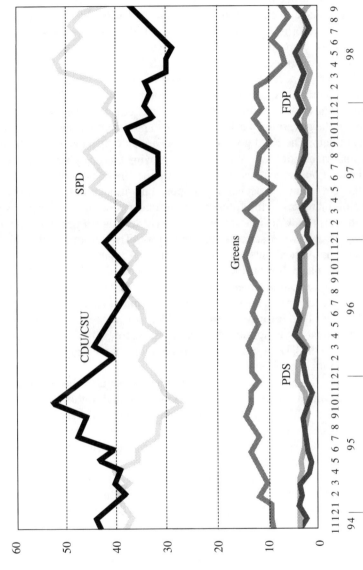

Source: Forschungsgruppe Wahlen: Politbarometer

compromise with the red–green majority in the Bundesrat. The planned tax reform was an example of a project that suffered the effects of being initiated too late. It lay too close to the election campaign, which got under way much earlier than usual, making it difficult to arrive at what would otherwise have been obvious compromises. Even had it been possible to pass a tax reform, however, its positive effects on the economic situation would have come too late to make any difference to the general election. The Kohl government's criticism of the SPD, that it had refused to permit the passage of necessary reforms, failed to convince the electorate. Indeed, on the contrary, the dispute over tax reform simply served to convince the public that the governing parties were not equal to the job. Even those reforms the governing parties were able to pass without Bundesrat approval did not help. The Kohl government was not able to get across to the public the importance of these reforms for improving Germany's attractiveness as a place for business investment. The 'Alliance for Jobs' broke apart because of the government's decision to impose cuts in sick pay. Plans to restrict pension increases in the future were misunderstood by pensioners as plans to cut pensions. Cuts in statutory insurance coverage of dental treatment for young people were seen as discriminatory. The reforms with which the governing parties pursued the objective of making Germany a more attractive place for business investment seemed to the population like systematic measures aimed at giving to the rich and taking away from the poor. The government was unable to communicate to the public the objectives the reforms were intended to achieve. Parallel to the improvement in its approval ratings (see Figure 3) the SPD succeeded in overtaking the CDU/CSU in public perceptions of its competence to resolve major political problems.[6]

In the case of the most pressing problem – the high level of unemployment – more competence was attributed to the SPD for dealing with it than to the CDU/CSU. The same applied with regard to perceived competence to maintain the security of the pension system, to deal with problems of health care, and to handle social security matters in general. Issues for which a larger measure of competence was attributed to the CDU/CSU, such as fighting crime, monetary and economic stability, or foreign and security policy, were either not 'in the news' or were viewed as in the process of being resolved.[7] The fact that shortly before the election the CDU/CSU succeeded in moving ahead of the SPD in perceived economic competence failed to have any significant effect. In 1998 the question of economic competence came nowhere near the importance it had had four years earlier. In any event, the German public showed much more confidence in Gerhard Schröder in this matter than it did in Helmut Kohl.[8]

The CDU/CSU's low level of perceived competence with regard to key issues doubtless contributed to the party's weak position in public approval ratings after mid-1996. However, to explain the enormous lead which the SPD had opened up, it is necessary to examine wider developments in the party landscape.

The second coalition partner, the FDP, had relatively modest approval ratings throughout the legislative term. In the monthly polls the Liberals, similar to the PDS, were usually just under the five per cent mark. For a party without ties to specific sociological groups the visibility of its leaders in the media is one of the most important prerequisites for good results. Wolfgang Gerhard's replacement of Klaus Kinkel as party chairman resulted in an improvement of media presence, but without attaining the intensity that is both necessary and possible for a party like the FDP. The polls taken in the run-up to the general election raised doubts as to whether the FDP would make it over the five per cent hurdle. These doubts were based on the fact that the polls were showing more and more clearly that the coalition partners of many years were not going to win this time. The FDP had always been able to rely on receiving 'second votes' from the ranks of CDU and CSU voters to ensure their common success. Despite the justified doubts with regard to the coalition winning the 1998 general election, the FDP, similar to the situation in 1994,[9] received 60 per cent of its votes from persons who indicated in a poll held shortly before the election by 'Forschungsgruppe Wahlen' that the CDU or CSU were their actual parties of preference.

The Greens made their best gains while SPD ratings were low (see Figure 3). They had good results in the state elections held during that time. As approval ratings rose for the SPD they declined for the Greens. However, the strong dip experienced in the early part of the election year was not a result of the growth in public approval for the SPD. As a result of clumsy presentation of energy policy plans they had made for their possible involvement in a future government the Greens came under fire from their own clientele, further contributing to the upward trend in approval ratings for the SPD.

THE ROLE AND IMPORTANCE OF LEADING CANDIDATES

The outcome of the 1998 *Bundestagswahl* will be analysed in the future from the standpoint of the influence the leading candidates for the CDU/CSU and the SPD had on the voting results attained by their parties. The question most often debated in this context is whether Helmut Kohl's candidacy damaged the CDU/CSU and, if this was indeed the case, whether the Christian Democrats would have achieved better results with Wolfgang

Schäuble. The night of the election Helmut Kohl accepted political responsibility for his party's election defeat and in doing so largely prevented the occurrence of a public debate over the question as to who was at fault. Needless to say, the question of whether a different set of candidates would have produced different results is of particular interest for purposes of scientific analysis. However, it is not a very easy question to answer.

Election researchers operate for the most part on the common assumption that the results of individual elections are not determined by any one single factor but rather by a combination of factors. Identification with a party, the assumptions made with regard to the ability of a given party to resolve important problems, and public perceptions of the leading candidate of a party are considered crucial determining factors in American research on elections.[10] These factors work together in combination without a voter having to be aware of the importance of any one individual factor. In the analysis of voting behaviour in Germany it is often argued that orientation towards a given party predominates in individual voting decisions, since in German general elections parties are voted for and not Chancellor candidates.[11] This is doubtless true for voters loyal to the two major parties as well as for most PDS voters, but not for floating voters, whose reactions can have a decisive influence on the outcome of an election. In the age of electronic media most voters get their information about an election campaign from television coverage.[12] However, the willingness of the population to follow complicated discussions of politics on television is quite limited. Since the German viewing public is strongly oriented towards entertainment, long and complex analyses of political issues are not a viable option. This situation is not much different in most other countries.

A charismatic and attractive looking politician will be particularly successful in getting his message across. Positive feelings for a politician are always connected with an assumption of competence. A politician will always use public approval to gain support for his policies without this mechanism having to be understood in detail. There can be no doubt that the leading candidates of the parties, the candidates for the chancellorship in particular, are of major importance for the election results of their parties, given that floating voters can be effectively reached through the media. However, as we know from past elections, approval ratings for a politician cannot simply be translated into votes and percentages.[13]

For a political system such as Germany's, whose institutional and social structures make it necessary in almost every instance to have coalition governments, tactical voting behaviour has to be taken into account as a further factor.[14] Tactical voting behaviour occurs when voters divide their first and second votes up among two different parties in such a way that the optimum is achieved for both parties. Thus in 1998, as in previous elections, a large number of CDU/CSU supporters cast their second votes for the FDP to help ensure that it got into the Bundestag. The same applies to first votes given to the PDS in their most successful constituencies in the east by persons who are actually SPD voters.

The leading candidates for the two major parties were not determined until fairly late in the game. Prior to the general election in 1994 Helmut Kohl had said on a number of occasions that this was going to be his last election campaign. On a television programme in April 1997 he declared his candidacy for the office of Chancellor once again. In assessing this event, which took the general public and large sections of the party rank and file by surprise, it is often forgotten that there were many in the CDU and the CSU who had urged Kohl to run again. At the same time, the situation in the SPD was characterised by the dualism of Oskar Lafontaine and Gerhard Schröder, the then premier of Lower Saxony. The Social Democrats had decided to wait until after the state election in Lower Saxony on 1 March 1998 to determine who the challenger would be. To everyone's surprise both politicians stuck to this condition and resisted public pressure to make the decision earlier. Based on public opinion polls taken at the time, the situation was quite clear. In a comparison between Kohl and Lafontaine, Kohl came out ahead. In a comparison between Kohl and Schröder, Schröder came out ahead by quite a large margin. After his victory in the state election and his immediate nomination as his party's candidate for the chancellorship, Schröder's lead continued to grow in the approval ratings and in response to the question as to preferred Chancellor. As expected, this lead diminished in the course of the election campaign but without the impression ever arising that Kohl could have caught up with Schröder.

In 1994 Kohl trailed behind his challenger, Rudolf Scharping, until May and June, at which time he moved into the lead and remained there. At the time there were a number of events that had a positive effect for Helmut Kohl and the CDU/CSU. The German presidential election was won by the CDU/CSU candidate. The European Parliament election went favourably for the CDU/CSU. Finally, Kohl's early prognosis of a forthcoming improvement in the economic situation was confirmed. There were no events of this kind on the agenda in 1998. The final determination of currency values with regard to the euro in May 1998 was at any rate not an event that brought about a fundamental change of mood in Germany, but it put an end to all speculation regarding this controversial issue.

What was the importance of the two leading candidates for the election results of their parties? Was public opinion with regard to Helmut Kohl and Gerhard Schröder a causal factor for the strong change in the results attained by their parties? Or was the desire for a change of government the primary

FIGURE 4

POPULARITY RATINGS (means of scale values +5 to –5)

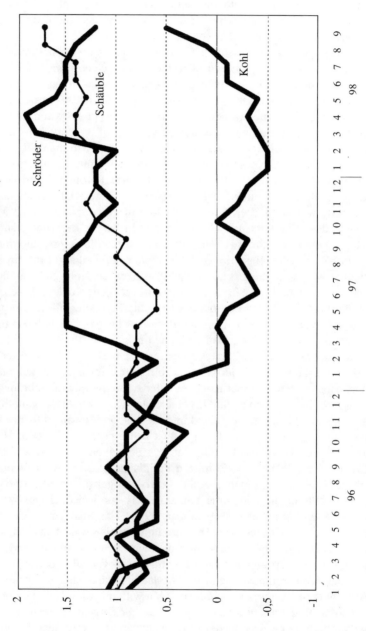

Source: Forschungsgruppe Wahlen: Politbarometer

FIGURE 5
PREFERRED CHANCELLOR

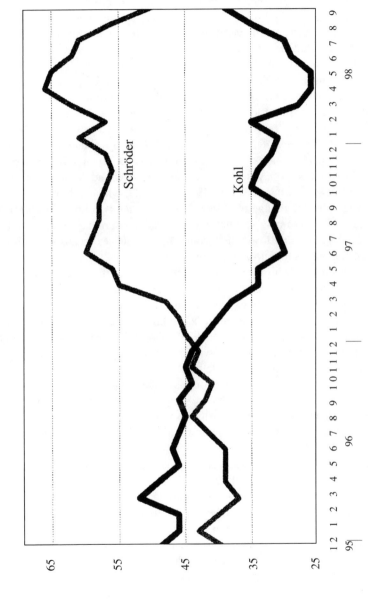

Source: Forschungsgruppe Wahlen: Politbarometer

determining factor and public opinion with regard to the candidates a secondary factor? In their analysis of the importance of the candidates for the outcome of the general election Gabriel/Brettschneider came to the conclusion that candidate effects were very strong among floating voters and that a larger percentage of these voters were in favour of Schröder. The authors concluded that 'Helmut Kohl helped to bring about one of the worst election defeats suffered by the CDU/CSU since 1949'.[15]

In connection with its reform plans, the CDU/CSU government had not reckoned with the possibility that a population conditioned by welfare state attitudes and expectations might not (or not yet) be able to understand the objectives of this reform policy. For floating voters the objective was to correct the policy trends of the recent past by changing the faces in government. In contrast to the situation in 1969, when Willy Brandt stood for a different policy towards eastern Europe and a different style of government, and in contrast to 1982 and 1983, when Helmut Kohl wanted to bring about a change in policy direction, what was involved in this third change of government was not new departures but rather restoration. It goes without saying that loyal SPD voters had greater expectations with regard to SPD policies than floating voters.

Schröder's election campaign corresponded to the general feeling that it was time for a change. One SPD campaign slogan, 'We're grateful Helmut. But 16 years is enough', expressed what many people felt. Helmut Kohl has his merits, but now we need a younger and more modern head of government. Schröder's statement, 'We won't do everything differently, but we'll do a lot of things better', was aimed at those voters who felt there was a need to correct mistakes made by the incumbent government.

Whether a different Chancellor candidate for the CDU/CSU would have led to a different election result may seem academic, but considerations of this kind are legitimate. Kohl's decision to run for office again was based on the assumption that he would be running against Oskar Lafontaine and not against Gerhard Schröder. When this assumption proved to be wrong it would still have been possible to change leading candidates, even though this would have been difficult to explain to the public. If Wolfgang Schäuble had taken Kohl's place as the leading candidate his approval ratings would doubtless not have continued to be as positive as they in fact turned out to be (see Figure 4). The political debates in the election campaign would have exposed Schäuble to strong party-political polarisation. As such, it would be naive to argue only on the basis of his poll results that Schäuble would have been the better candidate. On the other hand, Schröder's election campaign arguments would not have worked well against Schäuble. Nevertheless, it is unlikely that Schäuble could have brought about a majority for the governing coalition, although his candidacy may have served to minimise the losses suffered by the CDU/CSU.

One should beware of believing that everything that can be deduced logically from polls can be implemented politically. The political process has its own mechanisms and its own laws. After Kohl had announced his willingness to run again and the party's top leadership bodies had approved this, a change in the leading candidate was not possible any longer when the assumption his opponent was going to be Oskar Lafontaine turned out to be wrong. The confrontation between Kohl and Schröder was very much up Schröder's alley with regard to campaigning style. As such, it would be more correct to say that Gerhard Schröder won the general election as a result of an ably conducted election campaign and his approval ratings than to conclude that the election was lost only due to Helmut Kohl.

WHO VOTED FOR WHOM?

The analysis of voting behaviour in various demographic and sociological groups is of particular interest in every election, since one hopes on the basis of changes that occur to gain information about the motives of floating voters. The (for Germany) very strong changes during this general election led to the question of whether there was a trend that affected all groups in about the same way or whether specific changes in individual groups made it possible to draw conclusions regarding the reasons for the changes.

This analysis is based on an exit poll carried out by the Forschungsgruppe Wahlen. On the day of the election a total of 15,570 voters in western Germany and 5,424 in eastern Germany were interviewed as they were leaving their polling stations. The fact that these polls were taken right after the people in question had voted means that the responses are very reliable. The size of the sample makes it possible to deduce information about voting structures within groups that would not be possible with traditional polling methods. On the other hand, this exit poll, like any other, has its limitations. Results obtained with regard to the smaller parties need to be interpreted with a certain amount of reservation.

Age and Gender

Being part of a group defined in terms of age and/or gender is normally not connected with interest-related policy positions. From the outset, the Greens have been particularly successful among younger and highly educated voters, something that was always explained by the special interest this group had in Green policies. However, the voters' level of education was not included in the exit poll. When divided up into men and women no particular differences to the general trend were evident for the west. In the east, on the other hand, the CDU showed somewhat greater losses among women while the PDS showed gains.

TABLE 2.1

PARTY SUPPORT BY GENDER AND AGE IN WEST GERMANY RESULTS 1998
AND DIFFERENCES TO 1994

	SPD		CDU/CSU		Greens		FDP		PDS	
Total	42.3		37.0		7.3		7.0		1.2	
	+4.8		-5.1		-0.6		-0.7		+0.2	
Gender										
Men	42	+5	37	- 5	7	-1	7	-1	1	0
Women	43	+6	37	-6	8	-1	7	-1	1	0
Age Group										
18–24	37	0	35	0	11	-4	7	-1	2	0
25–34	45	+4	30	-3	11	-3	6	+1	1	0
35–44	45	+5	32	-5	12	0	6	-2	2	+1
45–59	44	+6	38	-8	6	+1	8	-1	1	0
60+	40	+6	45	-5	3	0	7	-2	1	0
Age and Gender										
18–24 Men	36	+1	35	-1	9	-4	7	0	2	0
18–24 Women	38	0	34	+1	12	-4	6	-1	2	0
25–34 Men	45	+7	31	-5	9	-4	7	+1	1	-1
25–34 Women	45	0	28	-1	13	-2	6	+1	1	0
35–44 Men	45	+4	32	-3	10	0	6	-2	2	0
35–44 Women	45	+7	31	-7	14	0	6	-2	1	+1
45–59 Men	43	+5	39	-6	5	+1	9	-1	1	0
45–59 Women	45	+8	37	-10	6	+1	8	0	1	0
60+ Men	40	+6	45	-6	2	0	8	-3	1	+1
60+ Women	41	+8	45	-8	3	0	7	-1	0	0

In a comparison of age groups there are clear differences between eastern and western Germany. In the west the CDU/CSU had most of its losses among those 35 and older, particularly among voters aged 45–59. The SPD had its greatest gains in the same age groups. The Greens had their highest percentages among voters up to the age of 44. In the two youngest groups they failed to do as well as they did in 1994. The FDP had very similar results in all groups. The CDU in eastern Germany suffered major losses in all age groups. These were above average among voters over the age of 35. In the same groups, and among the youngest voters, the SPD was able to improve its results significantly. There was a noticeable increase in voters for the PDS among the oldest group of voters.

TABLE 2.2

PARTY SUPPORT BY GENDER AND AGE IN EAST GERMANY RESULTS 1998
AND DIFFERENCES TO 1994

	SPD		CDU/CSU		Greens		FDP		PDS	
Total	35.1		27.3		4.1		3.3		21.6	
	+3.6		-11.2		-0.2		-0.2		+1.8	
Gender										
Men	37	+5	27	-10	3	0	4	0	19	0
Women	35	+3	27	-13	5	0	4	0	21	+4
Age Group										
18–24	31	+4	20	-9	8	-2	4	-1	20	-1
25–34	31	-2	25	-6	8	+2	5	0	19	-2
35–44	35	+4	25	-11	7	+1	4	-2	20	+1
45–59	38	+6	28	-13	5	+1	3	-1	22	+3
60+	39	+6	35	-11	1	0	3	0	21	+6
Age and Gender										
18–24 Men	31	+9	22	-9	5	-4	4	-2	18	-2
18–24 Women	31	0	17	-8	11	0	4	0	23	0
25–34 Men	30	-2	27	-8	7	+2	5	-1	17	0
25–34 Women	32	-2	23	-5	10	0	5	0	21	-3
35–44 Men	38	+5	26	-10	6	+1	3	-2	18	0
35–44 Women	32	+2	24	-13	7	+2	4	-1	24	+3
45–59 Men	41	+10	26	+16	4	+1	4	-2	18	+1
45–59 Women	35	+3	28	-10	6	+1	3	-1	22	+4
60+ Men	38	0	34	-2	0	-1	2	0	22	+2
60+ Women	39	+9	35	-15	2	0	4	-1	17	+6

Even with an overall sample of this size, the combination of age and gender results in group sizes, particularly in eastern Germany, that rule out any bold interpretations. But despite this limitation it can be said that in the west CDU/CSU losses among women above the age of 35 were greater than among men, while the SPD did particularly well among women in these age groups. The CDU/CSU continued to be the majority party only among the oldest voters. The losses the Greens suffered among younger voters were of about the same amount in all groups and, as such, were relatively higher among younger men than they were among younger women. In eastern Germany the joint comparison of age and gender did not produce any new knowledge with regard to the results attained by the CDU and the SPD. The losses suffered by the Greens among the youngest voters were to be found among young men. The largest gains for the PDS among the oldest voters came from women. The bulk of the changes that took place in both the west and the east involved voters over the age of 35. From this it can be assumed that what was involved were responses to reform legislation which these age groups feel more strongly affected by than younger age groups.

Jobs and Union Membership

The stability of German electoral behaviour in the past can be explained by the fact that certain sociological groups see the two major parties as representing their interests and for this reason the majority of them vote for the SPD and the CDU/CSU. As explained in detail elsewhere,[16] the SPD is seen as representing the interests of blue-collar workers, in which context it should be said that union membership greatly strengthens this tie. Established at the same time as the German party system, this affiliation has undergone considerable change in the course of the past few decades. On the one hand, social evolution has brought about a change in group sizes; on the other, interest-group-related factors are becoming more tenuous since their foundations are gradually being lost. By way of example, after the war blue-collar workers were the largest occupational group in West Germany, ahead of the self-employed (mostly farmers) and the white-collar workers. Today white-collar workers are the largest single occupational group, ahead of blue-collar workers and the self-employed, who are starting to grow in number once again, albeit from a low level. Reunification has led to an increase in the number of blue-collar and white-collar workers at the expense of the number of civil servants and self-employed.[17] Analyses of the first free elections held in eastern Germany showed that blue-collar workers there do not feel their interests are represented by the SPD as is traditionally felt in western Germany. Interest-group-related factors have faded in the course of time, that is, they have become weaker, since the reasons that led to their origin, such as the need for social protection and protection under labour law, no longer exist in the same way. Still, the effects of these traditional ties are found in the analysis of every election.

In his election campaign Gerhard Schröder stated, probably inspired by Tony Blair's 'New Labour', that the SPD represented the interests of the 'New Centre' and was aiming at attracting votes from the large group of white-collar workers. Strategically this was the correct thing to do, since there has always been a particularly large number of floating voters in this occupational group.

Analysis of the corresponding tables shows that the SPD succeeded in increasing its already high percentage of voters among blue-collar workers, particularly in western Germany, and in making gains in all occupational

TABLE 3.1

PARTY SUPPORT BY OCCUPATION RESULTS 1998 AND DIFFERENCES TO 1994

	SPD		CDU/CSU		Greens		FDP		PDS	
Total	40.9		35.1		6.7		6.2		5.1	
	+4.5		-6.3		-0.6		-0.7		+0.7	
Profession										
Blue-collar workers	48	+3	30	-7	3	-2	3	0	6	+1
White-collar workers	42	+6	40	-3	11	0	6	-2	6	0
Civil servants	22	+4	44	-8	10	+2	15	0	4	0
Self-employed	22	+4	44	-8	10	+2	15	0	4	0
Farmers	15	+1	69	+5	2	-2	9	0	3	0

TABLE 3.2

PARTY SUPPORT BY OCCUPATION IN WEST GERMANY RESULTS 1998
AND DIFFERENCES TO 1994

	SPD		CDU/CSU		Greens		FDP		PDS	
Total	42.3		37.0		7.3		7.0		1.2	
	+4.8		-5.1		-0.6		-0.7		+0.2	
Profession										
Blue-collar workers	53	+3	31	-4	4	-1	3	0	1	0
White-collar workers	43	+5	34	-6	9	-1	8	0	1	0
Civil servants	37	+4	41	-3	11	0	7	-1	2	+1
Self-employed	22	+5	46	-7	10	+2	17	+1	1	0
Farmers	10	-2	75	+10	2	-2	9	-1	1	0

TABLE 3.3

PARTY SUPPORT BY OCCUPATION IN EAST GERMANY RESULTS 1998
AND DIFFFERENCES TO 1994

	SPD		CDU/CSU		Greens		FDP		PDS	
Total	35.1		27.3		4.1		3.3		21.6	
	+3.6		-11.2		-0.2		-0.2		+1.8	
Profession										
Blue-collar workers	39	+4	27	-14	2	+1	3	0	17	+2
White-collar workers	35	+4	24	-8	7	+1	4	0	25	-1
Civil servants	35	+10	34	+4	10	+4	4	+2	15	-20
Self-employed	35	+15	43	-5	3	0	8	2	8	-8
Farmers	35	+13	43	-16	3	-4	8	+4	8	-1

groups. Their gains are particularly large among white-collar workers, that is, the largest occupational group. The CDU and CSU lost in all groups except for western German farmers and eastern German civil servants. The decline of the CDU in eastern Germany was particularly noticeable among blue-collar workers and farmers, while in western Germany CDU/CSU losses were particularly noticeable among white-collar workers and the self-employed. As a result of these changes the SPD became the majority party among blue-collar and white-collar workers in both western and eastern Germany. The Christian Democrats continue to be the majority party among the considerably smaller groups constituted by the self-employed and farmers, as well as among the civil servants in western Germany. The significant changes that have taken place in the voting behaviour of civil servants in eastern Germany at the expense of the PDS and to the benefit of all the other parties can be attributed to the structural changes that have taken place in public administration there.

The inclusion of union membership confirmed theoretical expectations. The SPD achieved higher percentages among voters who are union members but was able to gain just as much among voters who are not union members. The CDU/CSU lost votes among union members. Despite having a small base of union members to begin with, it still lost more among them than among non-members. It was clearly recognisable that the absence of union connections was advantageous for the FDP and that it had virtually no effect for the Greens.

TABLE 4

PARTY SUPPORT, OCCUPATION AND TRADE UNION MEMBERSHIP IN
WEST GERMANY RESULTS OF 1998 AND DIFFERENCES TO 1994

	SPD		CDU/CSU		Greens		FDP		PDS	
Total	42.3		37.0		7.3		7.0		1.2	
	+4.3		-5.1		-0.6		-0.7		+0	
Union membership										
Yes	60	+6	23	-7	7	+1	3	0	2	0
No	39	+6	40	-5	8	-1	8	0	1	0
Blue-collar and membership										
Yes	66	+6	19	-8	3	-2	2	0	2	0
No	46	+3	36	-4	4	-2	4	-1	1	0
White-collar and membership										
Yes	58	+6	21	-7	11	+1	4	0	2	0
No	41	+6	37	-5	9	-1	9	0	1	0

In summary, it can be said that the traditional ties between blue-collar workers and the SPD continue to apply with regard to western Germany. At the same time, the SPD has achieved its objective of improving its results among white-collar workers. Whether or not this is the 'New Centre' is more a political issue and not so much a question relating to the sociology of elections. On aggregate, the SPD was able to improve its position in western Germany among civil servants and the self-employed, groups who tend to show a stronger preference for the Christian Democrats. This speaks for a general trend in favour of the SPD in this election.

The changes noted in eastern Germany need to be assessed differently. Since there is no longer a traditional connection between blue-collar workers and the SPD in the east, the majority position of the SPD there is volatile, something that applies in principle to the election results of all the other parties as well. The fact that in eastern Germany the SPD managed to maintain the level of its overall average in all occupational groups speaks more for a general trend towards the SPD in this election than for the establishment of western German structures. In eastern Germany no party can be sure of the voters who have cast their ballots for it in the past. The only exception to this rule is the PDS which, as the former East German Communist Party, is the only party in eastern Germany with a loyal voter base. PDS losses among the civil servants and the self-employed were caused more by structural changes than by changes in voting behaviour in these groups.[18]

Religion and Church Affiliations

A relationship exists between Catholics and the CDU/CSU comparable to the one between blue-collar workers and the SPD. This relationship does not have a tradition that goes back as far as is the case with the SPD. When these parties were formed after the war they inherited voters from the former Centre Party ('Zentrum'). The Centre Party represented the political interests of the Catholic minority that lived in the predominantly Protestant, Prussian-dominated 'Kaiserreich'. The founding of the CDU as a non-denominational party committed to Christian values was intended to overcome the one-sided focus on Catholics, something which has worked only to a certain degree. The stronger a voter's connection is to the Catholic Church, the stronger it is to the CDU and CSU as well. The same thing applies with regard to Protestants, but to a much lesser extent. In eastern Germany these relationships exist only in part. In 1994 the CDU attained results among the few Catholic voters (four per cent of the total) similar to the results attained among Catholics in the west. In 1998 that was no longer the case. Although the CDU in eastern Germany did better among the Catholics living there as well as among Protestants (approximately 27 per cent) than it did among voters without a religion, this relationship is weaker than in western Germany and, as such, is not comparable.

Social change has diminished the importance of religious affiliations for the election results of the CDU and CSU. One out of every five persons in western Germany no longer has religious ties; at the same time, the frequency of church attendance is diminishing rapidly for both religions. In 1953 the number of Catholics who had strong ties to the church was 60 per cent; in 1994 it was 29 per cent and in the exit poll of 1998 it was down to 20 per cent.[19]

In this analysis there are once again nearly equal gains for the SPD compared with similar losses for the CDU/CSU. It is only in the combination of religious and church ties that the changes are somewhat more differentiated. The CDU/CSU maintained their dominant position among Catholics who have strong or not so strong church ties, showing average losses; in the insignificantly small group of Protestants with strong church ties there was virtually no change.

TABLE 5

PARTY SUPPORT, RELIGION AND CHURCH ATTENDENCE IN WEST GERMANY
RESULTS OF 1998 AND DIFFERENCES TO 1994

	SPD		CDU/CSU		Greens		FDP		PDS	
Total	42.3		37.0		7.3		7.0		1.2	
	+4.8		-5.1		-0.6		-0.7		+0	
Religion										
Catholic	36	+5	47	-5	6	0	6	-1	1	0
Protestant	48	+4	32	-5	7	-1	8	0	1	0
No religion	47	+7	22	-6	13	-1	7	-1	4	+1
Church attendance										
Often	21	+4	66	-3	4	+1	6	0	0	0
Sometimes	40	+5	43	-5	5	0	8	0	0	0
Never	47	+3	31	-3	8	-1	7	0	1	0
Religion and church attendance										
Catholic often	20	+6	70	-4	3	+1	5	-1	0	0
Catholic sometimes	36	+7	50	-4	4	-2	6	-1	0	0
Catholic never	43	+2	35	-2	8	-1	7	0	1	0
Protestant often	28	-2	48	+1	9	+1	9	0	1	0
Protestant sometimes	45	+5	36	-6	6	+1	9	0	1	0
Protestant never	50	+3	29	-3	8	+1	7	0	1	0

CONCLUSIONS

The 1998 general election was characterised in western Germany by a largely uniform trend in favour of the SPD and to the disadvantage of the CDU/CSU. This trend varied slightly in the various demographic and sociological groups, depending on the strength of the parties at the outset. It is worthy of note here in terms of the sociology of elections that prior structures were preserved in the various social milieus. The SPD did not manage to encroach on typical CDU/CSU structures. It was 'only' able to achieve improvements that were on the order of its overall average gains. The most noticeable changes were those among voters aged 35 and older. In western Germany this was the case particularly among women, a fact which bespeaks criticism of CDU/CSU reform legislation. In eastern Germany changes were stronger, given that sociological connections to the two major parties so typical for the west are absent there. As a consequence of this election gains and losses for the various parties will continue to be stronger in eastern Germany than in the west.

The voters who brought about the change of government in 1998 did not want to achieve a fundamental change of policies, but rather a correction of the policies that had been pursued up to then by letting a new group of people take over the reins of government. The desire to do this was very important among floating voters, which is why there was an increase in voter turnout, particularly in eastern Germany. It would seem probable that there might be more extensive ideas for policy change among the members of the red–green coalition than a mere correction of past policies. However, there is no evidence for this on the basis of the election results. The influence of the leading candidates on the electoral behaviour of floating voters was quite considerable in this election. The constellation of leading candidates was ideal for the SPD, since in the context of criticism that was being expressed against reform legislation passed by the government it was able to present a pragmatic and non-ideological Chancellor candidate. The fact that he was younger and more modern than the previous Chancellor was more than icing on the cake. In this regard Gerhard Schröder was very useful to the SPD. Helmut Kohl was unable to neutralise the 'Schröder effect' and to halt its damage to the CDU/CSU.

In the wake of the third general election to be held in all of Germany it can be seen that differences continue to exist between western and eastern Germany with regard to the party system. As in the past, there continues to be a four-party system in western Germany. Eastern Germany continues to have a three-party system. When joined together they result in a five-party system for Germany as a whole. Differences in voting behaviour between east and west have not grown larger. However, with the exception of voter turnout, nor have they grown any smaller.

NOTES

I am grateful to the Forschungsgruppe Wahlen e.V. Mannheim for their help.

Data of Figures: Monthly 1,250 respondents in Germany, representative for the German population 18 years and older.

1. R.J. Dalton, 'Unity and Division: The 1994 Bundestag Election', in R.J. Dalton (ed.), *Germans Divided. The 1994 Bundestag Elections and the Evolution of the German Party System* (Oxford, Washington, DC: BERG 1996), p.15.
2. K. Arzheimer and J.W. Falter, 'Annäherung durch Wandel? Das Wahlverhalten bei der Bundestagswahl 1998 in Ost-West-Perspektive', *Aus Politik und Zeitgeschichte*, B 52/1998, 18 Dec. 1998, pp.42–3.
3. Dalton, 'Unity and Division', pp.16–17.
4. W.G. Gibowski, 'Election Trends in Germany. An Analysis of the Second General Election in Reunited Germany', in G.K. Roberts (ed.), *Superwahljahr: The German Elections in 1994* (London: Frank Cass, 1996), p.36; also T. Emmert, M. Jung and D. Roth, 'Zwischen Konstanz und Wandel. Die Bundestagswahl vom 16. Oktober 1994', in M. Kaase and H.-D. Klingemann (eds.), *Wahlen und Wähler. Analysen aus Anlaß der Bundestagswahl 1994* (Opladen: Westdeutscher Verlag, 1998), p.79.
5. M. Küchler, 'Okonomische Kompetenzurteile und individuelles politisches Verhalten: Empirische Ergebnisse am Beispiel der Bundestagswahl 1983', in D. Oberndörfer, H. Rattinger and K. Schmitt (eds.), *Wirtschaftlicher Wandel, religiöser Wandel und Wertewandel. Folgen für das politische Verhalten in der Bundesrepublik Deutschland* (Berlin: Duncker & Humblot, 1985), pp.157–81.
6. M. Jung and D. Roth, 'Wer zu spät geht, den bestraft der Wähler. Eine Analyse der Bundestagswahl 1998', *Aus Politik und Zeitgeschichte*, B 52/98, 18 Dec. 1998, p.5.
7. Ibid., pp.8–9.
8. O.W. Gabriel and F. Brettschneider, 'Die Bundestagswahl 1998: Em Plebiszit gegen Kanzler Kohl?' *Aus Politik und Zeitgeschichte*, B 52/98, 18 Dec. 1998, p.28.
9. Gibowski, 'Election Trends in Germany', p.8.
10. A. Campbell *et al.*, 'The American Voter' (New York, 1960).
11. Emmert *et al.*, 'Zwischen Konstanz und Wandel', p.76.
12. K. Berg and M.-L. Kiefer, *Massenkommunikation V: Eme Langzeitstudie zur Mediennutzung und Medienbewertung 1964–1995* (Baden-Baden: Nomosverlag, 1996), p.187.
13. Gibowski, 'Election Trends in Germany', p.30.
14. Ibid., p.27.
15. Gabriel and Brettschneider, 'Die Bundestagswahl 1998', p.32.
16. F.U. Pappi, 'Sozialstruktur, gesellschaftliche Wertorientierungen und Wahlabsicht', in Max Kaase (ed.), *Wahlsoziologie heute* (Opladen: Westdeutsher Verlag, 1977) pp.195–229.
17. Gibowski, 'Election Trends in Germany', p.42, Table 4.
18. G. Eckstein and F.U. Pappi, 'Die politischen Wahrnehmungen und die Präferenzen der Wählerschaft in Ost und Westdeutschland: Ein Vergleich', in H.-D. Klingemann and M. Kaase (eds.), *Wahlen und Wähler. Analysen aus Anlaß der Bundestagswahl 1990* (Opladen: Westdeutscher Verlag, 1994), pp.397–421.
19. Emmert *et al.*, 'Zwischen Konstanz und Wandel', p.69.

Economic Conditions and the 1994 and 1998 Federal Elections

JÜRGEN MAIER AND HANS RATTINGER

The Bundestag election of 1998 ended in defeat for the ruling coalition of Christian Democrats (CDU/CSU) and Liberals (FDP). The longest governing period of a German Chancellor had come to an end. For the first time in the history of the Federal Republic, power at the federal level was exchanged between government and opposition as the direct result of a national election. The poor state of the economy, especially the high level of unemployment, is often cited as one of the most important factors for this defeat. Given the fact that the CDU/CSU–FDP coalition had created high expectations about economic growth in the course of German unification, one would expect a significant effect of the voters' perceptions of the state of the economy and the government's economic record on voting behaviour in the 1998 general election. This applies especially to the new Länder, where a second economic miracle and rapid equalisation of east and west German living conditions were promised.[1] At the same time, the personal impact of economic hardship was clearly more widespread in the east than in the old Länder.

The connection between the economic situation and voting behaviour can be analysed empirically both at the micro- and the macro-level.[2] Despite a great deal of research there is no certainty about the exact electoral effects of economic variables. Contradicting results are often accounted for by different designs of empirical analyses, which, beside the level of analysis,[3] also can vary with regard to the type of data.[4] In addition, different theoretical notions exist about the link between economic factors and political behaviour. One classic assumption, the so-called anti-government or 'incumbency' hypothesis, is based on the simple idea that a poor state of the economy will damage the government, while the opposition will benefit, and vice versa.[5] The hypothesis disregards that different social groups have different economic interests concerning this alleged reward and punishment mechanism. Opinions about the suitability of competing political parties to further these interests can turn out very differently, depending on the type of

Jürgen Maier, University of Jena; Hans Rattinger, University of Bamberg economic problem. According to a 'clientele' or 'policy' hypothesis, the electoral success of a government depends not only on the economic situation, but also on the type of most pressing problem: in this perspective, high unemployment tends to benefit parties of the left, while high inflation creates advantages for bourgeois parties.[6] Yet, because both mechanisms are not always mutually exclusive, it often cannot be clearly decided by empirical analysis which of these hypotheses applies.[7]

On the following pages we examine whether and in which measure economic conditions (more exactly, economic perceptions) have influenced the election result of 1998. To provide a comparative framework, a parallel analysis of the general election of 1994 is presented. Our starting point for the following empirical investigation is a short description of some indicators of perceptions of the economic situation at the time of the elections in 1994 and 1998. Next we attempt to ascertain to what extent economic perceptions can explain individual voter behaviour both in 1994 and 1998. Finally, we pursue the question of whether and in which way changing perceptions of economic conditions influenced electoral volatility.

Our data base consists of two surveys performed prior to the 1994 and 1998 elections. Both were carried out within the framework of a larger research project – 'Political Attitudes and Political Participation in Germany: A Long-Term Comparison of Determinants and Consequences', funded by the Deutsche Forschungsgemeinschaft (DFG) – of which the second author is one of the principal investigators. The first survey was carried out before the general election in 1994, with about 2,000 respondents each from east and west Germany. For 1998, polling also took place prior to the election, with about 1,000 respondents from the 'old' (west German) Länder, and 500 from the 'new' (east German) ones. The following analyses are exclusively based on interviews carried out before the voting in 1994 and 1998 respectively, even though the overall design of the data collection was much more complex, and also included post-election and panel components.

PERCEPTIONS OF THE ECONOMIC SITUATION

Three types of indicators are available to measure the voters' perceptions of the economic situation. The first category includes assessments of the general and individual economic situation. The perceived competence of the various political parties to solve economic problems belongs to the second category. The third category is made up of variables which gauge the extent to which people have been personally affected by economic hardship such as unemployment, involuntary change of a job or forced departure from the workforce into early retirement and so on.

Assessment of General and Individual Economic Conditions

In 1998, 22 per cent of the west German respondents described the general economic situation as bad or very bad; 26 per cent perceived it as good or very good; for more than half of them the state of the economy was neither good nor bad (see Table 1). Perceptions in the old Länder differ significantly from those expressed by the east German respondents, of whom 40 per cent reported a negative assessment of the current economic situation in 1998. Twelve per cent of the east German respondents described the situation as favourable, while 48 per cent chose the intermediate category of neither good nor bad. A comparison with the evaluations of the general economic situation in 1994 reveals that judgements about the state of the national economy have become only slightly more pessimistic in west Germany, whereas the downturn was much more pronounced in east Germany.

A further indicator of the assessment of the general economic situation is a retrospective question about how the economy has developed over the past one or two years. In 1998, 37 per cent of west Germans expressed the opinion that the economic situation had become worse, 18 per cent saw an improvement, while for the remaining 44 per cent the economic situation was unchanged. Retrospective assessments of the economic situation in the new Länder turned out to be quite similar to west Germany (35 per cent 'worse', 19 per cent 'improvement', and 48 per cent 'stable'). If the perceptions in 1994 are used as the base for comparison, it is evident that virtually no changes can be observed in the west, while retrospective evaluations of economic development have worsened considerably in the east.

When west German voters were asked about their expectations concerning the general economic situation over the next year before the 1998 election, 26 per cent appeared optimistic and believed that the situation would get better. One-fifth of the respondents expected a deterioration. The absolute majority (55 per cent), however, believed that the economic situation would not change. A similar distribution can be found in east Germany (23 per cent for 'better', 20 per cent for 'worse', and 57 per cent forecasting no change). Compared to 1994 expectations for the future development of the general economic conditions had turned to somewhat stronger pessimism in the old Länder in 1998, while expectations in the east had become considerably more sceptical than four years earlier.

Most respondents gave a positive evaluation of their personal economic situation in 1998 (see Table 1). Half of those interviewed in the old Länder portrayed their personal economic situation as good or very good, 12 per cent as bad or very bad, and 38 per cent as neither good nor bad. The distribution in the new Länder differed significantly from this. The

TABLE 1

ASSESSMENTS OF GENERAL AND INDIVIDUAL ECONOMIC CONDITIONS IN
EAST AND WEST GERMANY, 1994 AND 1998

	1994		1998	
	West	East	West	East
General economic situation, current				
% very bad	3.2[c]	4.7	3.3[c]	8.2
% bad	17.3	25.2	18.3	31.3
% so-so	51.1	53.4	52.4	47.9
% good	26.8	16.5	25.1	12.4
% very good	1.6	0.2	0.9	0.2
Mean (scale from -1 to +1)	0.03[c]	-0.09	0.01[c]	-0.17
General economic situation, retrospective				
% much worse	7.0[c]	3.7	6.9	6.8
% somewhat worse	31.2	14.9	30.4	26.0
% so-so	41.1	33.9	44.3	48.2
% somewhat better	20.1	44.5	17.5	18.6
% much better	0.7	3.0	0.8	0.4
Mean (scale from -1 to +1)	-0.12[c]	0.14	-0.13	-0.10
General economic situation, prospective				
% much worse	2.3[c]	0.7	2.0	2.6
% somewhat worse	13.4	5.4	17.6	17.4
% so-so	51.1	41.9	54.5	57.3
% somewhat better	31.1	48.5	25.0	22.4
% much better	2.1	3.5	0.9	0.4
Mean (scale from -1 to +1)	0.09[c]	0.24	0.03	0.00
Overall assessment of general economic situation[d]	0.00[c]	0.10	-0.03[c]	-0.09
Individual economic situation, current				
% very bad	1.7[a]	3.6	2.5[c]	4.0
% bad	8.3	10.6	9.4	15.2
% so-so	37.7	36.2	37.9	39.8
% good	46.7	44.6	46.6	35.6
% very good	5.7	5.1	3.6	5.4
Mean (scale from -1 to +1)	0.23[a]	0.18	0.20[c]	0.12
Individual economic situation, retrospective				
% much worse	2.7[c]	4.9	4.3	5.8
% somewhat worse	17.3	11.1	19.9	16.6
% so-so	60.3	41.7	59.6	57.2
% somewhat better	16.9	34.0	14.0	18.2
% much better	2.7	8.3	2.2	2.2
Mean (scale from -1 to +1)	0.00[c]	0.15	-0.05	-0.03
Individual economic situation, prospective				
% much worse	1.3[c]	1.1	1.2	1.8
% somewhat worse	8.4	6.0	11.1	10.2
% so-so	69.5	60.0	67.9	70.8
% somewhat better	19.3	29.1	17.8	15.0
% much better	1.6	3.8	2.0	2.2
Mean (scale from -1 to +1)	0.06[c]	0.14	0.04	0.03
Overall assessment of individual economic situation[d]	0.10[c]	0.16	0.06	0.04
N	1026	1001	1000	500

Notes: Level of significance of east–west differences: a: $p<0.05$, b: $p<0.01$, c: $p<0.001$.

d: Average of current, retrospective and prospective evaluations on a scale from -1 to +1.

proportion of those who described their situation as favourable was clearly lower (41 per cent). Negative evaluations of personal situation were clearly more widespread (19 per cent). As in the west, 40 per cent characterised their situation as partly good, partly bad. A comparison of the perceptions of the personal economic situation in 1994 and 1998 reveals that evaluations were only slightly more pessimistic in west Germany, while pessimism had clearly increased in the east.

A further indicator is the question about how the personal economic situation had changed in the last one or two years. Sixteen per cent of the west German respondents answered that their personal economic situation had improved somewhat or become much better in the last one or two years. Twenty-three per cent reported a deterioration, while 60 per cent portrayed their personal situation as unchanged. By contrast, one-fifth of the east Germans saw improvement of their personal economic situation, 22 per cent perceived a deterioration, and 57 per cent said that their own economic situation had not changed. Compared with the time before the 1994 election, these judgements deteriorated only slightly in the west. In the new Länder, evaluations of changes in personal economic conditions had been much less unfavourable four years earlier.

Expectations with regard to the future development of the economic situation turn out to be faintly optimistic. In west Germany one-fifth of the respondents believe in an improvement in their situation, 12 per cent expect a worsening, and 68 per cent forecast their situation to remain unchanged. In east Germany there are 17 per cent who expect a more favourable personal economic situation, 12 per cent who see a deterioration as probable, and 71 per cent hold the opinion that not much will change. In comparison to 1994, expectations in the new Länder have become somewhat more pessimistic, while change in the old Länder was marginal.

If these different indicators of perceptions of the general and individual economic situation are combined in an overall assessment, the nature of changes becomes very clear. As for the evaluation of the general economic situation, significant differences between east and west Germany existed both in 1994 and 1998. While these assessments stayed generally stable in the old Länder, perceptions of the general economic situation in the new Länder worsened considerably: the assessment in 1994 gave way to an even more pessimistic position in 1998. With regard to the personal economic situation in 1998, no systematic differences can be found between the two parts of the country: on the whole, these judgements turn out to be slightly positive in both west and east Germany. In 1994 more respondents had described their own economic situation favourably, with optimism more widespread in east Germany than in the old Länder. Thus, clearly favourable

assessments of personal economic situation gave way to more ambivalent
ones between 1994 and 1998.

Perceived Competence to Solve Economic Problems

In 1998 22 per cent of the population in the west and 21 per cent in the east
believed the Christian Democrats to be most capable of solving the
country's worst economic problems (see Table 2). This means, however,
that more than three-quarters of respondents in both parts of the country did
not believe that the CDU and CSU had the best concepts for overcoming the
country's economic problems. Moreover, most people who mentioned the
CDU/CSU as the most competent party did so for only one item, and very
rarely said that it was capable of solving the most pressing economic
problems. A comparison between 1998 and 1994 reveals only minor
changes; the level of economic competence attributed to the CDU/CSU
remained virtually unchanged.

The situation for the SPD is totally different. In 1998 32 per cent of west
Germans and 27 per cent of east Germans expressed the opinion that the
Social Democrats offered the best ideas to cope with economic problems.
More importantly, these percentages had significantly increased, for in 1994
only 19 per cent in the old and 21 per cent in the new Länder had shared this
view. On the other hand, just as with the Christian Democrats, the belief that
the SPD was competent to solve more than one of the economic problems
stated in the questionnaire was quite rare. The level of economic
competence attributed to the other parties was very low indeed. For the FDP,
Alliance '90/Greens and Republikaner these percentages hardly ever exceed
a maximum of two per cent in both 1994 and 1998. In the new Länder,
however, the PDS was considered to be economically competent by four per
cent in 1994 and by seven per cent in 1998.

If the economic problem-solving capabilities of the different parties are
aggregated according to their government or opposition status, the
opposition in 1998 had acquired a considerable lead over the governing
parties in both west and east Germany. This finding differs from 1994, when
the CDU/CSU and FDP government parties and the opposition parties had
scored more or less the same in both parts of the country.

Personal Experience of Economic Hardship

Questions about personal unemployment and the like often produce
underreporting, because of the fear of social stigmatisation. A further
methodological problem is that we are using population samples here, not
samples of the workforce, so that comparisons with official labour market
statistics are not meaningful. At the time of the 1998 general election,
around five per cent of the respondents in west Germany said they were

TABLE 2

PERCEIVED COMPETENCE FOR ECONOMIC PROBLEM SOLVING OF THE PARTIES
IN EAST AND WEST GERMANY, 1994 AND 1998[d]

	1994		1998	
	West	East	West	East
CDU/CSU				
% no competence for solving problems	77.6[b]	79.3	77.9[a]	79.4
% only competence for the second problem	7.4	3.8	4.1	5.2
% only competence for the first problem	13.5	15.7	15.6	11.4
% competence for first and second problem	1.5	1.2	2.4	4.0
SPD				
% no competence for solving problems	80.8	78.4	67.5[c]	73.2
% only competence for the second problem	5.4	5.2	5.2	1.8
% only competence for the first problem	13.2	15.9	25.8	19.8
% competence for first and second problem	0.7	0.5	1.5	5.2
FDP				
% no competence for solving problems	99.0	99.4	98.9	99.4
% only competence for the second problem	0.7	0.1	0.4	0.4
% only competence for the first problem	0.3	0.5	0.7	0.2
% competence for first and second problem	0.0	0.0	0.0	0.0
Alliance 90/The Greens				
% no competence for solving problems	98.2[a]	99.6	98.4	99.0
% only competence for the second problem	0.6	0.2	0.6	0.8
% only competence for the first problem	1.2	0.2	1.0	0.2
% competence for first and second problem	0.0	0.0	0.0	0.0
PDS				
% no competence for solving problems	99.8[c]	95.8	99.8[c]	93.0
% only competence for the second problem	0.1	1.1	0.0	0.2
% only competence for the first problem	0.1	3.0	0.2	5.2
% competence for first and second problem	0.0	0.1	0.0	1.6
Republicans[e]				
% no competence for solving problems	99.7	99.8	98.4[a]	97.2
% only competence for the second problem	0.2	0.0	0.5	0.0
% only competence for the first problem	0.1	0.2	1.1	2.4
% competence for first and second problem	0.0	0.0	0.0	0.4
Government[f]				
% no competence for solving problems	76.6[b]	78.7	76.8[a]	78.8
% only competence for the second problem	8.0	3.9	4.5	5.6
% only competence for the first problem	13.8	16.2	16.3	11.6
% competence for first and second problem	1.6	1.2	2.4	4.0
Opposition[g]				
% no competence for solving problems	78.5[a]	73.4	64.1[c]	62.2
% only competence for the second problem	6.3	6.5	6.2	2.8
% only competence for the first problem	14.5	19.6	28.2	27.6
% competence for first and second problem	0.7	0.6	1.5	7.4
N	1026	1001	1000	500

Notes: Level of significance of east–west differences: a: p<0.05, b: p<0.01, c: p<0.001.

    d: Combination of open-ended questions for the most important and the second most important problem in the federal republic with follow-up questions for the party best able to solve these problems.

    e: 1998: Republikaner, DVU, NPD

    f: CDU/CSU and FDP

    g: SPD, Alliance 90/Greens, PDS, Republikaner, and other parties

TABLE 3

PERSONAL EXPERIENCE WITH UNEMPLOYMENT, INVOLUNTARY
CHANGE OF THE WORKPLACE, AND INVOLUNTARY DEPARTURE FROM
THE WORKFORCE, 1994 AND 1998

	1994		1998	
	West	East	West	East
% currently unemployed	2.4^c	17.0	4.9^c	14.0
% previously unemployed^d	8.1^c	36.4	15.6^c	36.7
% involuntary change of the workplace^d	6.6^c	25.2	8.9^c	20.7
% involuntary departure from the work force^d	11.4^c	16.9	18.0^c	14.4
N	1026	1001	1000	500

Notes: Level of significance of east–west differences: a: $p<0.05$, b: $p<0.01$, c: $p<0.001$.

d: since the previous election.

unemployed (see Table 3). This percentage was twice as high as for the time prior to the previous election of 1994. An opposite trend appeared in the east German samples: in 1998, 14 per cent of the respondents declared themselves unemployed, while this share had been as high as 17 per cent in 1994.

Sixteen per cent of the respondents in the old Länder reported a loss of their job in the period 1994–98 – again a share almost twice as high as in the period between the elections of 1990 and 1994. In the new Länder the share of those affected by unemployment in the previous parliamentary term (1994–98) was considerably higher (around 37 per cent) than in the west, but had remained virtually constant if compared to the period 1990–94. Nine per cent of the west German respondents reported an involuntary change of their workplace between 1994 and 1998, two per cent more than in the period from 1990 to 1994. Again, there was an opposite trend at a much higher level in east Germany: the percentage declined from 25 (1990–94) to 21 per cent (1994–98). In west Germany about 18 per cent of the respondents said they had left the workforce involuntarily between 1994 and 1998. This is a significant increase compared to 1990–94, when 11 per cent of the west German respondents had been affected by this type of economic hardship. Once again, an opposite development is apparent in east Germany: while 17 per cent had claimed to have left the workforce against their will between 1990 and 1994, this portion was reduced to about 14 per cent for the period 1994–98, that is, it dropped below the comparable west German value.

Thus, east Germans were generally more likely to have experienced economic hardship such as (current and earlier) unemployment, forced change of the workplace or departure from the workforce than west Germans. If one compares the situation prior to the general election of 1998 to the years before the election of 1994, it is obvious, however, that the personal impact of such economic hardship has tended to decline somewhat in east Germany, while the west has 'caught up' in this respect.

PERCEPTIONS OF ECONOMIC CONDITIONS AS PREDICTORS OF VOTING BEHAVIOUR IN THE 1994 AND 1998 ELECTIONS

We now proceed from description and comparison of perceptions of economic conditions and of personal experience of economic hardship at the time of the 1994 and 1998 elections to the influence of such economic variables on voting preferences. In this exercise, voting preferences will be measured by the reported intention to vote for a particular party in the imminent general election. The attribution of economic competence to the parties and two indicators combining perceptions of general and individual economic conditions are introduced as explanatory variables. All indicators of personal experience with economic hardship are omitted from the models after preliminary testing, due to a consistent lack of significant explanatory power. In order to avoid overestimating the effect of economic factors, the party identification of respondents is entered as a further (causally prior) determinant.

The results of our multiple regression analyses show that the economic variables contributed very unevenly to the explanation of voting preferences (see Table 4). In 1998, the additional proportion of the variance explained by economic determinants over and above party identification ranged from zero (FDP) to six per cent (opposition) in west Germany, and from one (Alliance '90/Greens) to ten per cent (FDP) in east Germany. For 1994, the explanatory power of these variables was within a similar range.

If the variables measuring the parties' perceived economic problem-solving capacity are compared to variables measuring the general and the individual economic situation, the latter play only a secondary role as explanations for the voters' choice of a party. General economic perceptions exhibit significant effects on the vote in only three equations for 1998 (west: SPD, opposition; east: FDP) and in five for 1994 (west: CDU/CSU, Republikaner, opposition; east: PDS, opposition). Nevertheless, all these coefficients have the theoretically expected sign, that is, favourable evaluations of the general economic situation improved the likelihood of a vote for the incumbent government parties CDU/CSU and FDP. Negative assessments of the state of the national economy, on the other hand, favoured a vote for one of the opposition parties.

Perceptions of the personal economic situation exerted a significant influence on voting preferences to an even lesser degree than perceptions of the general economic situation. While one significant effect could be found

TABLE 4

EXPLANATION OF THE VOTE BY PERCEPTIONS OF ECONOMIC CONDITIONS
AND BY PARTY IDENTIFICATION IN EAST AND WEST GERMANY, 1994 AND 1998

	Intention to vote for[d]							
	CDU/CSU	SPD	FDP	All.90/Greens	PDS	Republi-kaner[e]	Govern-ment[f]	Opposi-tion[g]
West Germany, 1994								
R^2, complete model	57.8	57.7	33.0	42.0	-	53.0	58.6	51.5
R^2, only party ID	56.3	55.5	27.0	41.4	-	49.5	56.4	48.5
General economic situation[h]	0.05[a]	0.00	0.00	0.00	-	-0.09[c]	0.04	-0.05[a]
Individual economic situation[h]	-0.02	-0.01	-0.04	0.01	-	0.01	-0.03	-0.01
Economic competence[i]	0.13[c]	0.17[c]	0.26[c]	0.09[c]	-	0.17[c]	0.17[c]	0.19[c]
Party identification[j]	0.68[c]	0.66[c]	0.43[c]	0.61[c]	-	0.67[c]	0.67[c]	0.61[c]
East Germany, 1994								
R^2, complete model	56.6	45.2	61.4	43.3	54.1	-	55.6	44.3
R^2, only party ID	49.3	39.6	60.3	42.3	51.8	-	49.0	38.4
General economic situation	0.04	-0.01	0.01	0.04	-0.08[b]	-	0.05	-0.08[b]
Individual economic situation	0.04	0.04	0.03	-0.07[a]	-0.04	-	0.04	-0.02
Economic competence	0.29[c]	0.27[c]	-0.11[c]	0.09[c]	0.11[c]	-	0.26[c]	0.24[c]
Party identification	0.55[c]	0.51[c]	0.81[c]	0.63[c]	0.66[c]	-	0.56[c]	0.51[c]
West Germany, 1998								
R^2, complete model	54.1	40.8	20.3	37.9	-	14.3	53.2	41.6
R^2, only party ID	50.3	35.8	20.3	36.7	-	9.1	48.8	35.6
General economic situation	0.02	-0.07[b]	0.01	0.01	-	-0.01	0.03	-0.06[a]
Individual economic situation	0.01	0.01	0.03	0.01	-	0.03	0.02	0.00
Economic competence	0.23[c]	0.28[c]	0.03	0.12[c]	-	0.24[c]	0.25[c]	0.28[c]
Party identification	0.58[c]	0.45[c]	0.44[c]	0.57[c]	-	0.24[c]	0.56[c]	0.46[c]
East Germany, 1998								
R^2, complete model	53.1	42.2	60.1	67.1	46.4	-	57.2	42.9
R^2, only party ID	50.7	38.7	50.4	66.6	44.3	-	54.8	37.7
General economic situation	0.05	-0.06	0.08[a]	-0.01	0.03	-	0.06	-0.05
Individual economic situation	-0.01	0.12b	-0.03	-0.01	-0.04	-	-0.02	0.03
Economic competence	0.19[c]	0.19[c]	0.31[c]	0.09[b]	0.18[c]	-	0.19[c]	0.25[c]
Party identification	0.62[c]	0.53[c]	0.69[c]	0.78[c]	0.57[c]	-	0.62[c]	0.51[c]

Notes: Level of significance: a: $p<0.05$, b: $p<0.01$, c: $p<0.001$.

d: Dichotomous variable with values of zero (no intention to vote for this party) and one (intention to vote for this party).
e: 1998: Republikaner, DVU, NPD
f: CDU/CSU, FDP
g: SPD, Alliance 90/Greens, PDS, Republikaner, and other parties
h: Average of current, retrospective and prospective evaluations on a scale from -1 to +1.
i: Scale from zero (no competence regarding economic problems) to one (competence for all economic problems mentioned as important in response to an open-ended question).
j: Scale from zero (no identification with this party) to one (very strong identification with this party).

for east Germany both in 1994 and 1998 (1994: Alliance '90/Greens; 1998: SPD), evaluations of the personal economic situation were of little or no electoral relevance in the west. Moreover, the direction of the measured effect in the east is theoretically plausible only for 1994: the worse the personal economic situation was perceived to be, the more likely a vote was to be given to Alliance '90/Greens. For 1998 the significant positive correlation between the intention to vote for the SPD and the perceived individual economic situation has the 'wrong' sign.

In both elections, the economic problem-solving competence attributed to the parties was by far the most important economic determinant of voting preferences. Apart from a few minor exceptions (FDP, east Germany 1994, and west Germany 1998), there are only theoretically 'correct' and highly significant relationships with voting preferences. Generally, we observe that the tendency to vote for a party increased with its perceived level of economic competence. Two qualifications should be added with regard to this almost uniform relationship. First, the relative impact of this effect is strongest for the CDU/CSU, SPD and FDP. Second, the influence of economic competence ratings on the voting preferences in the old Länder increased from 1994 to 1998, while for the east a parallel development cannot be detected.

PERCEPTIONS OF ECONOMIC CONDITIONS AS PREDICTORS OF CHANGES IN VOTING BEHAVIOUR IN THE 1994 AND 1998 ELECTIONS

Finally, we turn to the group of voters who switched their vote from a government party in the previous (that is, 1990 or 1994) election to an opposition party in the current (1994 or 1998) one. More specifically, the question is whether and to what extent economic perceptions influenced voters of a government party in 1990 to switch to an opposition party in 1994 and to what extent vote switching from government to opposition parties could be observed between 1994 and 1998. Table 5 shows that the differences between vote switchers and the rest of the electorate with regard to economic perceptions were limited. As far as the west German respondents are concerned, neither the 1994 nor the 1998 survey revealed significant differences between vote switchers and the rest of the population in their evaluations of the general and individual economic conditions. In east Germany only a few perceptual differences can be detected. In 1994 retrospective judgements of the economic situation by voters who changed from the government to the opposition were more negative than those by the rest of the electorate. Also it can be recognised that expectations of the future development of the general and personal economic situation among

TABLE 5

INDICATORS OF ECONOMIC CONDITIONS BY CHANGE IN THE VOTE COMPARED
TO PREVIOUS ELECTION, 1994 AND 1998

	1994				1998			
	West		East		West		East	
	Govt. to oppos.[d]	Other[d]	Govt. to oppos.	Other	Govt. to oppos.	Other	Govt. to oppos.	Other
Assessment of the economic situation[e]								
General, current	0.0	0.0	-0.2	-0.1	0.0	0.0	-0.2	-0.2
General, retrospective	-0.2	-0.1	0.0[a]	0.2	-0.2	-0.1	-0.2	-0.1
General, prospective	0.0	0.1	0.2	0.2	0.0	0.0	0.1[a]	0.0
General, total[f]	-0.1	0.0	0.0	0.1	-0.1	0.0	-0.1	-0.1
Individual, current	0.3	0.2	0.1	0.2	0.2	0.2	0.2	0.1
Individual, retrospect.	0.0	0.0	0.1	0.2	0.0	-0.1	0.0	0.0
Individual, prospective	0.0	0.1	0.2	0.1	0.0	0.0	0.1[b]	0.0
Individual, total[f]	0.1	0.1	0.1	0.2	0.1	0.1	0.1	0.0
Economic competence[g]								
Government[h]	13.8	23.7	8.5[b]	22.4	22.7	23.1	22.2	21.3
Opposition[i]	37.9[a]	21.1	53.0[c]	24.3	27.3	36.3	33.3	38.3
Personal experience with economic problems								
% now unemployed	0.0	2.4	16.9	17.0	9.1	4.7	13.0	14.1
% previously unemployed	19.0	6.2	29.7	24.7	9.7	8.9	14.6	21.6
% involuntary change of workplace	14.3	7.9	40.5	36.0	9.7	16.0	50.0	35.0
% involuntary departure from workforce	4.8	11.6	13.5[a]	17.3	9.7	18.3	4.9	15.7
N	29	997	83	919	44	956	54	446

Notes: Level of significance: a: p<0.05, b: p<0.01, c: p<0.001.

   d: Government to opposition: In 1990 (1994) voted for a government party and in 1994
      (1998) intends to vote for a party of the opposition; other combinations: all other
      combinations of voting behaviour in 1990 (1994) and 1994 (1998) intention to vote.
   e: Scale from -1 to +1.
   f: Average of current, retrospective and prospective evaluations on a scale from -1 to +1.
   g: Percentage of those who believe the party or parties to be capable of solving at least
      one of the economic problems.
   h: CDU/CSU, FDP
   i: SPD, Alliance 90/Greens, PDS, Republikaner, and other parties.

former voters of the government, who now wanted to vote for one of the
opposition parties, were somewhat higher than among other voters.

   As to the perceived economic competence of government and
opposition parties, major differences between both groups of voters can
only be found for 1994. In east Germany, those who had voted for the
government in 1990 and wished to vote for an opposition party in 1994
clearly attributed less economic competence to the government parties than

TABLE 6

EXPLANATION OF CHANGES IN THE VOTE[d] BY PERCEPTIONS OF ECONOMIC
CONDITIONS IN EAST AND WEST GERMANY, 1994 AND 1998

	1994		1998	
	West	**East**	**West**	**East**
R^2	0.4	3.0	0.7	2.1
General economic situation[e]	0.04	0.06	0.06	0.08
Individual economic situation[e]	-0.05	-0.03	-0.04	-0.11[a]
Economic competence of government[f]	0.02	0.07[a]	0.02	0.10[a]
Economic competence of opposition[f]	0.03	-0.12[c]	0.06	0.06
N	1026	1001	1000	500

Notes: Level of significance: a: p<0.05, b: p<0.01, c: p<0.001.

    d: Measured by values of -1 (switches from a government party to an opposition party in the next election), +1 (switches from an opposition party to a government party in the next election), and zero (all other combinations).

    e: Average of current, retrospective and prospective evaluations on a scale from -1 to +1.

    f: Scale from zero (no competence regarding economic problems) to one (competence for all economic problems mentioned as important in response to an open-ended question).

did the rest of the electorate. Conversely, and this is valid in both west and east Germany, this type of government-to-opposition vote switcher attributed significantly more economic competence to the opposition than other groups of voters. Finally, those switching from the government to the opposition were practically not different from the rest of the electorate in their personal experience of economic hardship.

If one examines the influence of economic factors on changes of voting preferences in a multivariate model, economic perceptions are found to be more relevant in the new than in the old Länder (see Table 6). However, even for the east the ability to explain vote switching by economic perceptions is (with a maximum of three per cent explained variance) rather limited. A look at the significant effects shows that in 1994 economic competence alone played a role in explaining changes of voting preferences. Two complementary relationships emerge: for voters of one of the government parties in the first all-German general election in 1990 the probability of a vote for the government in 1994 increased with growing trust in the economic competence of CDU/CSU and FDP. Almost like a mirror image, there was an even stronger corresponding effect for the opposition parties: a strong belief in the economic competence of the opposition parties increased the likelihood of turning away from the government parties and switching to their opponents. For 1998 the picture is somewhat more complex. While the influence of judgements about the parties' economic competence remained stable in its direction and even grew slightly in comparison to 1994, an additional negative effect of perceptions of the personal economic situation can now be observed in the east. The probability of vote switching from government to opposition increased with an *improving* assessment of the respondent's personal economic situation. This latter finding contradicts theoretical expectations, however, so that it remains to be seen in the future whether this indicates a stable pattern or an idiosyncratic deviation.

CONCLUSION

The economic situation is often used as a criterion to assess a government's performance in office. This certainly applies to the government parties' political adversaries and the media. A similar yardstick is also often assumed to be used by the electorate. The empirical basis for such an assumption is the frequency with which economic problems, most of all the reduction of high unemployment, were mentioned as a central task by politicians of all political persuasions and by voters themselves in recent years. The 1998 defeat of the CDU/CSU and FDP has often been attributed to the unsatisfactory performance of the economy. Such a connection between the economic situation and voting preferences is confirmed by the analyses presented here, even though the relationship is weaker than might be expected. At the time of the 1998 Bundestag election, evaluations of the economic situation had deteriorated in both west and east Germany if compared to voter perceptions in 1994. Nevertheless, such evaluations of the general and individual economic conditions played only a minor role in explaining individual voting preferences. By contrast, relatively clear effects were discovered for the parties' perceived competence to solve economic problems. Of all *economic* variables analysed here, confidence in the parties' perceived capability to manage the economy emerges as the strongest determinant of voting preferences. From 1994 to 1998 its influence on voting preferences increased even further. Although the people in the new Länder are still personally more affected by economic hardship, the east–west differences in perceptions of economic conditions decreased from 1994 to 1998. In the new Länder, a higher level of scepticism about the economic problem-solving ability of both major parties still persists, but the consequences of these differences on voting behaviour, once again, are only of a limited nature.

NOTES

1. See W. Glastetter, G. Högemann and R. Marquardt, *Die wirtschaftliche Entwicklung in der Bundesrepublik Deutschland 1950–1989* (Frankfurt am Main: Campus, 1991).
2. See, for example, G. Kirchgässner, 'Economic Conditions and the Popularity of West German Parties: A Survey', *European Journal of Political Research*, 14 (1986), pp.421–39; idem, 'On the Relation between Voting Intention and the Perception of the General Economic Situation: An Empirical Analysis for the FRG, 1972–86', *European Journal of Political Economy*, 7 (1991), pp.497–526; H. Rattinger, *Wirtschaftliche Konjunktur und politische Wahlen in der Bundesrepublik Deutschland* (Berlin: Duncker & Humblot, 1980); idem, 'Allgemeine und persönliche wirtschaftliche Lage als Bestimmungsfaktoren politischen Verhaltens bei der Bundestagswahl 1983', in D. Oberndörfer, H. Rattinger and K. Schmitt (eds.), *Wirtschaftlicher Wandel, religiöser Wandel, Wertwandel: Folgen für das politische Verhalten in der Bundesrepublik Deutschland* (Berlin: Duncker & Humblot, 1985), pp.183–218; idem, 'Collective and Individual Economic Judgements and Voting in West Germany, 1961–1984', *European Journal of Political Research*, 14 (1986), pp.393–419; idem, 'Unemployment and Elections in West Germany', in H. Norpoth, M.S. Lewis-Beck and J.-D. Lafay (eds.), *Economics and Politics: The Calculus of Support* (Ann Arbor, MI: University of Michigan Press, 1991), pp.49–62; H. Rattinger and W. Puschner, 'Ökonomie und Politik in der Bundesrepublik Deutschland. Wirtschaftslage und Wahlverhalten 1953–1980', *Politische Vierteljahresschrift*, 22 (1981), pp.264–86; H. Rattinger and J. Krämer, 'Economic Conditions and Voting Preferences in East and West Germany, 1989–94', in C.J. Anderson and C. Zelle (eds.), *Stability and Change in German Elections: How Electorates Merge, Converge, or Collide* (Westport, CT: Praeger, 1998), pp.99–120. H. Jung offers a systematic overview of the literature on this theme: *Wirtschaftliche Einstellungen und Wahlverhalten in der Bundesrepublik Deutschland. Eine Quer- und Längsschnittanalyse von 1971 bis 1976* (Paderborn: Schöningh, 1982); idem, 'Ökonomische Variablen und ihre politischen Folgen: Ein kritischer Literaturbericht', in D. Oberndörfer, H. Rattinger and K. Schmitt (eds.), *Wirtschaftlicher Wandel, religiöser Wandel und Wertwandel. Folgen für das politische Verhalten in der Bundesrepublik* (Berlin: Duncker & Humblot, 1985), pp.61–95.
3. One must think here of the distinction between analyses on the individual level and examinations of the aggregate level. More infrequent, however, are context examinations, these being analyses that put the micro- and macro-levels in connection with each other.
4. Firstly, the used type of data must be differentiated here. Numerous examinations exist beside objective economic data (for example, unemployment rate, inflation rate) which base themselves on the analysis of subjective data, and thus most of all on the perceptions of the economic situation. Secondly, a distinction must be made according to the respective reference of the data: on one side the employed data could apply to the economic situation of individuals; on the other side the focus can be directed to the economic situation of aggregates (for example, social groups, nations).
5. See A. Downs, *An Economic Theory of Democracy* (New York: Harper & Row, 1957).
6. Empirical evidence for this correlation effect also exists for the Federal Republic. See, for example, D.A. Hibbs, 'On the Demand for Economic Outcomes: Macroeconomic Performance and Mass Political Support in the United States, Great Britain, and Germany', *Journal of Politics*, 44 (1982), pp.426–62; H. Rattinger, 'Arbeitslosigkeit, Apathie und Protestpotential: Zu den Auswirkungen der Arbeitsmarktlage auf das Wahlverhalten bei der Bundestagswahl 1980', in M. Kaase and H.-D. Klingemann (eds.), *Wahlen und politisches System. Analysen aus Anlaß der Bundestagswahl 1980* (Opladen: Westdeutscher Verlag, 1983), pp.257–318; idem, 'Collective and Individual Economic Judgements' (cf n.2).
7. A discussion of both theoretical approaches can be found in D.R. Kiewiet, *Macroeconomics and Micropolitics* (Chicago, IL: University of Chicago Press, 1983).

The East German Vote in the
1998 General Election

CORNELIA WEINS

The 1998 electoral campaign for the German Bundestag was quite a thrill. Since precise predictions as to how the three small parties in the Bundestag (FDP, Alliance '90/Greens, PDS) were going to fare were hardly feasible, and in view of the federal electoral system, virtually any coalition seemed possible. In the end, the electorate cast a clear vote, which came as a surprise. The SPD and the Greens ended the race more than six percentage points ahead of the governing CDU/CSU–FDP coalition (see Table 1) and gained the relative majority of votes even though the PDS entered the Bundestag.[1] For the Christian Democrats, this was the worst general election result since 1949. In east Germany, where the CDU had celebrated its greatest victory ever in the first free election of March 1990, its defeat was most pronounced. There, the Christian Democrats lost 11 percentage points – twice as much as in west Germany (approximately five percentage points). The parties of the extreme right, which had been able to mobilise a considerable share of the voters in the state election in Saxony-Anhalt at the end of May 1998, did even better in the general election.[2] Equally surprising was the result of the PDS: while in previous elections the successor party of the SED managed to enter parliament only by winning direct mandates in at least three constituencies, this time it succeeded in clearing the so-called 'five per cent hurdle'.[3]

The establishment of the PDS in the German party system[4] certainly represents most markedly the electoral differences between the east and the west of Germany. However, the particularities of east German electoral behaviour cannot be reduced to strong support for the PDS. Most striking is the high volatility of voter turnout and voter decisions. Above all, the outcome of the election in the east raises the question of which factors were responsible for the large-scale losses of the CDU. In this context, the voting behaviour of east German blue-collar workers should be particularly interesting. In the elections of 1990 and 1994, a disproportionate number of them voted for the CDU. Did they change this untypical – at least according

Cornelia Weins, University of Trier

TABLE 1

OFFICIAL RESULT OF THE 1998 GENERAL ELECTION
(*ITALICS: GAINS AND LOSSES IN PERCENTAGE POINTS COMPARED TO 1994*)

	East		West		Total	
SPD	35.1	*+3.6*	42.3	*+4.8*	40.9	*+4.5*
CDU/CSU	27.3	*-11.2*	37.1	*-5.0*	35.1	*-6.4*
The Greens	4.1	*-0.2*	7.3	*-0.6*	6.7	*-0.6*
FDP	3.3	*-0.2*	7.0	*-0.7*	6.2	*-0.7*
PDS	21.6	*+1.8*	1.2	*+0.2*	5.1	*+0.7*
Extreme right	5.0	*+3.7*	2.9	*+0.9*	3.3	*+1.4*
Other	3.6	*+2.5*	2.3	*+0.4*	2.6	*+1.0*
	100%		100%		100%	
Valid votes	9,520,646		39,787,866		49,308,512	
Turnout	80%	*+7.4*	82.8%	*+2.3*	82.8%	*+3.2*
Entitled to vote	12,131,155		48,631,596		60,762,751	

Source: Statistisches Bundesamt, Wiesbaden

Notes: SPD: Sozialdemokratische Partei Deutschlands; CDU: Christlich Demokratische Union Deutschlands; CSU: Christlich-Soziale Union in Bayern; FDP: Freie Demokratische Partei; PDS: Partei des demokratischen Sozialismus (former SED); The Greens: Bündnis '90/Die Grünen; extreme right: Die Republikaner, DVU: Deutsche Volksunion, NPD: Nationaldemokratische Partei Deutschlands.

to west German standards – voting behaviour and, if so, why? Most prominent among the factors influencing voting intention seems to be the candidate for the chancellery, and especially the renewed candidacy of Helmut Kohl – which is also supported by the latest discussion about the personalisation of politics. Besides these factors, issues such as the persistently high unemployment rate in east and west Germany need to be taken into consideration. It will have to be examined to what extent the voters' decisions were influenced by short-term factors, such as issues and candidates, and whether these factors exerted a greater influence in east than in west Germany, as could be assumed.

When analysing east German voting behaviour, the question arises which of the existing models of voting behaviour – all of which were developed in Western democracies[5] – apply to east Germany and which do not. This is of particular interest as far as cleavage theory[6] and the social-psychological[7] model of voting are concerned, as they assume voter–party ties mediated by cleavages or party identification, which cannot be assumed to exist in young democracies.[8] In part, the voting behaviour of the east German electorate in 1990 came as such a surprise because it did not match the expectations formed on the basis of a mechanical transfer of one explanatory model (cleavage theory) from west Germany, where it had been successful, to east Germany, where it did not apply.

DATA

The study is based on the 1998 analysis of the Bundestag election,[9] which contains two cross-sectional studies, one of which was conducted before and the other after the election.[10] Even though east Germans were over-sampled in both surveys, their absolute numbers in each survey[11] are too small to allow for separate analysis. Both data sets, therefore, had to be merged. The new data set now contains approximately 1,100 east German respondents. As the interviews generating these data were conducted at different times, this method yields systematic distortions which must be put up with in this analysis. Thus, the variable 'voting intention' is constructed on the basis of a (pre-election) survey question about whom the respondent is going to vote for in the upcoming general election, and the (post-election) recall question about whom s/he voted for in the past general election. This re-coded variable contains one category which was only included in the pre-election survey ('do not know') and one only employed in the post-election survey ('did not vote'). Since both categories were not used in both surveys,[12] they are excluded from this study. Therefore, the percentage of votes per party is determined on the basis of the number of valid votes, and not, as is the rule, on the basis of the number of persons entitled to vote. Thus, non-voters are not taken into account. This is the more regrettable as the proportion of non-voters in the east (see Table 1) varied strongly from one election to the next. As only a small number of east German respondents indicated that they intended to vote for the FDP or the Greens, these parties have been listed in the category 'Others'.

VOLATILITY AND PARTY SWITCHERS

The above-mentioned net changes of the parties' shares of votes already indicate the higher volatility of east German electoral behaviour. The Pedersen Index[13] – which, in this analysis, has been calculated for the changes of the shares of valid votes for the parties listed in Table 1 – is visibly higher in east Germany (11.6) than in west Germany (6.3).[14] This higher net volatility hints at a higher individual electoral volatility[15] in east Germany.[16]

Due to a lack of panel data, and with regard to the available cross-sectional data, our analyses have to rely on the recall question concerning the 1994 voting decision. As a consequence, individual voting shifts will most likely be underestimated as respondents tend to reconcile their present with their past behaviour. Due to the above-mentioned coding of voting intention,[17] for the purposes of this analysis it is only possible to examine the number of *party* changers, that is, persons who voted for different parties in the 1994 and 1998 general elections.

According to the findings on the basis of the recall question, 31 per cent of east Germans and 21 per cent of west Germans voted for different parties in 1994 and 1998. As expected, the individual stability in the east is thus lower than in the west. In comparison to the findings of Zelle[18] (for two subsequent general elections between 1969 and 1990), who observed between 13 and 18 per cent of party changers (1980–83), the proportion of west German party changers also appears to be relatively high.

As can be assumed from the election result, the CDU, in particular, lost many voters. In east Germany, 42 per cent of the 1994 CDU voters changed parties, and almost two-thirds of them now vote for the Social Democrats. Even the FDP and Alliance '90/Greens kept more voters than the CDU (SPD: 80 per cent; PDS: 82 per cent). In west Germany, the development was less dramatic for the CDU (24 per cent changed parties; 76 per cent still vote for the CDU), but the proportion of loyal voters is still very low when compared with Zelle's findings that between 1969 and 1990 89 to 93 per cent of CDU voters remained loyal to their party.[19] It would be most interesting to examine why voters changed parties and whether they did this for different reasons in the east and in the west, but, unfortunately, these questions cannot be answered as the small number of respondents does not allow for a separate analysis of the various groups of party changers.

It seems plausible to explain these fluctuations of electoral behaviour with respect to party affiliation as the result of the vote switchers' absent or weakly developed party identification. Strong party identification promotes a homogeneous view of the political world and thus reduces the probability that political events are perceived as standing in contradiction to one's own party affiliation. Therefore, strong party identification is likely to reduce vote switching.[20] In some Western societies, decreasing party identification is regarded as one of the causes for the increasing number of party switchers.[21] In east Germany, though, the situation is different: it can be assumed that due to the short time that has passed since German unification, party identification has not (yet) been developed to the same extent, or with the same intensity, as in the west. Although the employment of the party identification question comes with some difficulties in the east, as will be shown below, it is nevertheless used as an instrument due to a lack of alternatives.

As expected, the level of party identification in east Germany is lower than in west Germany. Only 63 per cent of east German respondents consider themselves 'psychologically attached' to a party, compared to 74

TABLE 2

PARTY CHANGE ACCORDING TO PARTY IDENTIFICATION

	Party Identification			
	No		Yes	
	East	*West*	*East*	*West*
Same party	46	60	77	84
Voting shift	54	40	23	16
	100	100	100	100
(Cases)	(178)	(256)	(529)	(1258)

Source: National Election Study 1998

per cent in the west. The intensity of party identification, though, is about the same in the east and the west. Party affiliations greatly stabilise the voting intention in both parts of Germany (see Table 2). However, identification with a party does not explain the different scope of party switching in the east and the west: irrespective of party identification, the proportion of party switchers is higher in east Germany than in west Germany. The intensity of party identification affects party switching differently in the two regions: while in west Germany, as expected, the likelihood of switching from one party to another decreases with increasing party identification, the relationship observed in east Germany is not linear.

DETERMINANTS OF VOTING BEHAVIOUR

Theories of Voting Behaviour and the East German Context

It can be assumed that short-term factors influencing voting behaviour, such as attitudes towards the candidates and/or issues relevant in an electoral competition, are more important in east than in west Germany because the voters in the east have less experience with the party system. Whether long-term determinants play a role in structuring east German electoral behaviour as well, and, if so, which ones, is contentious.

Cleavage theory, for instance, arguably fails to explain class-specific electoral behaviour in east Germany, but is well suited (as will be argued below) to elucidate differences in voting based on religious factors.[22] Similarly, it is highly disputed whether the concept of party identification – and thus the social-psychological model of voting behaviour – can be meaningfully applied to east German electoral behaviour.[23] For the social-psychological model, which much of German voting research is based upon, party identification represents the central long-term determinant of voting behaviour.[24] According to the original model, it affects the vote not only directly but also indirectly by serving as a filter with respect to the perception of the candidates and issues of an electoral competition (that is, the short-term factors of electoral behaviour).[25]

As to the applicability of this concept, Bluck and Kreikenbom observed that east Germans developed 'virtual party affiliations' even while they still lived under socialist rule in the GDR due to their interactions with west Germans and, in particular, their exposure to west German media.[26] Furthermore, in election surveys a large number of east Germans claim to identify with a party, which has also been interpreted as an indication that the concept of party identification applies in the new states.[27] However, previous analyses also reveal that the proportion of respondents identifying with a party is higher at times of election than at times when political mobilisation is low, and that party identification in the east is subject to short-term factors to a decidedly higher degree than in west Germany.[28] According to my own analysis of the Socio-Economic Panel[29] – which has been conducted in east Germany annually since 1991 and which has included the party identification (PI) question[30] since 1992 – between 1992 and 1997 only 33 to 41 per cent[31] of east German respondents claimed to identify with a party. These data deviate so strongly from the above-mentioned electoral study and the findings reported in the relevant literature[32] that there is reason to doubt the reliability of the PI question and, consequently, its validity.[33] The fact that the proportion of east Germans who identify with a party as well as the intensity levels of partisanship are decreasing also stands in contradiction to theoretical expectations.[34] This does not mean that in east Germany party identifications have not yet been developed. Nor does it mean that voting behaviour of east Germans is exclusively determined by short-term factors. For some east Germans, however, the PI question does not seem to measure stable affiliations which are independent of temporary party preferences. Therefore, the concept of party identification is not employed in this analysis. In order to avoid an overestimation of the effects of short-term factors, though, the ideological position is used as a stable determinant of electoral behaviour in the medium term.

THE SOCIAL BASES OF THE VOTE: CLASS AND RELIGION

In western European societies, the effects of class and religion as determinants of the voting decision are typically accounted for with reference to 'cleavage theory'. According to Lipset and Rokkan,[35] the western European party systems originate from profound social conflicts, which arose in the course of nation-building and the Industrial Revolution. Political parties developed along the 'cleavages' brought about by these social conflicts, transforming the concerns of social movements into political issues. According to Knutsen and Scarbrough, a cleavage is 'rooted

54 BUNDESTAGSWAHL '98

in a relatively persistent social division ..., engages some set of values common to members of the group' and 'is institutionalized in some form of organisation – most commonly a party, but also in churches, unions and other associational groups'.[36] Decades after their emergence, the original cleavages still characterised the party systems of western Europe. The cleavage structure of the early Federal Republic of Germany,[37] for instance, basically still corresponded to that of the German Empire even though there had been no free elections since the beginning of the 'Third Reich'.[38] Although the parties opened up ideologically[39] to attract new segments of the electorate, and despite the alleged 'individualisation' of the electorate, denomination and class[40] still influence the electoral behaviour of the western German population in a traditional way. The CDU's share of the vote is disproportionately high amongst Catholics, whilst workers have an above-average tendency to vote for the SPD.

Since class-specific electoral behaviour as observed in the west was automatically assumed to be found in the east as well, it came as a surprise when the majority of east German workers voted for the Christian Democrats in the 1990 elections.[41] It had been overlooked that the 'class structure' of the German Democratic Republic had differed fundamentally from that of the Federal Republic of Germany. Towards the end of socialist rule, workers had been positioned at the bottom of the 'state-socialist hierarchy of classes' (*staatssozialistische Klassenstruktur*).[42] This most certainly contributed to the alienation of workers from the government and the state party SED (which, after all, pretended to represent the interests of the workers). On the other hand, though, the concerns of the workers had not been manifested politically since independent unions or parties (apart from the SED) did not exist in the GDR. In sum, 'class differences' were not organised, and, thus, there was no such thing as a class cleavage in the sense defined above. Denominational and religious interests were an altogether different matter. Even under socialist rule, they had been organised by the two major churches, the Catholics and Protestants; therefore, it seems reasonable to assume that a religious cleavage existed and still exists in the area of the former GDR.[43]

Class

If only for their large numbers,[44] the voting behaviour of blue-collar workers[45] plays a central role in determining the election result in the east. In the 1990 general election – and, to a lesser degree, in 1994 – the Christian Democrats[46] won the largest share of votes among blue-collar workers. In 1998 this picture was practically reversed (see Table 3); the SPD became the favourite party for east German blue-collar workers, civil servants and white-collar workers below the managerial level.

TABLE 3
VOTE ACCORDING TO CLASS

	Blue-collar workers		White-collar w. & civ. servts below management		White-collar w. & civ. servts at manage- ment level		Self-empl. & farmers	
	East	*West*	*East*	*West*	*East*	*West*	*East*	*West*
CDU/CSU	17	28	31	26	27	32	40	47
SPD	47	61	46	57	35	42	23	21
PDS	22	1	18	2	24	3	15	2
Other	15	10	6	15	13	23	23	29
(Cases)	(120)	(182)	(88)	(195)	(82)	(278)	(40)	(131)

Notes: Calculation includes only persons with full-/part-time jobs.
  Aside from rounding, column totals add up to 100 per cent.

Source: National Election Study 1998

Thus, in the 1998 general election, class membership for the first time had a similar effect on the vote in both parts of the country. What this means for the federal party system depends to a large degree on what caused this development. Basically, it would be interesting to know whether in east Germany, eight years after reunification, parties and classes finally develop relations that lead to class-specific voting behaviour similar to that observed in west Germany. In the medium term the establishment of the west German pattern of interest group competition might support electoral behaviour based on socio-structural factors.[47]

From this viewpoint, the question arises whether the changed voting behaviour of blue-collar workers, shifting from the CDU to the SPD, can be attributed to unions increasingly being regarded as organisations representing their interests, thus creating a 'voting norm'. In order to answer this question, first of all, the nature and intensity of the attachment to the unions will have to be examined, and, secondly, its effect on the electoral prospects of the SPD. As the findings of Weßels and Schmitt indicate, neither in 1990 nor in 1994 did the classes differ as to their union ties. Obviously, identifying with an interest group only becomes relevant for voting behaviour when linked to a particular party. While considerably fewer east than west Germans perceived the SPD to be supported by the unions (43 per cent east, 79 per cent west) in 1990, east Germans were widely aware of this 'coalition' (63 per cent east, 79 per cent west) in 1994.[48] The perception of unions as the representatives of the people's interests and additionally as supporting the SPD improved the electoral prospects of the SPD in past elections, although to a lesser degree than in the western part of the country.[49]

Due to the small number of respondents, the variable 'class membership' has to be dichotomised for the purposes of this analysis. The category 'working persons type I' includes blue-collar workers, and white-collar workers/civil servants below the managerial level; the category 'working persons type II' includes self-employed persons and white-collar workers/civil servants at the managerial level. The variable 'union attachment' measures whether a respondent considers his/her interests to be represented by the unions. The 'voting norm' resulting from this attachment is operationalised by asking for the party with the greatest affinity to the unions. The 1998 data confirm earlier findings. By 1998, class-related patterns of representation have still not formed: 50 per cent of 'working persons type I' in the east consider the unions to represent their interests (55 per cent in the west) and 46 per cent of respondents of 'working persons type II' (44 per cent in the west). Of those who regard their interests to be represented by the unions, 71 per cent of the 'working persons type I' (81 per cent in the west) and 89 per cent of 'working persons type II' (94 per cent in the west) consider the unions close to the SPD. East Germans, thus, increasingly associate unions with the same party as west Germans.

As Table 4 shows, the electoral prospects of the SPD in both parts of the country are improved if voters consider the unions to represent their interests and perceive an ideological proximity between the unions and the SPD. However, the effects are still weaker in the east than in the west. Union affiliation improves the SPD's electoral results only by four percentage points among east German 'working persons type I' in comparison to nine percentage points among their west German counterparts.[50]

TABLE 4

VOTE ACCORDING TO CLASS AND REPRESENTATION BY UNIONS

	'Working persons type I'				'Working persons type II'			
	+		-		+		-	
	East	*West*	*East*	*West*	*East*	*West*	*East*	*West*
CDU/CSU	18	18	27	36	(18)	24	38	45
SPD	51	67	44	50	(31)	48	32	27
PDS	19	2	20	1	(41)	4	10	2
Other	11	13	9	13	(10)	24	20	26
(Cases)	(72)	(158)	(109)	(175)	(39)	(170)	(71)	(219)

Notes: +: respondents reply that unions represent their interests and unions are closest to the SPD;

-: respondents reply that unions do not represent their interests and/or unions are not closest to the SPD.

Calculation includes only persons with full-/part-time jobs.

Aside from rounding, column totals add up to 100 per cent.

Source: National Election Study 1998

The change in the electoral behaviour of east German 'working persons type I', consequently, does not result from the increasing recognition of unions as representatives of their interests. 'Working persons type I' consider their concerns to be attended to by the unions no more and no less than members of the other class. Moreover, the effect of 'union attachment' on the vote is still considerably weaker than in the west.

Religion

Religious life in east Germany has been shaped by the atheism of the socialist regime of the GDR. Today, the majority of east Germans does not belong to any religious community, almost one-third of the population is Protestant and approximately six per cent are Catholics.[51] The Protestant Church, in particular, suffered from severe membership losses during socialist rule. In 1946, approximately 80 per cent of the people living on east German territory were Protestant and almost 12 per cent were Catholic.[52] In the west, however, the religious structure has not undergone such a severe transformation despite secularisation and the ensuing loss of members which both official churches suffered. Today both denominations have nearly the same amount of members (approximately 43 per cent) while persons not belonging to any of the two denominations form a minority (eight per cent).

The confessional cleavage in west Germany still influences the electoral behaviour. Catholic voting is above average for the Christian Democrats, Protestants disproportionately vote for the Social Democrats. This voting behaviour has historical roots. In the German Empire, the conflict between Bismarck and the Catholic Church during the so-called '*Kulturkampf*' strengthened the Catholic Centre Party, the Zentrum. Until the fall of the Weimar Republic, the Zentrum remained a purely Catholic party. Even though the CDU was founded after World War II as a party open to all denominations, it inherited the Catholic electorate from the Zentrum.

The past elections showed that it is not decisive what denomination an east German voter is affiliated with, but whether s/he belongs to a religious community at all.[53] East German Protestant and Catholic voting alike is above average for the Christian Democrats.[54] It is assumed that this voting behaviour results from the dichotomy of 'spiritual' life under socialist rule, which only differentiated between atheists and religious persons and that the CDU is considered the party of religious voters nowadays. In west Germany, however, the 'line' is drawn between Protestants and Catholics, and the CDU is considered the party of the Catholics. Consequently, there seems to exist a religious cleavage in the east and a denominational cleavage in the west.[55] This does not mean that there are no denominational differences. In east Germany, too, the CDU is more successful amongst

TABLE 5

VOTE ACCORDING TO RELIGION/DENOMINATION

	East			West		
	No relig.	Cath./ Prot.		No relig.	Prot.	Cath.
CDU/CSU	18	42		22	29	45
SPD	41	38		42	53	38
PDS	26	8		3	2	1
Other	15	12		33	17	16
	100	100		100	100	100
(Cases)	(545)	(267)		(251)	(745)	(677)

Note: West: other religions (1.5 per cent) excluded

Source: National Election Study 1998

Catholics than amongst Protestants.[56] In view of the small number of Catholics in east Germany, though, this hardly has any consequences for the outcome of an election.

As Table 5 illustrates, religious affiliation in east Germany mainly affects the electoral prospects of the CDU and the PDS. While religious persons vote is above average for the CDU, the Christian Democrats gain the support of only 18 per cent of non-religious voters. The PDS, on the other hand, wins 26 per cent of the votes cast by non-religious persons, and a mere eight per cent of the votes cast by religious persons. When we distinguish between denominations, we see that the CDU, with 38 per cent, lost Protestant support (in 1990: 52 per cent; in 1994: 57 per cent[57]), whereas Catholic support seems to have remained constant.[58]

IDEOLOGICAL POSITION

A person's general ideological convictions are frequently categorised in terms of 'leftist' and 'rightist' and measured on a scale from 'left' to 'right'.[59] It can be assumed that citizens of the GDR and the FRG were both familiar with the terms 'left' and 'right' with respect to the classification and evaluation of political issues.[60] The opposite ideological orientations of the two German states are probably responsible for the fact that east Germans today take a more leftist position on this scale than west Germans.[61] As another consequence of the different developments the two German states took, 'leftist' values should be embedded differently in their social structures. Put simply, it can be assumed that the members of the former socialist 'service classes' (*Dienstklassen*),[62] who had benefited from the social order and who had been more thoroughly moulded by the GDR educational system, tend to hold leftist positions. On the other hand, east German blue-collar workers, who had been located at the bottom of the 'socialist class hierarchy',[63] should take a more detached view of the prevalent GDR ideology, and, therefore, should now be rather more conservative. The ideological standpoint seems to be of particular importance with respect to the electoral prospects of the PDS, the successor to the former state party SED. This is indicated by the findings of Klein and Caballero,[64] who claim that the PDS does not so much attract east German voters who were objectively or subjectively deprived in the course of German reunification – as has frequently been assumed – but is more likely to be supported by persons sharing its ideological position. In west Germany, Alliance '90/Greens and the SPD are located on the left side of the party spectrum, whereas the FDP and the Christian Democrats are located on the right. Since their formation in the 1970s and 1980s, the Greens have been competing with the SPD, with the SPD representing 'old-left' (materialist) values, and the Greens 'new-left' (post-materialist) values.[65]

In this survey, east Germans position themselves about 0.7 points left of west Germans on the 'left–right' scale (see Table 6). East and west Germans generally agree as to the ideological positioning of the parties, with the exceptions of the PDS and Alliance '90/Greens.[66] As expected, east German workers place themselves right of the east German average, whereas west German workers, as expected, position themselves slightly left of the west German average. With regard to its ideological proximity to the voters, the SPD's chances of winning the election are better than those of any other party in both parts of the country.[67]

TABLE 6

POSITIONING ON THE LEFT–RIGHT SCALE (MEAN)

	East	(Cases)	West	(Cases)
Self-positioning:				
All respondents	4.8	(985)	5.5	(1,940)
Blue-collar workers	5.3	(130)	5.4	(210)
Positioning of parties:				
CSU	8.2	(982)	8.2	(1,930)
CDU	7.3	(997)	7.4	(1,944)
FDP	6.8	(962)	6.5	(1,888)
SPD	4.1	(1,005)	4.2	(1,952)
Greens	4.1	(966)	3.5	(1,908)
PDS	2.4	(1,000)	3.4	(1,796)

Note: scale ranges from 1 ('left') to 11 ('right')

Source: National Election Study 1998

TABLE 7

VOTE ACCORDING TO SELF-POSITIONING ON THE LEFT–RIGHT SCALE

	Extreme left	Left	Centre	Right	Extreme right
East:					
CDU	9	18	42	61	41
SPD	39	55	37	17	3
PDS	44	16	7	5	3
Other	8	12	14	18	54
(Cases)	(211)	(296)	(152)	(84)	(37)
West:					
CDU/CSU	8	19	41	68	64
SPD	60	60	43	18	17
PDS	4	1	1	1	1
Other	28	21	16	13	19
(Cases)	(303)	(512)	(366)	(280)	(129)

Notes: Extreme left includes scale points 1 to 3; left 4 and 5; centre 6; right 7 and 8, extreme right 9 to 11.
Aside from rounding, column totals add to 100 per cent

Source: National Election Study 1998

The ideological position has the expected influence on the voting intention (Table 7). Respondents who position themselves at the left end of the scale (points 1 to 3) prefer the PDS to the SPD in the east, whereas in the west the SPD and also the Greens (approximately 26 per cent; respective data are not indicated in the table) are the favoured parties. In the east even the 'moderate leftist' vote for the PDS is below average. The CDU, on the other side of the spectrum, attracts voters in the east and in the west who consider themselves more conservative. Furthermore, a large percentage of respondents who place themselves at the extreme right of the scale also prefer right-wing extremist parties (west: 11 per cent; east: 50 per cent[68]). The ideological position mainly figures in the explanation of the stability of the voting intention. Short-term fluctuations of the voting behaviour are usually explained by issue and candidate orientations.

ISSUES

The voting decision is not affected by just any issue. An issue only influences the voting decision if a voter is aware of it, considers it important and if one party is preferred in view of its position or competence in handling this issue.[69] The 1998 electoral campaign was dominated by the persistently high unemployment rate in east and west Germany.[70] In

September, the month of the election, more than 16 per cent of the east German labour force and almost nine per cent of the west German labour force were registered by the Federal Employment Agency (Bundesanstalt für Arbeit) as seeking employment. Unemployment was the number one issue under public discussion in 1998.

This is also reflected by the results of this survey. To the open question on the most important current problem of the FRG, the reply most frequently given is 'unemployment' (east: 42 per cent; west: 54 per cent), followed by 'job creation' (east: 34 per cent; west: 11 per cent). 'Social justice' ranks third among the problems considered most important (four per cent) in the east and 'immigrants' (three per cent) in the west. When all unemployment-related answers ('unemployment', 'job creation', 'youth unemployment' and 'stop job losses') are considered together, 80 per cent of the east German and 68 per cent of the west German respondents judge unemployment to be the most important issue.

Unemployment is a classic valence issue,[71] that is, the objective of political action, in this case 'full employment', is not under discussion. As voters and parties do not disagree on the aim to be achieved, the subject of dispute is rather which party is most capable of solving the problem fully and efficiently. Valence issues, thus, pose questions about the parties' problem-solving competence. In consequence, differences in voting behaviour result from the differences in the voters' perception of which party is most capable of reducing unemployment. In both parts of the country, the SPD enjoys a clear lead in this respect (see Table 8).

TABLE 8

PROBLEM-SOLVING COMPETENCE WITH RESPECT TO THE MOST
IMPORTANT PROBLEM (COLUMN PERCENTAGES)

		Most important problem	
		Unemployment	Other
CDU/CSU	East:	17	23
	West:	25	32
SPD	East:	38	31
	West:	45	33
PDS	East:	7	13
	West:	1	1
Other	East:	3	11
	West:	1	5
All the same	East:	9	6
	West:	5	4
None	East:	25	16
	West:	19	17
Cases	East:	765 (=77%)	22 (=23%)
	West:	1,355 (=68%)	630 (=32%)

Note: Aside from rounding, column totals for each region add up to 100 per cent.

Source: National Election Study 1998

East and west Germany, however, differ in one decisive respect: one-quarter of the east German voters who consider unemployment to be the most urgent problem consider none of the parties capable of solving the problem. This perception may be a result of the situation on the labour market, which is particularly severe in east Germany. Moreover, east Germans, more than west Germans, believe job creation to be the government's responsibility. Almost two-thirds of east Germans believe job creation to be 'definitely' the responsibility of the government (approximately 43 per cent in the west). In view of the alarming situation on the labour market, and the public notion in the east that it is the government's job to do something about it, it does not come as a surprise that east Germans are less satisfied with the government's performance on this issue than west Germans. Almost half of the east German respondents, in this respect, are 'absolutely dissatisfied' with government performance (west: 25 per cent), and more than one-third of the voters are 'rather dissatisfied' (west: 37 per cent).

As *the second most important problem* in the FRG, east Germans most frequently name 'internal security' (14 per cent) followed by 'social justice' (13 per cent). In the west it is again 'unemployment' (11 per cent), followed by 'foreigners' (ten per cent). As the percentages indicate, these answers are more scattered than those referring to the most important problem. No matter the topic of the second most important problem, the SPD is considered by above-average percentages of Germans to be the party best capable of solving it in both parts of the country.

The fact that many east Germans diagnose a lack of 'social justice' points to their rejection of the social inequalities which accompany the increasing differentiation of the social structure brought about by the problems of transformation. This, however, is not only an east German grievance: when asked about the nation's most important and second most important problem, 'social justice' ranks fourth among west German respondents.

It can be assumed that the general evaluation of the competence of the governing coalition is based on its performance during the past legislative period. On an 11-point rating scale from -5 (dissatisfied) to +5 (satisfied), east Germans assess the government's achievements more negatively (-0.89) than west Germans (-0.41).

CANDIDATES

The renewed candidacy of Helmut Kohl for the office of Federal Chancellor is held to be one of the major causes of the defeat of the CDU in the 1998 general election.[72] While his opponents in the 1990 (Oskar Lafontaine) and

TABLE 9

PREFERRED CHANCELLOR

	East	West
Kohl	26	31
Schröder	49	51
Neither of these two	25	18
	100	100
(Cases)	(1,014)	(2,048)

Source: National Election Study 1998

1994 (Rudolf Scharping) elections had led the electoral competition at the beginning by a wide margin, but then rapidly lost their lead as election day drew closer,[73] Helmut Kohl was way behind Gerhard Schröder as the preferred candidate for the chancellery during all of the 1998 campaign.[74]

The results of the present survey also support the finding that Gerhard Schröder enjoyed a clear advantage over Kohl. About half of the respondents in the east and the west prefer Schröder as Chancellor, whereas Kohl is preferred only by about one-third of the respondents and fares slightly worse in the east than in the west (Table 9). Since unemployment is considered to be the most important problem in the east and the west, the candidate's perceived economic competence is particularly important. On a rating scale from −2 ('does not apply at all') to +2 ('applies fully') the respondents could indicate to what extent they consider each of the two candidates to have 'reasonable ideas' on 'how to stimulate the economy'. In both parts of Germany, Schröder is rated as more competent than Kohl (see Table 10). Furthermore, Gerhard Schröder is perceived to be by far a more likeable and energetic person than Helmut Kohl. East and west Germans, however, differ in their evaluation of Helmut Kohl's political trustworthiness. East Germans have less confidence in him than west Germans, and, more importantly, less than in Schröder. This assessment may be a consequence of the promises Helmut Kohl could not keep with respect to the economic and social effects of German unification on the individual citizen. According to these results, Kohl's candidacy diminished the electoral prospects of the CDU, particularly in the east.

GENERAL MODEL

Up to this point, various factors affecting voting intention were analysed bivariately. In order to assess the relative importance of each factor, it is necessary to estimate the impact of all factors simultaneously in a

TABLE 10

ASSESSMENT OF THE CANDIDATE'S CAPACITIES (MEDIAN)

		Kohl	Schröder
Reasonable ideas to	*East:*	0.09	0.57
stimulate the economy	*West:*	0.14	0.54
Likeable	*East:*	0.23	0.62
	West:	0.17	0.56
Politically trustworthy	*East:*	0.26	0.43
	West:	0.53	0.43
Energetic	*East:*	0.50	0.95
	West:	0.51	0.92

Notes: scale ranges from -2 (does not at all apply) to 2 (applies fully)
Cases: East: approx. 1,085; West: approx. 2,196

Source: National Election Study 1998

multivariate analysis. In the bivariate analysis, the CDU/CSU, the SPD and the PDS were examined separately. Since we are mainly interested in explaining the defeat of the CDU (and, consequently, of the governing coalition) in what follows, we distinguish only between the government and the opposition. The following variables serve as predictors: religion, class membership, representation of interests by the unions, ideological position, satisfaction with government performance, and competence to solve the problem of unemployment. 'Satisfaction with government performance' measures the general evaluation of the competence of the CDU/CSU–FDP coalition. The perception of unemployment as the most important problem only influences the voting intention if the various parties are judged to differ with respect to their problem-solving capabilities. In order to explain the election result for the *governing coalition* it is important whether an *opposition party* is judged competent to do away with unemployment. Therefore, the variable is coded as '1' when unemployment is considered the most important issue and an opposition party was thought competent of solving it. In all other cases the variable takes the value of '0' (see Table 11 concerning the encoding of the other variables).[75]

The results of logistic regression models[76] are presented in Table 11. The independent variables used in the analysis reduce the errors in predicting the voting intention in both regions by approximately 60 per cent (Pseudo-R^2), and the model fits the data extraordinarily well.[77] Neither class membership nor union affiliation prove to be significant in the east.[78] However, this also holds true for class membership in the west. An east/west comparison can be conducted on the basis of the logit coefficients, b, or the effect coefficients, exp (b).[79] These coefficients show that both short-term factors in the model, 'preferred candidate for the chancellery' and 'unemployment',

TABLE 11

THE EFFECT OF SOCIAL, IDEOLOGICAL AND SHORT-TERM FACTORS
ON CASTING A VOTE FOR THE GOVERNMENT OR OPPOSITION
(LOGISTIC REGRESSIONS)

	East			West		
	b	exp(b)	exp(b s)	b	exp(b)	exp(b s)
Class[1]	-.312	.732	.871	-.336	.715	.870
		[1.366]	[1.148]		[1.399]	[1.143]
Unions[2]	-.212	.809	.802	-.308**	.735	.707
		[1.236]	[1.247]		[1.361]	[1.415]
Denom./relig.[3]	-.836**	.434	.680	-.440*	.644	.806
		[2.304]	[1.470]		[1.553]	[1.240]
Left–right[4]	.271**	1.312	1.696	.312**	1.367	1.884
Government performance[5]	-.330**	.719	.396	-.333**	.717	.377
		[1.390]	[2.522]		[1.395]	[2.650]
Unemployment[6]	-2.014**	.134	.371	-1.479**	.228	.493
		[7.462]	[2.698]		[4.386]	[2.028]
Preferred Chancellor[7]	-3.300**	.037	.234	-2.854**	.058	.262
		[27.027]	[4.281]		[17.241]	[3.813]
Intercept	2.983			2.412		
$-2LL_0$	838.921			1,971.957		
$-2LL_1$	304.223			785.779		
Pseudo-R^2	.637			.607		
(Cases)	(702)			(1,493)		

Notes: ** $p<0.01$, * $p<0.05$; b: logit-coefficient, s: standard deviation
vote: 0: opposition, 1: government (CDU/CSU and FDP)

1 0: other, 1: "working class I" (see definition above)
2 scale from -2 ('oppose own interests') to +2 ('represent own interests')
3 East: 0: catholic/protestant, 1: no religion; West: 0: catholic, 1: protestant/other/no religion
4 scale from 1 ('left') to 11 ('right')
5 scale from 1 ('satisfied') to 11 ('dissatisfied')
6 0: other, 1: unemployment is most important problem and opposition party has competence
7 0: Kohl, 1: Schröder/other

Source: National Election Study 1998

affect the voting intention in the east more strongly than in the west. If unemployment is considered the most important problem, and the competence to solve the problem is attributed to an opposition party, the estimated odds (see Table 11, columns exp(b)) of casting a vote in favour of a governing party multiply by 0.134 in the east and 0.228 in the west; that is, they decrease strongly. Even more striking is the effect of the 'preferred candidate for the chancellery'. If a candidate other than Helmut Kohl is preferred for the office of Chancellor, the odds of voting for one of the governing parties are only 0.037 times in the east and 0.058 times in the west what they are if Kohl is preferred. This is a very strong effect. Obviously, Kohl's decision to run for the office of Chancellor again contributed a great deal to the downfall of his party, especially in the east. The standardised effect coefficient, exp(b s), indicates which factors have the greatest effect on the voting intention.[80] In the eastern states of Germany, the preference for the future Chancellor exerts the greatest influence on the voting intention, followed by the opposition's competence to solve the problem of unemployment and the voters' satisfaction with government performance. In the western states of Germany, the preference as to the future Chancellor represents also the most important predictor of voting intentions, followed by the assessment of government performance and, ranking third, competence to solve the problem of unemployment.

If the analysis (excluding 'class membership' as predictor) is conducted only for east German 'working persons type I', which includes blue-collar workers, the findings are quite telling as to what was motivating this group's voting behaviour (due to the small number of respondents, n=190, though, this result has to be interpreted with caution). The candidates for chancellery, and the attribution of problem-solving competence with regard to unemployment, seem to have an even stronger effect on the voting intention of this group than on east Germans in general.

CONCLUSIONS

In the 1998 election, the east German vote was again characterised by a particularly high degree of volatility – mainly to the disadvantage of the CDU. In the east, the Christian Democrats lost a considerably higher percentage of votes than in the west. This study, therefore, first of all tried to clarify what the major determinants of the CDU's defeat were, especially in the east. In view of the high volatility, the study secondly examined whether short-term factors affecting voting behaviour played a more important explanatory role in the east than in the west.

Gerhard Schröder's advantage over Helmut Kohl as the preferred candidate for Chancellor was outstanding in both parts of the country, and, furthermore, this factor exerted a strong influence on voting intention. The negative effect of Kohl's candidacy was clearly stronger in the east than in the west. In view of these results, one may tend to attribute the high losses of the Christian Democrats in the main to the renewed candidacy of Helmut Kohl. However, such a far-reaching interpretation is not warranted by the presented data.[81] East and west Germans considered the SPD more capable than the CDU to solve the problem of unemployment, which was the major issue in the 1998 election. As expected, this assessment of competence had a stronger effect on voting behaviour in the east than in the west. In addition, the CDU's starting position in the east, in general, is worse than that of the SPD as the east German voters on average position themselves rather to the 'left' of the ideological centre, and a high percentage do not belong to any religious community. The CDU's defeat in the east was partially due to the vote of the blue-collar workers. For the first time, their vote was above average for the SPD rather than for the CDU as it had been in previous elections. For the future electoral prospects of the SPD and the CDU it will be decisive whether this change in voting behaviour is of a permanent nature or just a passing phenomenon. As the findings (with respect to union affiliation, ideological position and the importance of short-term factors for voting behaviour) indicate, it cannot yet be concluded that the present parallels point to a permanent adaptation to west German patterns of class-specific voting behaviour in the east.[82] In comparison to the short-term factors, socio-structural determinants exerted only a surprisingly minor influence on the results of the election in both parts of Germany.[83] However, short-term factors seem to be more important in the east than in the west. In the future, therefore, east German voting behaviour can be expected to be as volatile as in previous elections.

NOTES

I should like to thank Annette Schmitt, Kai Arzheimer, Ulrich Teusch and Jürgen R. Winkler for their invaluable comments and Jürgen W. Falter for making the data sets available to me.

1. The CDU/CSU–FDP coalition won the 1994 election only 0.3 percentage points ahead of the SPD, the PDS and the Greens. The CDU/CSU, though, benefited from the rule according to which a party receives all the seats won directly in the constituencies of a state even if the number of directly won seats exceeds the number of seats it deserves proportionally (*'Überhangmandateregelung'* – surplus mandates). In 1998, the SPD profited from this rule. On the results of both elections, cf. K. Gaspers, 'Endgültiges Ergebnis der Wahl zum 13. Deutschen Bundestag am 16. Oktober', *Wirtschaft und Statistik*, 11 (1994), pp.879–87; and K. Gaspers and H.-C. Herbertz, 'Endgültiges Ergebnis der Wahl zum 14. Deutschen Bundestag am 27. September 1998', *Wirtschaft und Statistik*, 10 (1998), pp.803–12.
2. Unfortunately, due to a lack of pertinent data it is impossible to examine the parties of the extreme right (see below).
3. A party enters Bundestag if it gains more than five per cent of the valid second votes or if its candidates win at least three constituencies directly. A candidate enters parliament directly, if s/he receives the majority of the valid first votes in a constituency (so-called 'basic mandate clause'/*'Grundmandateklausel'*). In 1994 the PDS won four direct mandates in (four constituencies of) East Berlin and thus, as a result of the basic mandate rule, sent as many representatives to parliament as it deserved in proportion to its total share of second votes (4.4 per cent).
4. After the state elections of 27 September 1998 in Mecklenburg-West Pomerania, the local PDS formed a governing coalition with the Social Democrats.
5. See the survey of R.J. Dalton and M. Wattenberg, 'The Not so Simple Act of Voting', in A. Finifter (ed.), *Political Science: The State of Discipline II* (Washington, DC: APSA, 1993), pp.193–218.
6. S.M. Lipset and S. Rokkan, *Party Systems and Voter Alignments* (New York: Free Press, 1967).

7. A. Campbell *et al.*, *The American Voter* (unabridged edition, Midway Reprint, Chicago, IL: Chicago University Press, 1980, first published 1960).
8. T. von Winter, 'Wählerverhalten in den östlichen Bundesländern: Wahlsoziologische Erklärungsmodelle auf dem Prüfstand', *Zeitschrift für Parlamentsfragen*, 2 (1996), pp.298–316.
9. J.W. Falter, University of Mainz, O.W. Gabriel, University of Stuttgart, and H. Rattinger, University of Bamberg, conducted the primary research work. The data sets are to be made available to the public by the Central Archive for Empirical Social Research, ZA, in Cologne. The author is, of course, responsible for the analysis and the interpretation of the data.
10. The few respondents who were not entitled to vote were excluded from the analysis.
11. The pre-election survey contains 527 respondents from east Germany and 1,106 respondents from west Germany; the post-election survey contains 580 east Germans and 1,124 west Germans (including respondents less than 18 years old).
12. In the pre-election survey, respondents were asked how likely they were to participate in the up-coming election. Their replies could have served to construct the category of 'non-voters'. This question was not taken into account (for example, by constructing a non-voter category), though, because not all of the categories could be unambiguously interpreted.
13. M.N. Pedersen, 'Changing Patterns of Electoral Volatility in European Party Systems, 1948–1977: Explorations in Explanation', in H. Daalder and P. Mair (eds.), *Western European Party Systems* (London: Sage, 1983), pp.32–4.
14. The difference would be even more pronounced if the non-voters were taken into account in the calculation of the index since voter turnout in the east fluctuated more strongly than in the west. For the respective 1994 and 1998 data, see K. Arzheimer and J.W. Falter, 'Annäherung durch Wandel? Das Wahlverhalten bei der Bundestagswahl 1998 in Ost-West-Perspektive', *Aus Politik und Zeitgeschichte*, B52 (1998), pp.33–43.
15. M. Kaase, *Wechsel von Parteipräferenzen. Eine Analyse der Bundestagswahl 1961* (Meisenheim: Anton Hain, 1967); and C. Zelle, *Der Wechselwähler. Politische und soziale Erklärungsansätze des Wählerwandels in Deutschland und den USA* (Opladen: Westdeutscher Verlag, 1995).
16. On the relation between aggregate volatility and individual voting shifts, see S. Bartolini and P. Mair, *Identity, Competition, and Electoral Availability* (Cambridge: Cambridge University Press, 1990), pp.27–34.
17. In the following I will always use the term 'voting intention' although the variable also include the retrospective voting decisions as explained above.
18. Zelle, *Der Wechselwähler*, p.127.
19. Rates of voters who remained loyal to the same party in subsequent general elections between 1969 and 1990, see Zelle, *Der Wechselwähler*, p.129.
20. Campbell *et al.*, *American Voter*, pp.133ff.
21. I. Crewe, 'Introduction: Electoral Change in Western Democracies: A Framework for Analysis', in I. Crewe and D. Denver (eds.), *Electoral Change in Western Democracies* (New York: St. Martin's Press, 1985), p.14.
22. T. Emmert and D. Roth, 'Zur wahlsoziologischen Bedeutung eines Modells sozialstrukturell verankerter Konfliktlinien im vereinten Deutschland', *Historische Sozialforschung*, 20, 2 (1995), pp.137, 156.
23. The methodological criticism of the model and the question of whether the concept is useful in the west German context are here not taken into consideration. On the first issue, see H.B. Asher, 'Voting Behavior Research in the 1980s: An Examination of Some Old and New Problem Areas', in A. Finifter (ed.), *Political Science: The State of the Discipline* (Washington, DC: APSA, 1983), pp.339–88; on the second issue, see Winter, 'Wählerverhalten', pp.306–7.
24. Campbell *et al.*, *American Voter*, p.121.
25. Ibid., pp.128–36.
26. C. Bluck and H. Kreikenbom, 'Quasiparteibindung und Issues', in O.W. Gabriel and K.G. Troitzsch (eds.), *Wahlen in Zeiten des Umbruchs* (Frankfurt am Main: Peter Lang, 1993), pp.455–70.

27. See, for example, H. Rattinger, 'Parteiidentifikationen in Ost- und Westdeutschland nach der Vereinigung', in O. Niedermayer and K. von Beyme (eds.), *Politische Kultur in Ost- und Westdeutschland* (Berlin: Akademie Verlag, 1994), pp.77–104; and H. Rattinger, 'Parteineigungen in Ostdeutschland vor und nach der Wende', in H. Bertram (ed.), *Ostdeutschland im Wandel. Lebensverhältnisse – politische Einstellungen* (Opladen: Leske & Budrich, 1995), pp.231–53.
28. Arzheimer and Falter, 'Annäherung durch Wandel', p.41; U.W. Gehring and J.R. Winkler, 'Parteiidentifikation, Kandidaten- und Issueorientierungen als Determinanten des Wahlverhaltens in Ost- und Westdeutschland', in O.W. Gabriel (ed.), *Politische Orientierungen und Verhaltensweisen im vereinigten Deutschland* (Opladen: Leske & Budrich, 1997), p.484.
29 J.P. Haisken-De New and J.R. Frick, *DTC. Desktop Companion to the German Socio-Economic Panel Study (GSOEP). Version 2.2 – September 1998* (Berlin: German Institute for Economic Research (DIW), 1998).
30. The question-wording is 'Viele Leute neigen in der Bundesrepublik längere Zeit einer bestimmten Partei zu, obwohl Sie auch ab und zu eine andere Partei wählen. Wie ist das bei Ihnen: Neigen Sie – ganz allgemein gesprochen – einer bestimmten Partei zu? Wenn ja, welcher?'.
31. 1992: 36 per cent; 1993: 33 per cent; 1994: 35 per cent; 1995: 41 per cent; 1996: 37 per cent; 1997: 35 per cent (weighted).
32. On the basis of data provided by the *Politbarometer*, Gehring and Winkler, 'Parteiidentifikation', p.481, observed that the number of east Germans identifying with a party varies between almost 45 per cent (November 1993) and more than 60 per cent (March 1991). And these rates are actually lower than those reported by Rattinger, 'Parteiidentifikationen', p.83, on the basis of electoral surveys.
33. It must be added that the proportion of west German 'party identifiers' as recorded by the Socio-Economic Panel is also lower than in other surveys.
34. Gehring and Winkler, 'Parteiidentifikation', pp.480–82; and Hans Rattinger, 'Partei-identifikationen', p.83.
35. S.M. Lipset and S. Rokkan, 'Cleavage Structures, Party Systems, and Voter Alignments: An Introduction', in S.M. Lipset and S. Rokkan (ed.), *Party Systems and Voter Alignments* (New York: Free Press, 1967), pp.1–64.
36. O. Knutsen and E. Scarbrough, 'Cleavage Politics', in J.W. Van Deth and E. Scarbrough (eds.), *The Impact of Values* (Oxford: Oxford University Press 1995), p.494.
37. Compared with other European states, Lipset and Rokkan consider the cleavage structures of France and Germany – due to the party system changes – as rather unstable.
38. J.W. Falter, 'Kontinuität und Neubeginn. Die Bundestagswahl 1949 zwischen Weimar und Bonn', *Politische Vierteljahresschrift*, 22, 2 (1981), pp.236–63.
39. The CDU opened up to attract members of all denominations, and at the 1959 Godesberg party convention the SPD decided to transform from a socialist into a social-democratic party.
40. W. Müller, 'Sozialstruktur und Wahlverhalten. Eine Widerrede gegen die Individualisie-rungsthese', *Kölner Zeitschrift für Soziologie und Sozialpsychologie*, 49, 4 (1997), pp.747–60.
41. Due to the large percentage of blue-collar workers in the GDR and the political tradition of the Weimar Republic the SPD was predicted to win the election.
42. H. Solga, *Auf dem Weg in eine klassenlose Gesellschaft? Klassenlagen und Mobilität zwischen Generationen in der DDR* (Berlin: Akademie Verlag, 1995), p.209.
43. R.J. Dalton and W. Bürklin, 'The Two German Electorates: The Social Bases of the Vote', *German Politics and Society*, 13, 1 (1995), p.90.
44. About 43 per cent in the east and 37 per cent in the west of all employed persons are blue-collar workers. See G.A. Ritter and M. Niehuss, *Wahlen in Deutschland 1990–1994* (München: Beck, 1995), p.16.
45. The term 'class' is used in a purely descriptive sense unless otherwise stated.
46. M. Jung and D. Roth, 'Kohls knappster Sieg. Eine Analyse der Bundestagswahl 1994', *Aus Politik und Zeitgeschichte*, B51–2 (1994), p.11; K. Schmitt, 'Sozialstruktur und Wählerverhalten', in O.W. Gabriel (ed.), *Politische Orientierungen und Verhaltensweisen im vereinigten Deutschland* (Opladen: Leske & Budrich, 1997), p.436.

47. B. Weßels, 'Gruppenbindung und rationale Faktoren als Determinanten der Wahlent-scheidung in Ost- und Westdeutschland', in H.-D. Klingemann and M. Kaase (eds.), *Wahlen und Wähler. Analysen aus Anlaß der Bundestagswahl 1990* (Opladen: Westdeutscher Verlag, 1994), p.155.
48. Schmitt, 'Sozialstruktur', p.443.
49. Weßels, 'Gruppenbindung', pp.137 and 141; Schmitt, 'Sozialstruktur', pp.442–3.
50. Due to the small number of relevant respondents the results for east German employees in leading positions ('working persons II') cannot be interpreted.
51. Ritter and Niehuss, *Wahlen*, p.14.
52. G. Braun, 'Daten zur demographischen und sozialen Struktur der Bevölkerung', in Martin Broszat and H. Weber (eds.), *SBZ-Handbuch* (Munich: Oldenbourg, 1993), p.1072.
53. Schmitt, 'Sozialstruktur', p.438.
54. W.G. Gibowski, 'Election Trends in Germany: An Analysis of the Second General Election in Reunited Germany', *German Politics*, 4, 2 (1995), p.44.
55. Weßels, 'Gruppenbindung', p.150, and Emmert and Roth, 'Zur wahlsoziologischen Bedeutung', p.137.
56. Dalton and Bürklin, 'The Two German Electorates', pp.88ff.
57. Schmitt, 'Sozialstruktur', p.438; and Dalton and Bürklin, 'German Electorates', p.91.
58. Due to the small number of east German Catholics in the data set (n=34) the results were not explicitly presented.
59. On the contents and meaning of the terms 'left' and 'right', see H.-D. Klingemann and D. Fuchs, 'The Left–Right Schema', in M.K. Jennings et al., *Continuities in Political Action* (Berlin/New York: Walter de Gruyter, 1989), pp.203–34.
60. F.U. Pappi and G. Eckstein, 'Die Parteipräferenzen und Koalitionsneigungen der west- und ostdeutschen Wählerschaft, *Kölner Zeitschrift für Soziologie und Sozialpsychologie*, 48, 4. (1996), p.656.
61. See the self-assessment of east and west Germans in E. Roller, 'Positions- und performanzbasierte Sachfragenorientierungen und Wahlentscheidung: Eine theoretische und empirische Analyse aus Anlaß der Bundestagswahl 1994', in M. Kaase and H.-D. Klingemann (eds.), *Wahlen und Wähler. Analysen aus Anlaß der Bundestagswahl 1994* (Opladen: Westdeutscher Verlag 1998), p.195.
62. Solga, *Klassenlose Gesellschaft?*, p.68.
63. Ibid., pp.215–19.
64. M. Klein and C. Caballero, 'Rückwärtsgewandt in die Zukunft. Die Wähler der PDS bei der Bundestagswahl 1994', *Politische Vierteljahresschrift*, 37, 2 (1996), pp.241, 245.
65. Even though the left–right scale is applied, we do not assume that the party system can be reduced to this one dimension.
66. See also Roller, 'Sachfragenorientierungen', p.195, and K. Arzheimer and M. Klein, 'Die Wähler der REP und der PDS in West- und Ostdeutschland. Ein empirischer Vergleich', in U. Backes and E. Jesse (eds.), *Jahrbuch für Extremismus und Demokratie* (Bonn: Bouvier, 1997), p.45.
67. A. Downs, *An Economic Theory of Democracy* (New York: HarperCollins, 1957), pp.114–41.
68. Due to the small number of east Germans (n=37) who positioned themselves at points 9 to 11 on the left–right scale this result must be interpreted with much caution.
69. Campbell et al., *American Voter*, p.170.
70. On the election year 1994, see Gibowski, 'Election Trends', pp.28–9.
71. Roller, 'Sachfragenorientierungen', for a detailed analysis of issue orientations.
72. See the analyses of M. Jung and D. Roth, 'Wer zu spät geht, den bestraft der Wähler', *Aus Politik und Zeitgeschichte*, B52 (1998), pp.3–18; O.W. Gabriel and F. Brettschneider, 'Die Bundestagswahl 1998: Ein Plebiszit gegen Kanzler Kohl?', *Aus Politik und Zeitgeschichte*, B52 (1998), pp.20–32.
73. Gehring and Winkler, 'Parteiidentifikation', p.487; and Gibowski, 'Election Trends', p.34.
74. Jung and Roth, 'Wer zu spät geht', p.10.
75. The categorical independent variables are dummy encoded, whereas the 11-stage scales are retained in their original form (that is, interval scale level was assumed).
76. A. Agresti, *An Introduction to Categorical Data Analysis* (New York: John Wiley, 1996), pp.103–35.

77. 96 per cent of the east German respondents and 93 per cent of the west German respondents with intention to vote for an opposition party were correctly classified as well as 82 per cent of the east German respondents and 85 per cent of the west German respondents with intention to vote for a government party.

78. The significance was calculated on the basis of the Wald Statistic, see Agresti, *Categorical Data Analysis*, p.109.

79. To compare effect coefficients lower than one with effect coefficients greater than one, the reciprocal value is given in parentheses in Table 11.

80. The standardised effect coefficients can only be used for comparisons within the model (that is, not for east–west comparisons) since their size depends on the standard deviation.

81. In addition (as in all empirical analyses) the results have to be evaluated relative to the model. Thus it cannot be excluded that the 'candidate effect' measures a factor which is not included in the model. The same applies to the other independent variables.

82. See also Arzheimer and Falter, 'Annäherung durch Angleichung', p.43.

83. Weßels, 'Gruppenbindung', pp.150–52.

Parties, Leaders and Issues in the News

HOLLI A. SEMETKO AND KLAUS SCHOENBACH

The news media are nowadays at the centre of the electioneering process in modern democracies. Politicians gear their daily campaign activities around the deadlines of television news, and most people experience the campaign through television. In Germany, television continues to be the medium able to reach the largest portion of the population.[1] In 1995, 83 per cent of Germans were exposed to television each day, 75 per cent to radio, and 65 per cent to newspapers. In Germany overall 60 per cent were reached by political content on television, compared with 57 per cent for radio, and 46 per cent for newspapers, and the figures for east Germans' exposure to political content on television were considerably higher (75 per cent) than west Germans' (65 per cent).

In this article, we focus on how the 1998 German campaign was presented in television news. There are two macro-level aspects of the national media system which may have an important bearing on the way in which the election was presented in the news. The first concerns the balance between public and commercial (private) broadcasting. How dominant is public service broadcasting in Germany in comparison with private outlets? The second concerns the rules and traditions surrounding party access to broadcasting. How have these forms of access developed? We address these questions briefly before turning to our content analysis of the 1998 campaign.

GERMAN MEDIA SYSTEM CHARACTERISTICS

The balance between public and commercial broadcasting has changed in Germany, as in most European countries, over the past decade.[2] In the late 1970s and up into the mid-1980s, we could still speak of a broadcasting system that was entirely public service in the west. West Germany's public broadcasting system was financed by a mixture of licence fees and advertising revenue. In the west, private channels were introduced in the mid-1980s financed entirely by advertising. As audiences shifted from public to private channels, advertisers put more revenue into the private

Holli A. Semetko and Klaus Schoenbach, University of Amsterdam channels and the competition between the public and private channels intensified.

The form of financing broadcasting systems has important implications for the range and quality of political programming on offer.[3] On a continuum ranging from entirely state-owned at one end to entirely market-driven on the other, the US is perhaps the best known example of a market-driven system, with many European countries having moved recently from entirely state-owned to the centre of the continuum. The more public service-dominant the system, the more likely it is that prime-time television will include a broad range of political news and current affairs programming; the more commercially driven the system, the more market pressure for ratings and hence the more reluctant prime-time television will be to replace popular entertainment programming for political information programming.[4] This predisposition for more or less political programming, stemming from the balance of public service versus commercial in the broadcasting systems, is also likely to be reflected in the amount of election-related programming during campaigns

Although in Germany there was an initial concern that the launch of private television in the mid-1980s would have a negative impact on news by bringing in American-style reporting, in fact that did not happen. The news on the private channels initially tried to be more entertaining and sensational but soon resembled the German public channels far more than originally anticipated.[5]

The rules, traditions and practices surrounding party access to broadcasting during election campaigns have also changed as the broadcasting system changed. An important, related, characteristic is the political autonomy of broadcasting from government and political parties. As competition and the number of channels increased, in Germany and elsewhere, there was also a diversification of income sources and a corresponding lessening of control by political authorities. The more commercial the broadcasting system, the less opportunity for government or political parties to exert direct influence over broadcasting organisations. Public service channels in Germany are subject to oversight by mostly state-level boards comprised of socially relevant groups including representatives of the political parties in each state parliament. The German private channels are licensed and oversight is dealt with by independent commissions, with responsibilities similar to that of, for example, the Independent Television Commission in Britain. German public broadcasters' concerns over possible repercussions in the broadcast councils could have consequences for the quantity and quality of election-related programming.

One crucial difference between the German public and private channels is in the ways in which journalists advance in their careers. In the public channels, career advancement is related to a concept of political 'sympathy' that requires journalists to affiliate with one or another of the two main parties.[6] Major positions in the newsroom are occupied by senior news executives who are not only exceptionally well qualified professionally, but also appropriately qualified politically.[7]

Political parties can nowadays purchase advertising time on private television, whereas that was previously forbidden, and they continue to receive an allocation of free time for advertising on the public channels. Political programmes on the public channels are also expected to be balanced over the course of the campaign with respect to the visibility of political parties. Popular assumption, however, has it that ARD and RTL are more sympathetic to the SPD and ZDF and SAT1 to the CDU/CSU/FDP.

Political debates among the top candidates featured as key events from the 1972 to 1987 election campaigns. These were valuable and unique opportunites for parties to reach voters. Baker, Norpoth and Schoenbach, in comparing the 1972 and 1976 debates, found that politicians who displayed a more positive style of debate were more likely to be perceived as the 'winner' of that debate.[8] Baker and Norpoth's study of the 1972 debate found that electors did learn more about the candidates and parties from this event, and that this had a particular impact on evaluations of the opposition party.[9] Schrott's analysis of the electoral impact of the 1972, 1976, 1980 and 1983 debates suggested that debates do make an important difference to electoral outcomes.[10] Controlling for party identification and other factors, citizens were significantly more likely to vote for the candidate they believed had won the debate. Thus, winning debates not only improved the candidates' images, but also their chances of getting elected. Because the German debates were usually held only a few days prior to the election, their short-term effects may have further enhanced their importance to the voting decision. Perhaps concerned about the possible negative impact of debates, incumbent Chancellor Helmut Kohl refused to participate in any after 1987. There were thus no Chancellor debates in the 1990, 1994 or 1998 Bundestag election campaigns.

Our study of the December 1990 Bundestag election campaign in newly reunited Germany drew on a content analysis of 15 high-circulation newspapers across the country and main evening television news programmes on public service and leading private channels, as well as a representative panel survey of voters in the western part of the country during the 'hot phase' of the campaign – the final eight weeks when the parties' campaigning activities were in full swing.[11] Two key findings are important here. One concerns the effects of the campaign: significant changes in public opinion about the incumbent coalition were a consequence of the visibility of politicians in the news. Another concerns the content of the news: there was a significant difference between the Chancellor candidates, and between the government and opposition parties, in terms of their visibility in the news. The visibility bonus of the incumbent coalition in television news showed that the main opposition party could not expect the same amount of time or space in the news, whereas in other democracies the broadcast news media made special efforts to provide equal or balanced coverage of the leading parties and candidates at election time. There was no equal opportunity for the opposition parties to communicate to voters via the main evening news, and this was buttressed by a low level of attention paid to the 1990 campaign in the press. The imbalance between the government and opposition parties in the news was not due to biased or evaluative remarks by television reporters, however, for these comments were almost always neutral or simply descriptive. We concluded that this was not a problem of ideology or partisanship among news programmes or a reflection of the personal political preferences of television news executives. The visibility bonus existed on all television news channels, so, if the parties of government were to change, it was potentially just as likely that such an advantage would begin for the new parties in power. We argued that in the 1990 election it was television news reporters' professionalism, in reporting largely without evaluations and in selecting only those stories that satisfied certain news value criteria, that made mere visibility a bonus in 1990. A scandal or a running negative news story could have meant that the visibility bonus had negative consequences for perceptions of the parties in power, but there were none in 1990.

How visible was the 1998 election campaign and its issues in the news? How were the candidates and the parties reported? We content-analysed the main evening news programmes on ARD, ZDF, RTL and SAT1 which were broadcast between the hours of 6.30pm and 8.15pm each evening and are the German equivalents of US network evening news or Britain's ITN News at 6.30pm. We also content-analysed the first two pages of the largest circulation newspaper in the country, the *Bild*. The newspaper customarily deals with the most important political information on those pages, and devotes the third page to local news. The content analysis focused on the 'hot phase' of the campaign for the seven weeks before election day, from 10 August to election day, 27 September 1998. All stories that mentioned German parties or politicians were selected for coding. This resulted in a total of 524 television news stories, and 384 newspaper stories. Coding was conducted by a team of three trained graduate students. The intercoder reliability ranged from 0.92 to 0.96.

We focus on the main evening news programmes because these have the highest audience ratings, these audiences are more representative of the public at large demographically and in terms of political interest, and they are a common basis for cross-national comparison. Audiences for the later evening current affairs news programmes each evening on ARD and ZDF, such as *Tagesthemen* or *Heute Journal* (Germany's *Newsnight* equivalents), are quite different, in terms of size and demographic characteristics, and are more politically interested.

AN EXCITING ELECTION

An astute follower of German politics will not be able to recall an election in recent years that received more attention in the news than this one. The campaign itself was mentioned much more often in the news than the historic 1990 election, which was the first national election after reunification, when the vast majority of news stories about politics in the final six weeks before election day simply ignored the election campaign.[12]

One reason the campaign preceding the December 1990 election was barely visible in the news was that the result was largely a foregone conclusion. At the start of the 'hot phase', some six weeks before election day, more than 80 per cent of the population believed the incumbent coalition would return to power. Another reason why the 1990 campaign was barely visible had to do with journalists' responses to the opposition Chancellor candidate, Oskar Lafontaine, whose public support had lagged well behind Helmut Kohl's since May 1990, when the SPD was split by Lafontaine's insistence that the party seek to prevent the passage of the unification treaty in the Bundesrat. According to one ZDF TV news producer who was interviewed during the 1990 campaign (not an SPD man himself), 'even SPD journalists were not willing to fight for Lafontaine', and so there was less coverage of the 1990 SPD campaign in the news. Other journalists who were more sympathetic to the SPD in 1990, however, suggested that the likelihood of Helmut Kohl's victory provided a 'chilling effect' that discouraged them from making a case to bring more coverage of the campaign or the SPD's campaigning activities into television news.[13] As a consequence, the coverage of the 1990 election campaign in the news was extremely limited, while the coverage of day-to-day activities of the government and the Chancellor continued as usual even in the final two weeks preceding the vote.

In 1998, it could not have been more different. First, it was a much more competitive election, with polls showing a change of government as the most likely outcome for many months leading up to election day. The victory of the SPD and its Minister President candidate Gerhard Schröder in the Lower Saxony elections in March 1998 signalled the beginning of an exciting and unusually long and interesting Bundestag election campaign. The official 'hot phase' began in August, six weeks before election day, and the Bundestag campaign heated up further in the last two weeks when the CSU won and the SPD lost by an unexpectedly large margin in the state elections in Bavaria. The 1998 Bundestag election was thus far more competitive, and hence far more interesting in terms of sheer news values. Gerhard Schröder was also an altogether different challenger than Oskar Lafontaine had been. Schröder kept the SPD united. At the same time, with his relative youth, vigour and telegeneic qualities, he stood in stark contrast to Kohl. As potential Chancellor, then, Schröder in 1998 also ranked high in news value terms.

CAMPAIGN VISIBILITY

The 1998 Bundestag election campaign was actually mentioned in quite a considerable number of the political stories on television news in the final weeks before the vote: 53 per cent. There was considerable variation among channels, though, and the private channels mentioned the campaign far more often than the public channels. A full 71 per cent of political stories on RTL mentioned the election campaign, compared with 58 per cent on SAT1, 47 per cent on ZDF, and 40 per cent on ARD. Campaign-related stories were also, on average, longer than those that were not campaign-related. The average length of a story that mentioned the election campaign was 96 seconds on RTL, 147 seconds on SAT1, 116 seconds on RTL and 107 seconds on ARD, whereas the average length of a story that did not mention the campaign was 77 seconds on RTL, 88 seconds on SAT1, 70 on ZDF, and 67 on ARD.

In the *Bild*, a full 38 per cent of political stories on the first two pages mentioned the election campaign. A look at the headlines in the *Bild* and on television news shows how the emphasis was on the opinion polls, the closeness of the race, and the possible coalition outcomes. Table 1 gives the front page headlines in the *Bild*, a newspaper that traditionally supported the incumbent coalition and in particular the CDU and Helmut Kohl, in the final couple of weeks along with election headlines from ZDF and RTL main evening news.

The election-related headlines on ZDF and RTL were somewhat less sensational and evaluative than those in the *Bild*. The news on 14 September, for example, focused on the outcome of the Bavarian Landtag elections, in which the CSU, the Bavarian sister party of the CDU, performed better than expected and the SPD lost more votes than expected. As a result, this race was labelled in the *Bild* as one that provided momentum to the CDU/CSU's race across the country, making the national election campaign 'wide open', and the Bavarian CSU Minister President Stoiber was described as 'triumphant'. Television news headlines claimed

TABLE 1
BILD, ZDF AND RTL ELECTION-RELATED HEADLINES
14–27 SEPTEMBER 1998

14 September

BILD: Riesenschub für Kohl: Stoiber triumphiert in Bayern, SPD verliert, Bundestagswahl wieder offen
Major push for Kohl: Stoiber triumphant in Bavaria, SPD loses, Federal election campaign wide open

ZDF: Nachlese: Bonn am Tag nach der Landtagswahl in Bayern
Second harvest: Bonn one day after the State Parliamentary election in Bavaria

RTL: Endspurt in Bonn: Der CSU-Sieg in Bayern macht die Bundestagswahl jetzt richtig spannend
Final push in Bonn: The CSU victory in Bavaria makes the federal election really exciting

15 September

BILD: Arbeitslosen- und Sozialhilfe zusammenlegen? Pläne der CDU/CSU im Falle eines Wahlsieges
Combine unemployment payments and social benefits? The plans of the CDU/CSU if they win

RTL: Volldampf im Osten: Im Endspurt vor der Wahl kämpfen die Parteien um jede Stimme in den Neuen Landern
Full steam ahead in the East: in the final push before the election the parties fight for every vote in the new states

16 September

RTL: Wahlkampf pur: In Bonn eskaliert der Streit um eine Erhöhung der Mehrwertsteuer
Pure Campaigning: The row escalates over proposed increases to the value added tax

18 September

BILD: Wahl-Prügel: Der Kanzler, die SPD, die FDP: alle hauen auf Frau Nolte (die Ministerin, die den neuen Steuer-Streit auslöste)
Election Thrashing: The Chancellor, the SPD, the FDP: all beat up on Mrs. Nolte

ZDF: Politbarometer: Der Abstand zwischen Opposition und Regierung wird kleiner
Politbarometer: the gap between the opposition and government is narrowing

19 September

BILD: Wahl: Es wird gaaaanz knapp
8 Tage bis zur Wahl: der Abstand schrumpft nach Angaben von Meinungsforschungs-instituten
Election: It will be reeeeaaaaaallllly close
8 days before the election: the distance shrinks according to public opinion research institutes

21 September

BILD: 6 Tage bis zur Wahl: dimap-Prognose, Doppelte Staatsbürgerschaft, Grüner fordert neue Nationalhymne, Kohl gegen große Koalition, Stollmann läßt sich von L. Späth beraten, Lafontaine will bei illegaler Beschäftigung hart durchgreifen
6 days before the election: dimap's (one institute's) forecast, Dual citizenship, Greens want a new national anthem, Kohl against grand coalition, Stollmann advised by Lothar Spaeth (SPD shadow cabinet minister for economics advised by former CDU Minister President of Baden-Württemburg), Lafontaine wants to take strong measures against illegal employment

TABLE 1 (Continued)

ZDF: Wahlkampf: Im Endspurt setzen Regierung und Opposition auf die Zweitstimme
Election Campaign: government and opposition's final push for the second ballot vote

RTL: Solidarität aus Bonn: Mit Abscheu und Empörung reagieren deutsche Politiker auf die Veröffentlichung des Clinton-Videos
Solidarity from Bonn: German politicians react to the publication of the Clinton video with disgust and indignation

22 September

ZDF: ZDF-Interview: Herausforderer Schröder im Wahlkampfendspurt
ZDF Interview: Challenger Schröder's final push in the election race

23 September

ZDF: ZDF-Interview: Bundeskanzler Kohl zur Frage einer möglichen großen Koalition
ZDF Interview: Chancellor Kohl addresses the question of a possible grand coalition

RTL: Hochspannung vor der Wahl: Kohl schließt eine große Koalition nicht mehr kategorisch aus
High voltage before the election: Kohl does not categorically rule out a grand coalition

24 September

BILD: Kohl: 'Große Koalition prinzipiell möglich'
Kohl: 'Grand coalition possible in principle'

ZDF: Wahlkampfbilanz: Die Parteien mobilisieren ihre letzten Reserven
Election in the balance: Parties mobilize last reserves

RTL: Wahlkampfbilanz in Bonn: 3 Tage vor der Wahl sehen sich alle Parteien als Sieger
Summing up the election campaign: 3 days before the election each party considers itself the winner

25 September

BILD: 2 Tage bis zur Wahl: Wählertäuschung durch Lafontaine? Wirtschaftsprognose Kohls, FDP-Wahlkampf,
2 days before the election: Voters deceived by Lafontaine? Kohl's economic forecast, FDP campaign

ZDF: 2 Tage vor der Wahl: Haushaltsstreit im Bundesrat
Two days before the election: A row about the budget in the Second Chamber

RTL: Noch 48 Stunden bis zur Entscheidung: Kohl und sein Herausforderer treten ein letztes Mal vor die Wähler
With only 48 hours before the decision: Kohl and his challenger meet the voters for the last time

26 September

BILD: Jede Stimme zahlt, auch Ihre. Letzte Umfragen: Kopf-an-Kopf-Rennen
Every vote counts, yours too. Last polls: head-to-head race

ZDF: Wahlfieber: Wer hat morgen die Nase vorn?
Election fever: Who will win tomorrow?

RTL: Kopf-an-Kopf-Rennen: 1 Tag vor der Wahl wird der Abstand zwischen Union und SPD geringer
Head to Head: One day before the election the gap between the Union and the SPD narrows

that the Bavarian outcome made the federal election now 'really exciting'. But this apparent boost was short-lived. A controversial statement about value-added tax policy by CDU Minister Nolte caused a major embarassment to the governing coalition, and this very problematic story featured in all television news outlets and on page 1 of the *Bild* only ten days before the vote. From then on, many of the stories focused on the narrowing gap between the CDU and the SPD, and provided conflicting accounts of the election outcome possibilities. On 19 September, the day after the bad news about Minister Nolte, the front page of the *Bild* reminded voters that the election result would be '*gaaaanz knapp*' ('reaaaally close'). The front page on the 21st announced that Kohl was against a grand coalition, but only a few days later, on the 23rd, after Kohl's interview aired on ZDF, it said that Kohl thought a grand coalition was possible. On the day before the vote, the *Bild* urged voters to go to the polls and devoted its front page to the theme 'every vote counts'. Television news described the country as having 'election fever' and claimed the race was 'head-to-head'.

The election campaign made it into the headlines regularly despite the news value of other events in the world, not least the developments in the story of US President Clinton and former White House intern Monica Lewinsky. The Clinton–Lewinsky affair reached a high point in the news in the final weeks before election day, when the President testified on videotape before a grand jury, and this was subsequently leaked to the media. German electors, like most Europeans and Americans, were fed an almost daily dose of the Bill and Monica story in the seven weeks before election day. In fact, there were many days in August and September when this long-running story made the headlines and the election did not.

THE ELECTION AND VARIOUS THEMES IN THE NEWS

Each political news story was coded for up to six subjects or themes, in order of predominance. These give us an indication of the visibility of various issues in the news. It also shows the extent to which the election campaign was a focus in a story, which means that the story went beyond simply mentioning the campaign (as discussed above) to actually deal with the campaign in a major way. The election campaign in comparison with other themes in television news during the period under study is presented in Table 2.

Table 2 shows that the campaign itself, in other words the activities of the parties and the Chancellor candidates on the campaign trail, at evening rallies and at press conferences, accounted for the largest portion of political themes in the news on all the channels. The opinion polls were in a separate category. Overall, the campaign accounted for some 24 per cent of themes in television news and opinion polls some eight per cent. The economy was the most important substantive issue, accounting for 15 per cent of themes in television news, and the party manifestos and records accounted for 14 per cent of themes. These figures are displayed in the last column in Table 2. The economy was the single most important issue in the campaign on all channels, and on television this was followed by foreign affairs, and social welfare. Less attention was paid to other issues – education, law and order, the environment, infrastructure. These seven substantive issues together accounted for about half (45 per cent) of all themes in television news.

TABLE 2

THEMES IN POLITICAL TV NEWS STORIES 10 AUG.–27 SEPT. 1998
(% OF ALL THEMES)

	ARD	ZDF	RTL	SAT.1	Total
Political system	4	3	3	3	3
Campaign	17	21	28	30	24
Polls	1	5	18	9	8
Manifestos/platforms	13	14	15	16	14
Social welfare	13	8	6	5	8
Environment	3	3	1	3	3
Economy	17	19	13	12	15
Infrastructure	2	1	1	3	2
Law and order	4	3	2	3	3
Education	7	2		1	3
Foreign affairs	14	15	7	12	12
State profiles	1	2		1	1
Ex-DDR	3	1	2	1	2
Other	3	4	3	2	3
Number of themes	237	249	209	209	904
N (political stories)	154	145	111	114	524

Note: columns may not sum to 100 percent due to rounding

Source: K. Schoenbach and H.A. Semetko, Media Content Analysis of the 1998 German Bundestag Campaign

TABLE 3

THEMES IN FRONT-PAGE NEWS IN THE *BILD* 10 AUG.–27 SEPT. 19980
(% OF ALL THEMES)

Political system	7
Campaign	29
Polls	3
Manifestos/platforms	8
Social welfare	9
Environment	2
Economy	15
Infrastructure	2
Law and order	5
Education	6
Foreign affairs	8
State profiles	2
Ex-DDR	2
Other	4
Number of themes	538
N (political stories)	384

Source: K. Schoenbach and H.A. Semetko, Media Content Analysis of the 1998 German Bundestag Campaign

There were important differences between the public and private channels in reporting the election. Taking together the key seven substantive issues – economy, social welfare, environment, infrastructure, law and order, education, foreign affairs – there was a clear difference in emphasis by the public and private channels. These substantive issues accounted for 59 per cent of themes on ARD and 50 per cent on ZDF, in comparison with 31 per cent on RTL and 38 per cent on SAT1. The editorial decisions taken at each channel thus had considerable influence over the presentation of the dynamics of the campaign and the issues. Campaign events were far more important on the private channels, with some 30 per cent of themes on SAT1, 28 per cent on RTL, 21 per cent on ZDF, and only 17 per cent on ARD. The private channels also chose to report the opinion polls more often. On RTL, for example, opinion polls accounted for 18 per cent of themes in the news, compared with less than half that on SAT1, under five per cent on ZDF and under one per cent on ARD.

In comparison with television, the *Bild* paid less attention to the manifestos and platforms of the political parties, and less attention to the polls, though rather more attention to the events on the campaign trail, as can be seen in Table 3. The rank order of the other substantive issues in this newspaper were economy, social welfare, foreign affairs, education, law and order, the environment, and infrastructure.

POLITICAL PARTIES AND LEADERS IN THE NEWS

We were interested in the visibility of the Chancellor candidates and the political parties, relative to one another, in the news. We coded up to ten actors in each political story. In the 524 television news stories, there were a total of 2,295 actors. In the 384 *Bild* stories, there were a total of 1,221 actors. We also measured the amount of time devoted to politicians' soundbites or quoted statements in television news.

Helmut Kohl was more visible than his challenger in all the news outlets here, but the visibility bonus was less than it had been in 1990. Overall, Kohl appeared in 37 per cent of political stories in comparison with 26 per cent for Gerhard Schröder on television, as can be seen in Table 3. Although this gap was still considerable, it was down five percentage points from what it had been in 1990, when Kohl appeared in 22 per cent of stories and Lafontaine in six per cent. In the *Bild*, Kohl appeared in 25 per cent of stories, and Schröder appeared in 15 per cent, in comparison with 1990 when the comparable figures were 32 per cent for Kohl and 17 per cent for Lafontaine.[14]

There was another aspect to visibility, however, in which Helmut Kohl was actually less visible than Gerhard Schröder, and that was in terms of the average time devoted to soundbites or quoted remarks. Soundbites refers to the actualities in the news, when the candidate is seen and heard speaking on the screen. Other quoted remarks (*'indirekte Rede'*) are statements by the candidates that are given by the news reader. Taken together, these soundbites and quoted remarks represent the amount of time available to the two leaders to get their message across on television news, in their own words. Although Schröder made fewer appearances in the news than Kohl, the average length of a statement from Schröder was 30 seconds compared to 19 seconds for Kohl. In 1990, by contrast, the situation was reversed. The average length of a statement from Kohl was 30 seconds compared to 19 seconds for Lafontaine.[15]

In 1998, the CDU/CSU and FDP party actors were also more visible than the SDP and Green Party actors in all news outlets studied here, although the gap between the CDU/CSU and the SPD was smaller than it had been in 1990. In 1998, the CDU/CSU actors appeared in 89 per cent of stories, and the FDP in 37 per cent, the SPD in 67 per cent, the Greens in 34 per cent, and the PDS in 14 per cent, with some mixture of the three opposition parties in an additional two per cent. Table 4 displays the actors in television news in 1998.[16]

There was considerable variation among media outlets, however, with respect to the presentation of parties and leaders in the news. Two points are especially noteworthy. First, RTL devoted a greater portion of news to the two Chancellor candidates and the main parties than any other channel. Second, ARD devoted considerably less attention to the Chancellor candidates and political actors from the main parties. In comparison with ARD, which gave the least attention to the candidates and parties in comparison with all the TV news programmes, the political actors were even less visible in stories in *Bild*. The figures for the *Bild* are presented in Table 5.

These differences in the visibility of the political party actors did not translate into positive or negative news on television. There was little in the way of explicitly positive or negative statements about political actors in television news. For every political actor in television news, we coded any evaluation as neutral or straight/descriptive, positive, negative, or a mixture of positive and negative. German television news was largely descriptive/neutral. Taking all television news programmes together across all channels, 84 per cent of evaluations of political actors were descriptive or neutral, only 12 per cent were negative, and three per cent were positive, with less than one per cent mixed. The only news programme that varied considerably from this was ARD, which carried more negative news than the other programmes. ARD's coverage of political actors included 81 per cent of descriptive or neutral evaluations, 17 per cent negative evaluations, and two per cent positive evaluations.

TABLE 4

PARTY ACTORS IN POLITICAL NEWS STORIES ON TELEVISION*
10 AUG.–27 SEPT. 1998 (%)

	ARD	ZDF	RTL	SAT.1	Total
Kohl	26	35	46	43	37
CDU/CSU	79	91	95	97	89
FDP	30	39	51	33	37
Government	21	15	14	17	17
Schröder	15	26	43	24	26
SPD	50	71	78	75	67
Green	30	26	47	36	34
SPD+Green	2	5	4	4	3
PDS	12	10	27	11	14
SPD+Green+PDS	4	1		1	2
Other parties	10	6	12	11	9
N (political stories)	154	145	111	114	524

Note: *Proportion of stories in which the actor was one of the first ten actors in the story. Columns are not additive because multiple responses were possible.

Source: K. Schoenbach and H.A. Semetko, Media Content Analysis of the 1998 German Bundestag Campaign

TABLE 5

ACTORS IN FRONT-PAGE NEWS IN THE *BILD**
10 AUG.–27 SEPT. 1998 (%)

	Bild
Kohl	25
CDU/CSU	72
FDP	25
Government	14
Schröder	15
SPD	44
Green	19
SPD+Green	1
PDS	6
SPD+Green+PDS	1
Other parties	7
N (political stories)	384

Note: *Proportion of stories in which the actor was one of the first ten actors in the story. Columns are not additive because multiple responses were possible.

Source: K. Schoenbach and H.A. Semetko, Media Content Analysis of the 1998 German Bundestag Campaign.

Overall, television news in 1998 was more evaluative and less descriptive than it had been in 1990, when 96 per cent was descriptive, one per cent positive and two per cent negative.[16] Interestingly, there was no real difference between the evaluations of the candidates and parties. The government was not criticised more heavily than the opposition, or vice versa.

CONCLUSION

The 1998 German Bundestag election was a watershed not only because it marked the first time since the existence of the Federal Republic that the German electorate voted to oust an incumbent government, or because it marked an end to the leadership of Helmut Kohl and the coalition of CDU/CSU and FDP parties, which had held office since 1982. It was also remarkable for beginning an even more media-centred era in German politics with a new Chancellor recognised for his abilities to come across exceptionally well on television.

The 1998 Bundestag election was the most reported federal election campaign in decades. With this emphasis on the campaign, German election news on television appeared to be moving in the direction of the UK or the US, with the associated hoopla and horse race elements. The 1998 campaign was more exciting in terms of news values not only because the polls showed that the SPD's chances of winning were greater than in any previous campaign in recent decades, but also because its leader presented a formidable alternative to the incumbent Chancellor. The SPD itself was also united throughout its campaign, and strategically had learned a lot from Tony Blair's leadership and the Labour Party's successful bid for power in the British 1997 general election.

There was a clear difference between the public and private channels in the emphasis on the campaign in the news. The private channels devoted far more attention to the campaign and the opinion polls than the public channels, and correspondingly less to the substantive issues over which the campaign was being fought. There was nevertheless still a strong similarity between German public and private television coverage in the predominantly neutral or descriptive coverage of politicians. In comparison with the US, where election news about presidential candidates was often negative, German television news was predominantly neutral or descriptive.[17] That said, the amount of negative coverage of German politicians increased over the past decade, but this trend was in fact not more evident on the private channels. In 1998, the highest percentage of negative evaluations of politicians appeared on the public service channel ARD.

Although the Chancellor's visibility bonus continued to exist in 1998 in terms of the number of stories in which the candidates appeared, it was not as great as in previous campaigns. It also disappeared entirely, and was actually reversed, in terms of the amount of time the candidates were seen speaking in television news.[18]

In conclusion, we observed major changes over the past decade in Germany's broadcast media system, which has become more commercial and more competitive than ever before. This may have had consequences for the reporting of the 1998 election, and we observed more attention to the events and the polls in comparison with the substantive issues on the private channels, whereas on the public channels this was reversed. But the 1998 national election campaign satisfied all possible news value criteria – with an outcome that was predicted to be quite close, a formidable challenger to the incumbent Chancellor, and a campaign that followed years of negative news for the incumbent parties. The CDU's visibility bonus in the news was not as great as it had been in the past, and it was not really a bonus considering the negative news that was generated in the campaign. This negative news was not a consequence of television journalists' evaluations, however; it stemmed instead from the statements of political actors who appeared in the news. So journalists left it to the politicians to criticise one another and selected more of such news in 1998 than they had in 1990. But even in 1998, the vast majority of the news contained no explicit positive or negative evaluations, only neutral or descriptive accounts of events and issues. In comparison with the main evening news reporters in the US or the UK, who are quick to offer their opinions on the candidates each day, German television reporters largely refrained from explicit evaluations.

NOTES

We should like to thank the Amsterdam School of Communications Research at the University of Amsterdam, and the University of Music and Theater in Hannover for providing support for this study. We are grateful to Marina Caspari, Andreas Genz, Melanie Schneider and Edmund Lauf for their research assistance on the project. We should also like to thank the reviewers for valuable comments on an earlier version of this manuscript.

1. K. Berg and M.-L. Kiefer (eds.), *Massenkommunikation V: Eine Langzeitstudie zue Mediennutzung und Medienbewertung 1964–1995* (Baden-Baden: Nomos Verlagsgesellschaft, 1996), pp.40, 183.
2. K. Brants and K. Siune, 'Public Broadcasting in a State of Flux', in K. Suine and W. Truetzschler (eds.), *Dynamics of Media Politics: Broadcasting and Electronic Media in Western Europe* (Beverly Hills, CA and London: Sage, 1992), pp.101–15.
3. J.G. Blumler and T.J. Nossiter (eds.), *Broadcasting Finance in Transition* (Oxford: Oxford University Press, 1990).
4. J.G. Blumler, M. Brynin and T.J. Nossiter, 'Broadcasting Finance in Transition', *European Journal of Communication*, 1, 3 (1986), pp.343–64.
5. B. Pfetsch, 'Convergence through Privatization? Changing Media Environments and Televised Politics in Germany', *European Journal of Communication*, 11, 4 (1996), pp.427–51.
6. H.A. Semetko, 'Journalistic Culture in Comparative Perspective: The Concept of "Balance" in U.S., British and German TV News', *Harvard International Journal of Press/Politics*, 1, 1 (1996), pp.51–71.
7. See H.A. Semetko and K. Schoenbach, *Germany's 'Unity Election' Voters and the Media* (Cresskill, NJ: Hampton Press, 1994).

8. K.L. Baker, H. Norpoth and K. Schoenbach, 'Die Fernsehdebatten der Spitzenpolitiker vor den Bundestagswahlen 1972 und 1976' [The Television Debates of Leading Politicians in the Bundestag Election Campaigns, 1972 and 1976], *Publizistik*, 26 (1981), pp.530–40. See also K. Schoenbach, 'The Role of Mass Media in West German Election Campaigns', *Legislative Studies Quarterly*, 12 (1987), pp.373–94.

9. K.L. Baker and H. Norpoth, 'Candidates on Television: The 1972 Electoral Debates in West Germany', *Public Opinion Quarterly*, 45 (1981), pp.329–45.

10. P.R. Schrott, 'The West German Television Debates, 1972–1983' (unpublished Ph.D. thesis, State University of New York, Stony Brook, 1986); P.R. Schrott, 'Electoral Consequences of 'Winning' Televised Campaign Debates', *Public Opinion Quarterly*, 54 (1990), pp.567–85.

11. H.A. Semetko and K. Schoenbach, 'The Campaign in the Media', in R. Dalton (ed.), *The New Germany Votes: Unification and the Creation of the New German Party System* (Providence, RI and Oxford: Berg, 1993), pp.187–208.

12. Semetko and Schoenbach, *Germany's 'Unity Election'*, p.66. See also Chapter 5. Additional sources on media coverage in recent German elections include K. Schoenbach, 'Mass Media and Election Campaigns in Germany', in F.J. Fletcher (ed.), *Media, Elections and Democracy* (Toronto and Oxford: Dundurn Press, 1992); K. Schoenbach and H.A. Semetko, 'Medienberichterstattung und Parteienwerbung im Bundestagswahlkampf 1990', *Media Perspektiven*, 7 (1994), pp.328–40; B. Pfetsch and K. Voltmer, 'Geteilte Medienrealitaet? Zur Thematisierungsleistung der Massenmedien im Prozess der deutschen Vereinigung', in H.-D. Klingemann and M. Kaase (eds.), *Wahlen und Waehler: Analysen aus Anlass der Bundestagswahl 1990* (Opladen: Westdeutscher Verlag, 1994); R. Schmitt-Beck and P. Schrott, 'Dealignment durch Massenmedien? Zur These der Abschwaechung von Parteibindungen als Folge der Medienexpansion', H.-D. Klingemann and M. Kaase (eds.), *Wahlen und Waehler: Analysen aus Anlass der Bundestagswahl 1990* (Opladen: Westdeutscher Verlag, 1994).

13. Semetko and Schoenbach, *Germany's 'Unity Election'*, see Chapter 5.

14. Ibid., p.51, Table 4.4. The period under study in 1990 was 1 October to 2 December, in comparison with 10 August to 27 September 1998, approximately eight weeks in each election campaign. See also the findings from the 1998 election content analysis discussed in M. Schneider, K. Schoenbach and H.A. Semetko, 'Kanzlerkandidaten in den Fernsehnachrichten und in der Waehlermeinung: Befunde zum Bundestagswahlkampf 1998 und frueheren Wahlkaempfen', *Media Perspektiven*, 5 (1999), pp.262–9; M. Caspari, K. Schoenbach and E. Lauf, 'Bewertung politischer Akteure in Fernsehnachrichten: Analyse der Berichterstattung in Bundestagswahlkaempfen der 90er Jahre', *Media Perspektiven*, 5 (1999), pp.270–74.

15. Ibid., p.52, Table 4.5.

16. Ibid., p.53, for comparable figures for 1990.

17. For trends in US news, see T. Patterson, *Out of Order* (New York: Vintage, 1993).

18. To learn more about how German coverage of politics during election campaigns compares with the most recent general election in Britain, see P. Norris *et al.*, *On Message: Communicating the Campaign* (London: Sage, 1999); H.A. Semetko, M. Scammell and T.J. Nossiter, 'The Media's Coverage of the Campaign', in A. Heath, R. Jowell and J. Curtice (eds.), *Labour's Last Chance? The 1992 Election and Beyond* (Aldershot and Brookfield, VT: Dartmouth, 1994), pp.25–42. Effects of the British press on voters is discussed in J. Curtice and H.A. Semetko, 'Does It Matter What the Papers Say?', in A. Heath, R. Jowell and J. Curtice (eds.), *Labour's Last Chance? The 1992 Election and Beyond* (Aldershot and Brookfield, VT: Dartmouth, 1994), pp.43–64; H.A. Semetko *et al.*, *The Formation of Campaign Agendas: A Comparative Analysis of Party and Media Roles in Recent American and British Elections* (Hillsdale, NJ: Lawrence Erlbaum, 1991). See also J.G. Blumler, M. Gurevitch and T.J. Nossiter, 'The Earnest Versus the Determined: Election Newsmaking at the BBC, 1987', in I. Crewe and M. Harrop (eds.), *Political Communications: The General Election of 1987* (Cambridge: Cambridge University Press, 1989), pp.157–74.

The Boundaries of Stability:
The Party System Before and After the
1998 Bundestagswahl

STEPHEN PADGETT

The 1998 *Bundestagswahl* stands out as one of the few examples in post-war German electoral history of *Machtwechsel* (government turnover) precipitated by the electorate rather than changes in the coalition behaviour of the parties. Yet the drama of the 1998 election does not in itself mean dramatic party system change. The alternation of parties in government is one of the defining properties of liberal democracy and takes place in the most stable party systems. *Machtwechsel* is not, therefore, the main focus of this article. Instead we are concerned with what the election reveals about underlying party system trends. On every recognised dimension of analysis, it will be argued, the evidence of the 1998 election points towards the increasing complexity, fluidity and openness of the party landscape. This explains the defining characteristic of the 1998 election: the unpredictability of the outcome. Despite consistent electoral projections from the five main opinion polls, the composition of the new government remained uncertain until late into election night. This uncertainty, it will be argued further, was not merely the outcome of situational factors, but is endemic to the structure of the German party system at the turn of the millennium. A structural analysis of the party system, however, requires conceptual foundations, and it is with these that we begin.

PARTY SYSTEM ANALYSIS

The determining characteristics of a party system have long been established in the literature.[1] The most basic variable is the number of parties in the system, with a fundamental distinction between the Anglo-Saxon 'duopoly' and the multi-party systems predominant in western Europe.[2] Refinements in the multi-party model include the introduction of a second, related variable: the distribution of electoral strength between large and small parties. The dynamics of a concentrated multi-party system

Stephen Padgett, University of Liverpool

dominated by one or two large parties will be quite different from a diffuse system composed of several fairly evenly balanced medium sized parties. These two variables have been combined in an aggregation index,[3] arrived at by dividing the vote share accruing to the dominant party by the number of parties in the system. Aggregation is of decisive importance in coalition formation. Aggregated systems contain a high potential for the formation of majority two-party coalitions (one large party plus one small 'make-weight'). In the disaggregated system on the other hand the likelihood of multi-party coalitions increases.

The electoral landscape also determines party system dynamics. Stability is imparted by societal cleavages which have the effect of structuring the electorate and ordering the party system. In the absence of socially rooted partisanship, electoral behaviour is individualised in an open political market, resulting in a more variable pattern of interaction between parties and a looser systemic configuration, with more potential for system change. A weakening in 'the long term bases of party support'[4] and a concomitant increase in electoral volatility[5] are common themes in the literature. These tendencies are not necessarily reflected in radical party system change. Institutional parameters (like electoral rules operating against the entry of new parties) may dampen the effects of system change. Moreover, by adapting to a changing environment, established parties are able to retain their dominant position in the system.[6] Nevertheless, whilst the composition of the party system may remain relatively unchanged, electoral competition is intensified in an open political market. Electoral uncertainty, it has been argued, accentuates vote-seeking behaviour,[7] leading parties to gravitate towards the political centre, where most votes are concentrated.

The ordering of parties on the ideological spectrum is a major variable in shaping party system dynamics. Methods of approach vary from content analysis of election programmes to expert evaluation of party positioning. Classification revolves around a continuum from polarisation to centre-oriented systems, with some evidence of a secular trend towards convergence in the centre.[8] This type of interpretation, however, may conceal more complex tendencies. First, the orientation of mainstream parties towards the centre coexists in some countries with systemic polarisation resulting from the emergence of small parties of left and right. Second, ideological co-ordinates are subject to increasing diversity as the left–right dimension is cross-cut by conflicts between old and new politics[9] or the axis between authoritarianism and libertarianism.[10] Attempting to come to terms with the more pluralistic and multifaceted value configurations of post-modern societies, it may be argued, parties exhibit an increasingly multivalent ideological profile.

The mode of interaction between parties constitutes a further dimension of analysis. A party system is more than the sum of its parts. Its dynamic emerges out of networks of inter-party relations, the strategic positioning of parties in relation to one another, and the resultant patterns of competition and co-operation. The analysis of party strategy departs from Downs'[11] assumption that parties are motivated primarily by electoral considerations (vote-seeking). This type of analysis has been modified, however, to incorporate the strategic dilemma which parties may face between broadening their electoral catchment on the one hand, and consolidating their core electorate on the other.[12] The rational actor model has also been expanded to incorporate a policy-seeking orientation (especially amongst the rank and file) towards the pursuit of particular objectives.[13] A vote-seeking strategy which is incompatible with the values of the membership milieu risks the negative electoral consequences of intra-party conflict. In multi-party systems, these strategic considerations are further complicated by the logic of coalition building, which may exert an ideological pull at odds with that of a vote-seeking electoral strategy. Moreover, coalition strategy can itself pose a dilemma between the pursuit of alignments most likely to capture government office, and policy-seeking preferences for 'ideologically connected' coalitions.[14] In a disaggregated party system, it will be argued below, subject to electoral de-alignment and ideological diversification, these dilemmas are intensified, with inter-party relations becoming more multifaceted and complex and an increasing potential for party system instability.

THE STRUCTURE OF THE PARTY SYSTEM

Aggregation provides a measure of the concentration of the party system around the large parties. *Volkspartei* domination has been one of the defining characteristics of the post-war party system, reaching its height in 1976 when the SPD and CDU/CSU collectively polled 91.2 per cent of the vote. Since then, the *Volkspartei* share of the vote has been subject to a progressive decline, falling to 77.3 per cent in 1990. Decline was precipitated, of course, by new party system entrants: the Greens in 1983, followed by the PDS in 1990. As we can see from Table 1, the combined effects of *Volkspartei* decline and the increase in the number of parties in the system are reflected in a sharp decline in the aggregation index. On the evidence of the 1994 election, the decline in the *Volkspartei* share of the vote appeared to have bottomed out at around 77.9 per cent. In the 1998 election, however, it suffered a further setback, falling to 76.1 per cent, the lowest level of *Volkspartei* support since 1953.

Aggregation provides a key indicator of the coalition potential of the party system. A decline in the share of the vote accruing to the largest party,

TABLE 1

PARTY SYSTEM AGGREGATION

(Largest party share of vote / no. of parties in the Bundestag)

	1976	1980	1983	1987	1990	1994	1998
Largest party share	48.6	44.5	48.8	44.3	43.8	41.4	40.9
No of parties	3	3	4	4	5	5	5
Aggregation Index	16.2	14.8	12.2	11.1	8.8	8.3	8.2

along with an increase in the number of parties in the system, reduces the potential for coalitions based on the one-plus-one model (one *Volkspartei* plus one small party coalition make-weight) on which all coalition governments except the 1966–69 grand coalition have been based since the 1950s. In the 1990s, this model has become more difficult to sustain. In 1994, the *electoral* margin of the Christian-Liberal coalition was wafer-thin, the government parties polling a mere 0.3 per cent more than their rivals. The electoral margin in 1998 was slightly more comfortable, but still narrow, with 47.6 per cent against 46.4 per cent for the opposition parties. In both 1994 and 1998, coalition majorities were inflated by additional seats (*Überhangmandate*) resulting from the operation of the dual ballot electoral system which tends to over-reward the largest party. In the 1990s, consequent upon the disaggregation of the party system, the customary model of 'one-plus-one' coalitions hangs in the balance.

Additional complexity is introduced into coalition calculations by the dual structure of a party system differentiated between east and west.[15] The party system in the west replicates the four-party model of the 1980s, with the SPD and CDU/CSU polling around 80 per cent of the vote and the FDP and Greens at around seven per cent. By contrast the party system in the east approximates to a three-party system, with around 83 per cent of the vote divided between the SPD, CDU/CSU and PDS. Squeezed between the three larger parties and an exceptionally high fringe party vote of 8.6 per cent, the FDP (especially) and the Greens have a marginal existence in the east. The dual party system is reflected in divergent patterns of coalition formation in Land governments, and adds complexity to inter-party relations and the strategic positioning of the parties in relation to each other.

Whilst the 1998 election shows that it is still possible for the parties to operate in a five-party system according to customary patterns of one-plus-one coalition behaviour, the marginality of the model is underlined by a sharp increase in the 'fringe' party vote. Across Germany, almost six per cent of the vote went to small extra-parliamentary parties, more than half of which was accounted for by the extreme right-wing Republikaner and the DVU. In the east, this tendency was particularly pronounced, with 8.6 per cent of the electorate voting for an extra-parliamentary party. The split between the two parties, and fissiporous tendencies in the Republikaner, restricted the capacity of the extreme right for attaining parliamentary representation. Nevertheless, the far right is closer than previously in the Federal Republic to making a realistic challenge for representation. Indeed, it may already be regarded as a relevant force in the party system, exerting an influence on the CDU/CSU through its threat to their right flank. More disaggregated than previously, with a dual structure differentiated between east and west and with a sixth political force exerting an influence, the party system after the 1998 *Bundestagswahl* thus appears to be nearing the margins of stability.

THE ELECTORAL DIMENSION

On the electoral dimension, the central question emerging from the 1998 *Bundestagswahl* is whether the shift to the left which brought Gerhard Schröder to power is indicative of a long-term, structural realignment of the electorate, or merely a reflection of the situational effects of political circumstances which were uniquely favourable to the SPD. To answer this question we need to examine the structural characteristics of the 1990s electorate, and the dynamics of electoral change. 1998 was only the second post-war election in which the SPD has succeeded in breaking the electoral hegemony of its main rival. The dominance of the CDU/CSU has appeared to be embedded in the structure of the electorate, reflecting the fundamentally conservative value orientations of the electorate.[16] In the more fluid and open electorate of the 1990s, it might be argued, the structural advantage of the centre-right is less firmly entrenched.

In the 1990s electorate there is strong evidence of the dealignment of socially structured partisanship, and the decline of partisan identification.[17] The resultant increase in electoral volatility in the 1990s can be seen from Table 2, showing a sharp rise in the Pedersen Index of electoral change. With the exception of the 'realigning' election of 1983, the index for elections between 1965 and 1987 falls between 3.7 and 5.65, against an index averaging around 7.3 for the 1990s. The table suggests that the dynamics of electoral change in 1998 are of a different character to the realignment of 1983. In the latter election, the sharp rise in the Pedersen Index stands out sharply from the relative stability which preceded it and which asserted itself thereafter as the new electoral landscape was consolidated. By contrast, electoral change in the 1990s has remained at a high plateau, indicating a permanent state of electoral flux.

TABLE 2
ELECTORAL VOLATILITY (PEDERSEN INDEX)

	1976	1980	1983	1987	1990	1994	1998
Ptcptn	90.7	88.6	98.1	84.3	77.8	79.0	82.3
CDU/CSU	48.6	44.5	48.8	44.3	43.8	41.4	35.2
SPD	42.6	42.9	38.2	37.0	33.5	36.4	40.9
FDP	7.9	10.6	7.0	9.1	11.0	6.9	6.2
Greens		1.5	5.6	8.3	5.1	7.3	6.7
PDS					2.4	4.4	5.1
Other	0.9	0.5	0.5	1.3	4.2	3.6	5.9
Pedersen Index*	3.7	4.5	8.4	5.7	7.3	7.1	7.5

Note: * Calculated from +/- party share of vote for CDU/CSU, SPD, FDP, Greens (from 1980), PDS (from 1990), and a residual category, 'others'.

An explanation for electoral instability can be found in the structure of the party vote. Both the *Volksparteien* retain a *Stammwählerschaft* in their traditional milieux in the west. Thus, some 66 per cent of trade union member manual workers in the west voted SPD in 1998. In the absence of traditional voting ties in the east, SPD voting amongst this group was weaker at 45 per cent. Nevertheless, over the whole of Germany, the party was still able to claim the allegiance of some 61 per cent of this milieu.[18] Similarly, the CDU/CSU stronghold amongst church-going Catholics remains intact. This confessional group is confined largely to the west, where 70 per cent of church-attending Catholics voted for the CDU/CSU in 1998.[19] The *impact* of socially rooted partisanship, however, has been eroded by a secular decline in both of these social groups relative to the wider electorate. In 1994, church-going Catholics made up just 14 per cent of the CDU/CSU electorate. Trade union member workers constituted a mere 13 per cent of SPD voters, falling further to 11 per cent in 1998.[20] The confinement of socially structured partisanship to these relatively small and declining milieux leaves the 1990s party system subject to sharp swings in electoral behaviour.

Elections are won and lost, of course, through shifts of electoral allegiance amongst unattached or weakly attached voters. The electoral shift which brought the SPD to power in 1998 centred on two particularly fickle voting groups. First, as can be seen from Table 3, there was a large-scale

TABLE 3

VOTING BEHAVIOUR OF 'CORE ELECTORATE' 1994–98

	SPD	CDU/CSU	FDP	Greens	PDS	Others
Trade union	94	55	30	2	4	5	5
member workers	98	61	19	2	3	6	9
Regular church attending	94	14	74	6	2	0	4
Catholics (west)	98	20	70	5	3	0	3

Source: Forschungsgruppe Wahlen, Mannheim, *Bundestagswahl 1994: eine Analyse der Wahl zum 13. Deutschen Bundestag am 16. Oktober 1994* (Mannheim: FGWM, 1994), pp.21–5; Forschungsgruppe Wahlen, Mannheim, *Bundestagswahl 1998: eine Analyse der Wahl vom 27. September 1998* (Mannheim: FGWM, 1998), pp.21–9.

shift amongst white-collar workers, with the CDU/CSU lead of seven percentage points decisively reversed, and the SPD establishing a commanding ten-point lead. Age was also significant, with a strong shift to the SPD amongst the middle aged. In 1994 the SPD was the largest party amongst the under 35s, whilst the CDU had the advantage amongst the 45–60s, and an even more decisive lead amongst the over 60s. A key factor in the 1998 election was a big shift in the 45–60s, where the SPD wiped out a CDU advantage of 8.5 percentage points to establish a seven-point lead of its own.[21] This pattern of electoral change suggests the key to the centre-left majority was the middle aged middle class, responding to the SPD's reorientation to the *neue Mitte*.

A second trend making a substantial contribution to the SPD's victory was the exodus of manual workers from the CDU in the east. Although its initial advantage in this group had been eroded in 1994, the party had retained 41 per cent of the manual worker vote against 35 per cent for the SPD. In 1998 the CDU suffered losses of around 14 percentage points here, the SPD establishing an advantage of 39 per cent to the CDU's 27 per cent.[22] Thus the 1998 election was won in the centre-oriented, middle aged middle class in the west, and manual workers in the east, groups of weakly attached voters whose loyalties to the SPD can be expected to be shallow. Far from signifying a *structural* realignment of the electoral landscape, the centre-left victory of 1998 appears to be a classical example of a *situational* response to the political and economic conjuncture. On the other hand, in an electorate subject to the decline of socially structured partisanship, the balance between the parties can be expected to fluctuate more than it has in the past. Thus, whilst the centre-left majority cannot be taken as indicative of a long-term electoral realignment, nor can the centre-right be complacent about the reassertion of its structural advantage.

TABLE 4

VOTE SPLITTING (1983 / 1998)

(First vote of Green / FDP second voters %)

		SPD	CDU/CSU	Greens	FDP
	90	28	5	62	2
GREEN	94	33	7	56	1
	98	54	6	37	1
	90	16	34	2	46
FDP	94	10	55	2	32
	98	11	61	1	26

A further electoral trend of some significance for the party system is the emergent pattern of vote splitting. The practice has increased in the 1990s, with 18 per cent of first voters for both *Volksparteien* giving their second vote to another party, against only 12 per cent in 1990.[23] The corollary can be seen in even sharper relief from Table 4. Amongst those who give their second vote to Greens or the FDP, there is an increasing tendency to cast their first vote for the SPD or CDU/CSU respectively. In each case, the incidence of vote splitting amongst Green and FDP voters has almost doubled over the three 1990s elections. In 1998 a majority of Green second voters and approaching two-thirds of those of the FDP gave their first vote to the 'neighbouring' *Volkspartei*. This pattern of 'milieu-specific' vote splitting, it may be concluded, is symptomatic of a 'two-block' party system configuration in which electoral choice is perceived by a significant part of the electorate in terms of a choice between red–green and Christian-Liberal camps.

Political circumstances in 1998 were, of course, very favourable to the SPD and the Greens. The exhaustion of the Christian-Liberal coalition, and a Chancellor for whom the fifth election was one too many, provided the centre-left with a window of opportunity. Reorientating itself in the campaign to the centre, and with a Chancellor candidate equipped with the media skills to exploit the opportunities, the SPD was optimally poised to maximise its advantage. This 'situational' interpretation is well supported by the available data. Polls showing satisfaction with government and opposition gave the SPD a decisive lead over the government, with positive endorsement of its performance contrasting sharply with 1994 when the SPD's lead was whittled away in the four months before the election. Significantly, public perceptions of the SPD's performance rose sharply in March when Schröder's Chancellor candicacy was announced. The 'candidate effect' was also decisively in the SPD's favour, with Schröder establishing a clear two-point lead over Kohl (on a scale from -5 to +5) although this narrowed to 0.7 by the election. Schröder's influence was also evident in public perceptions of the economic competence of government and opposition, with the SPD taking the lead in March, although this became less decisive as the election neared and was even reversed in the immediate run-up to polling day.[24] With all these factors favouring an SPD-led government, it is hard to disbelieve the situational explanation for the centre-left majority. This kind of interpretation gains further credibility from data suggesting that large sections of the electorate remained undecided until the final days of the campaign. Fully 19 per cent of the electorate were undecided four days before the poll, with 15 per cent arriving at their decision only on election day itself.[25]

There is little, then, to suggest that the centre-left majority was a reflection of long-term structural changes in the electoral landscape. The evidence points towards a de-structured electorate, with the main party's *Stammwählerschaft* accounting for only one-third of the electorate. The decisive changes appear to have taken place in the centre-orientated middle class in the west along with the working class in the east, both social groups characterised by fickle voting behaviour. In a destructured electorate, change is accounted for by the situational effect of perceptions about party performance, economic competence, and the relative merits of the respective Chancellor candidates. Shifting electoral foundations thus suggests a party system with a permanently high potential for change.

THE IDEOLOGICAL DIMENSION

On the ideological dimension, the party system shows two countervailing tendencies over the last decade. On the one hand, the emergence of the PDS on the left and the Republikaner and DVU on the right means that the ideological range of the system has widened. On the other, the ideological distance between the *Volksparteien* has narrowed. These tendencies can be seen from Figure 1, which is based on expert interpretations of party locations on a left–right scale from 0 to 10.[26] In 1984, party locations ran from the Greens at 2.8 to the CSU at 7.9, a range of 5.1. By 1995 the range had widened to 7.8, with the PDS at 1.5 and the Republikaner at 9.3. A reverse tendency can be seen in the ideological distance between SPD and CDU/CSU locations narrowing from 4.6 to 3.5. Analysis of party election programmes shows a similar pattern of ideological convergence, the distance between SPD and CDU/CSU programmes narrowing from between 30 and 43 points in the period 1976–83 to around 24 points in 1987 and 1990. A pronounced divergence in 1994 is followed by a reassertion of convergence in the 1998 election.[27]

FIGURE 1

IDEOLOGICAL RANGE OF THE PARTY SYSTEM (1984; 1995):
EXPERT INTERPRETATIONS
(left / right scale of 0-10)

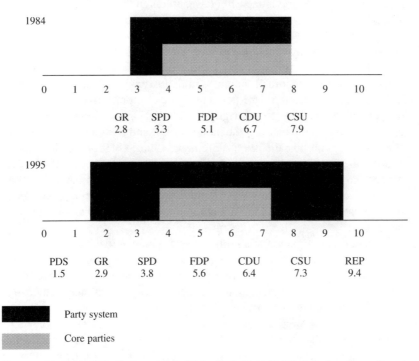

Sources: for 1984, F.G. Castles and P. Mair, 'Left–Right Political Scales: Some Expert Judgements', *European Journal of Political Research*, 12 (1984); for 1995, J. Huber and R. Inglehart, 'Expert Interpretations of Party Space and Party Locations in 42 Societies', *Party Politics*, 1 (1995).

Party programmes in the 1998 election conformed to this pattern of convergence. Paradoxically, whilst the SPD programme emphasised political change, and although, as Schröder noted in his victory speech, the rhetoric of the centre-right parties had attempted to polarise the country between Christian-Liberal and red–green camps,[28] the campaign lacked sharply focused policy alternatives. On the major issues, CDU and SPD programmes bore striking similarities. Both offered a cut in the basic rate of tax to 15 per cent, although the Christian Democrats outbid their rivals in anticipating bigger reductions in the highest tax rates. Similarly, both major parties were committed to reducing state debt by rolling back the demands on government. Employment policies were high on the agenda of both parties, although the CDU's commitment to 'employment-related wage agreements' was different in tone from the SPD's pledge to 'creating jobs by stimulating growth'.[29] Each party was committed to an overhaul of German nationality and citizenship laws, although the CDU reform stopped short of the SPD's provisions for dual nationality.[30]

As we saw above, convergence between the *Volksparteien* around the centre of the party system coexists with a widening of its ideological range towards the poles. Although this latter tendency is modest in Bundestag elections it is rather more pronounced in the party systems in the Länder. In the 1998 federal election, 15.1 per cent of the electorate voted for a party to the left of the SPD or to the right of the CDU/CSU. Some recent Land elections, however, have seen the parties of left and right taking over 20 per cent of the vote in the west (Bremen, 1995: 18.3 per cent; Baden-Württemberg, 1996: 21.2 per cent; Hamburg, 1997: 21.4 per cent) and over 30 per cent in the east (Berlin, 1995: 30.5 per cent; Saxony-Anhalt, 1998: 36.5 per cent; Mecklenburg-West Pomerania, 1998: 31.6 per cent).[31] Does this indicate the ideological polarisation of the German electorate and party system?

Such an interpretation should be treated with caution. To the left of the *Volksparteien*, the PDS and the Greens are too ideologically diverse to be classified as 'polar parties'. Certainly, the 1998 election programme of the PDS advocated 'a complete change in the political landscape' rather than merely a change of government, with an economic policy related to a 'redistribution of wealth from top to bottom'. As in 1994, however, its advocacy of 'fundamental political change' is tempered by the softer themes of the new left: ecology, gender issues and participatory democracy.[32] Above all, however, the programme stamped the PDS as a party of east German interests, rather than a left alternative. For their part, the Alliance '90/Greens programme reflected the growing dominance of the pragmatic 'realo' wing of the party, its aspirations towards government, and the moderating influence of Alliance '90 in the east. Thus the maximalist demands ratified by the Magdeburg conference of March 1998 were significantly scaled down in the final draft of a programme in which the traditional Green themes of environmental protection, social welfare and international co-operation were not irreconcilable with a social democratic agenda. Remarkably, the section of the programme dealing with participatory democracy was briefer than that concerned with strengthening public security through 'preventative policing'.[33] In view of the ideological diversity of the PDS programme, and the assimilation of the Greens into the political mainstream, it is difficult to interpret voting for either party as a manifestation of polarisation on the left.

With their xenophobic and authoritarian tendencies, a stronger case can perhaps be made for regarding Republikaner and DVU voting as evidence of polarisation. Yet even here the conclusion requires qualification. There is compelling evidence that the parties of the extreme right mobilise the protest votes of the economically marginal, especially the young unemployed. In the Saxony-Anhalt election of April 1998, for instance, the DVU mobilised this constituency around a campaign based on the failure of the established parties to address regional economic decline, taking around 30 per cent of the under-30s vote, and 34 per cent of the unemployed, against an overall poll of 12.9 per cent. Over half (53 per cent) of its supporters were previous non-voters. Some 76 per cent of its voters had a negative perception of economic prospects.[34] Whilst there is some evidence that the parties of the extreme right attract those with authoritarian tendencies, this profile of DVU support is suggestive of protest rather than ideologically motivated voting. This conclusion is corroborated by the results of the Bundestag election in Saxony-Anhalt, when the combined support for the parties of the extreme right crumbled to around five per cent, a pattern consistent with the tendency of Land elections to attract protest voting which evaporates in federal elections. Whilst reservations about polarisation on the left stem from the programmatic character of the parties then, scepticism concerning polarisation on the right is bound up with questions of voter motivation.

Whilst there is little evidence in the 1998 election to suggest an ideological polarisation of the party system, another tendency stands out quite strikingly. In responding to the social pluralism of the electorate, parties are becoming more *multivalent* in their ideological composition. This tendency is particularly pronounced on the left. With the multifaceted ideological profile observed above, the PDS embraces traditional social democrats, the new left, and GDR nostalgists in the east, as well as a small constituency of the 'hard left' in the west. A similar ideological diversity is evident in the 'Green spaghetti' of fundamentalists, ecological socialists, libertarians, moderate left-realos and socially conservative environmenta-lists, compounded by the heterogeneous civil rights orientation of Alliance '90 in the east.

Ideological multivalence was the key to the SPD's success in 1998. Its programme balanced Keynesian social democracy with commitments to a competitive market economy and tax reductions in an attempt to extend its appeal from its traditional constituency to the political centre, whilst at the same time, with its proposals for an ecological energy tax and a radical reform of the citizenship laws, reaching out to the new left. In media-oriented societies, however, policy programmes are less important than 'image-making' via the new technologies of political marketing. In a *thematic* rather than policy-oriented campaign, the SPD crafted its image around five key motifs: a combination of *innovation* and *order* in the economy and labour market, *justice* in the social state, advocacy on behalf of *families*, and an emphasis on *youth and the future*.[35] Underlying these motifs was an image of the party as a confident and competent agent of political change. Thus eschewing conventional ideological positions, the SPD was able to project a multifaceted appeal to a pluralistic society.

The parties of the centre-right, by contrast, have become embedded in narrow ideological milieux. In a tired and lacklustre campaign, the CDU's focus on the Chancellor and economic performance failed to resonate beyond the party's hard-core electorate, whilst the attempt to demonise the red/green axis merely backed the party further into a conservative, Christian-bourgeois corner. The FDP suffered from a similarly unidimensional ideological stereotyping. Although its *programme* made genuflections towards social liberalism ('Liberal is social' ... 'equal rights to participate in society'),[36] the party's *image* revolved around the neo-liberal agenda of tax reduction and deregulation which the FDP had pursued throughout the 1994–98 parliament. Occupancy of the *ideological* centre is crucial to a party whose *raison d'être* is rooted in a *functional* role as the central pivot of the party system. The 1998 election suggests that in becoming indelibly stereotyped on the right, the FDP has lost the property of ideological bivalence which enables it to play this role. Contrasting sharply with the multifaceted profile of the parties of the left, the ideological confinement of the CDU/CSU and FDP places them at a pronounced disadvantage in terms of strategic positioning, and it is to this dimension of the party system that we now turn.

INTER-PARTY RELATIONS

The tendencies identified above have far-reaching implications for the interaction of parties within the system. First, in an enlarged multi-party system, the patterns of inter-party competition and co-operation become more multifaceted, with differentiation between systemic configurations in east and west adding to the complexity. Second, the decline of socially structured partisanship in a more fluid electorate means that the parties are less able to rely on the support of a stable core of voters, opening up and intensifying electoral competition. Third, with a less sharply defined social profile, party identities are more fluid, allowing them more scope for strategic manoeuvre. In short, with a fluid electorate and an open party system, strategic flexibility assumes paramount importance, involving a combination of electoral positioning and coalition alignment.

The success of the SPD in 1998 might be attributed to the party's dexterity in repositioning itself towards the centre whilst at the same time being in a position to embark upon a coalition with the Greens on the left. In so doing, the party exploited an unusually favourable systemic configuration. The new German party system, it has been argued, contains a pronounced asymmetry of coalition opportunities.[37] Whilst the CDU is restricted to coalition with the FDP or a grand coalition, the SPD has a wider range of options, with openings to either the CDU or the FDP on the right, or the Greens on the left. Moreover, with the emergence of an SPD–PDS coalition axis in the eastern Länder, the taboo on co-operation with the PDS is growing weaker, opening up new strategic opportunities on the left. This wide range of coalition options, however, is accompanied by a strategic dilemma. Should the party consolidate the coalition alignment on the left, perhaps broadening it to include the PDS, or should it retain its orientation towards the *neue Mitte*? From a strategic point of view, the SPD should try to do both, but this will be a difficult balancing trick to sustain.

Although the Social Democrats left their coalition options open in the 1998 campaign, the expectation was that the outcome would be an SPD-led grand coalition, a 'safer' prospect for the centre-oriented voters than a red–green government. It will be harder in the next election for the party to remain 'on the fence', since government parties are expected to make their coalition intentions clear in advance of the election. Additionally, the SPD's coalition behaviour in intervening Land elections will already have signalled the party's intentions to the electorate. Fighting the next election for a renewal of the red–green coalition, particularly with the shadow of the PDS as a potential coalition make-weight hovering in the wings, the SPD will inevitably find it less easy to mobilise those change voters in the centre who were a decisive component in the centre-left majority in 1998. Retaining a credible commitment to the *neue Mitte*, on the other hand, may entail government policies which strain the compromise capacity of the Greens to (or beyond) its limits.

Managing the centre-left majority will thus place heavy demands upon the strategic dexterity of the SPD. Its success in 1998 appears to signal the resolution of the debilitating internecine conflict of the 1980s and early 1990s, with the SPD torn internally between the centre, traditional social democrats and the new left, and vacillating between competition and co-operation with the Greens.[38] In government, the resilience of the settlement will be severely tested. A leadership team of Schröder and Lafontaine was well-equipped to appeal to the diverse social and cultural milieux on which the centre-left majority rests. The resignation of the latter may be the signal for the emergence of a left opposition within the government parties. The relatively modest scale of the vote (76 per cent) confirming Schröder as Lafontaine's successor as party Chairman may be indicative of this tendency. Much will depend upon the performance of the red–green government, and the indications of the first six months are already suggestive of the difficulties. Untidy compromises on nuclear fuel reprocessing, energy taxes, and the liberalisation of citizenship laws have undermined key elements of the red–green reform agenda, without convincing centre-orientated voters of the government's reliability. The scale of centre-left majority in 1998 reflects the broad social and ideological spectrum which it embraces. The test for the SPD will be holding this pluralistic coalition together.

For the Greens, the new party system configuration also presents strategic dilemmas. The Hesse election of February 1999 was the fifth successive Land election in which the Greens experienced losses, particularly amongst younger voters. The response of the pragmatic 'realo' wing of the party is to broaden the Green agenda to embrace economic issues and employment, whilst at the same time streamlining the cumbersome structures of internal party democracy. This strategy, however, risks provoking a fundamentalist backlash and may also weaken the distinctive character of the party. This conflict intensifies the dilemma the Greens faced on entering government. The smoothness with which coalition negotiations were concluded (and ratified by the party's membership assembly) is indicative of the ascendancy of the pragmatic 'realos' and the stabilisation of internal party life. Nevertheless, Joschka Fischer and Jürgen Trittin will have to balance 'responsibility' with the need to retain a distinctive profile in the coalition, ensuring that the Greens do not become merely the new left appendage of the social democratic government. The strategic dilemma may be sharpened by electoral competition with the PDS, which now has the monopoly over the left opposition. In the longer term, the Greens will need to assert their independence in order to avoid coalition 'capture' by the SPD, either by opting for periods of opposition, or even by opening up the possibility of coalition with the CDU.

The strategic dilemmas of the centre-left appear as nothing compared to those of the Christian Democrats. Having lost the structural dominance which it has exercised in the post-war party system, the CDU after the 1998 election is faced with the need for a strategic reappraisal. Rescued from the full effects of its electoral decomposition by unification in 1990 and by economic upswing and an ineffectual opposition in 1994, the party has failed to respond to a long-term decline in its capacity for electoral mobilisation, and is now reduced to the ghetto of its core Christian-bourgeois electorate. Revitalisation entails reasserting its hold over the electoral centre, but it is by no means clear how this is to be achieved now that the SPD has reaffirmed its character as a modern, progressive *Volkspartei*. One strategy would be to combine neo-liberal solutions to Germany's structural economic difficulties with a revamped version of the

Christian Democratic ethic of social solidarity, relying on the failure of the government's neo-corporatist approach. Less steeped in the Christian social tradition than its predecessors, the new generation of leaders emerging around Wolfgang Schäuble may be amenable to this type of appeal. There are, however, a number of risks attached to this strategy. First, it would alienate the labour wing of the party, and the Catholic worker element in the CDU's fragile electoral alliance. Second, there is as yet no evidence that the electorate is prepared to embrace the inevitable welfare losses accompanying neo-liberal economics. Finally, a centre-orientated strategy might also leave the party vulnerable to extremist parties on the right.

The bankruptcy of the CDU in terms of coalition strategy was underlined in the 1998 election by the strategic disorientation of the leadership. Having dismissed the possibility of a grand coalition throughout the campaign, Chancellor Kohl appeared to change position four days before the election, only to recant subsequently under pressure from his campaign team. Disorientation reflects the isolation of the CDU in the party system of the late 1990s. Reliance on coalition partnership with the FDP is particularly damaging given the electoral marginality of the latter and the ever-present risk that it may fail to overstep the electoral hurdle. One long-term strategy periodically addressed by party managers is to 'stalk' the Greens, playing on their need for an alternative to the SPD. However, although there is already some co-operation at the local level (especially in North Rhine-Westphalia and in southern Germany where the Greens are more conservative), and whilst relations in the Bundestag are not uncordial, the two parties are divided by fundamental differences in the value orientation of their membership and core electorate.[39] Whilst the possibility might be attractive to 'office seeking' leaders in both parties, a black–green coalition remains a distant option. For the CDU, then, electoral regeneration is the only way to escape party system isolation.

Central to any discussion about changing inter-party relations in the new German party system is the future of the Free Democrats. The *raison d'être* of the FDP has been its functional role as the pivot around which the party system revolves. The role depends upon the party maintaining a central position in the system, open to coalition with both left and right, its long-term changes in choice of coalition partner reflecting seminal shifts in electoral opinion and precipitating government alteration between the *Volksparteien*. There are three reasons for concluding, on the evidence of the 1998 election, that its capacity to play this role may now be exhausted. First, with a *Stammwählerschaft* of no more than around 2–3 per cent,[40] electoral survival depends upon the vote-splitters who give their first vote to the CDU, 'loaning' their second to the FDP. Dependent on this electoral life-support system, a change in coalition orientation would be electoral suicide. Second, the FDP no longer has the dual orientation to the right on economics and the left on social issues. In the 1990–94 Bundestag it was still able to assert its liberal agenda of tax-cuts and deregulation. These were also the dominant themes in an election campaign which focused on demonising a red–green coalition. Without a social-liberal axis, a coalition alignment on the centre-left is unthinkable. A final factor militating against this sort of realignment relates to the structure of the new party system. With the Greens offering the alternative to the SPD in the west, and the PDS in the east, the centre-left is already a crowded platform, offering little political space to a born-again social liberal FDP.

CONCLUSION

The conclusion to be drawn from the above analysis is that on each of the dimensions of analysis outlined at the beginning of this article, the German party system is nearing the margins of stability. Disaggregation weakens the *Volksparteien* as the central pillars of the system, with potentially serious consequences for coalition formation. In both the 1994 and 1998 elections, workable government majorities depended heavily on an idiosyncrasy of the electoral system. Whilst the party configuration in the east can be expected to continue producing *Überhangmandate*, further tendencies towards disaggregation will prejudice the customary formula for coalitions consisting of one of the *Volksparteien* plus one minor party.

The 1998 election illustrates very clearly the effects of the decline in socially structured partisanship, corroborating the contention that a more fluid electoral landscape intensifies vote-seeking behaviour amongst the parties. The repositioning of the SPD towards the centre, and its exploitation of the new technologies of political marketing, cannot but be seen in these terms. The analysis of electoral change in 1998 identifies the key voters on whom the SPD victory depended as the middle aged, middle class in the west and manual workers in the east, notoriously fickle voting groups for whom electoral choice revolves around judgements about party competence, candidates and short-term party preference. This analysis suggests that the centre-left majority was situational in character rather than the result of any structural realignment of the electorate. In the next election, the campaign strategy of the SPD is likely to be replicated by the CDU, further escalating the pitch of electoral competition.

On the ideological dimension, the party system shows tendencies originating in the electoral landscape. Both the indicators we have examined – expert evaluations and a reading of the parties' 1998 election programmes – point towards a convergence of the *Volksparteien* in the centre. This tendency, however, coincides with a widening of the ideological range of the party system. The ideological diversity of the Greens and the PDS suggests caution in interpreting this in terms of polarisation. Nevertheless, the ideological range of the red–green coalition is significantly wider than its predecessor, and its management will require considerable political skill.

All three parties of the left, exhibit a multivalent ideological character. Indeed, the success of the SPD in 1998 can be attributed in large part to an image which cleverly combined the politics of the *neue Mitte*, traditional social democracy, and the new left, a synthesis personified by its leadership team of Schröder and Lafontaine. The tensions inherent in translating this hybrid ideological appeal into a coherent programme were evident in the first six months of the government, and were graphically illustrated by the dramatic resignation of Lafontaine in March 1998. Ideological stereotyping, on the other hand, leaves the parties of the centre-right in an electoral ghetto, escape from which, for the CDU at least, can only come through programmatic diversification.

In an enlarged multi-party system divided between east and west, with an open and fluid electoral landscape, and with parties assuming multivalent identities, inter-party relations become correspondingly more multifaceted and complex. All the parties face strategic dilemmas. The strategic dominance of the SPD in the 1998 party system, it has been argued, will be very difficult to sustain in the longer term. Not only will it have to reconcile the vote-seeking strategy of the *neue Mitte* with the policy-seeking inclinations of its membership, it will also have to balance a centre-oriented electoral strategy with the management of a red–green coalition. For the Greens, the dilemma is to reconcile government responsibility with the maintenance of a distinctive electoral appeal, while at the same time avoiding coalition capture by the SPD. On the centre-right the dilemmas are even more acute. The CDU faces the difficult task of reconciling its Christian social traditions with a neo-liberal approach to Germany's structural economic problems, in order to fashion a credible appeal to the political centre which can be distinguished from that of the SPD. The FDP, on the other hand, faces the almost insuperable problem of reconciling the disjuncture between its vocational role as a centre party and its ideological positioning on the right.

The FDP having lost the ability to sustain its former functional role, and with at least four coalitionable parties in the system, it is clear that the old triangular model of inter-party relations is defunct. It is less clear, however, that the dynamics of the new German party system conform to the 'two-block' model which has been offered as the alternative. The formation of the first red–green coalition is, of course, itself suggestive of a two-block party system, as is the evidence presented above showing the increase in milieu-specific vote splitting. There is less evidence, however, of the sort of ideological patterns characteristic of a two-block system; strong ideological affinities between parties *within* blocks, alongside polarisation *between* the two camps. Rather than polarisation, we have seen parties exhibiting increasingly ambivalent ideological profiles. Moreover, despite the rhetoric of the 1998 campaign, it is less than clear that the strategic thinking of the parties is confined within the rigid configurations of the two-block model. Indeed, most of the evidence points towards a much more fluid pattern of inter-party relations, and a party system with a high potential for flux.

NOTES

1. For an overview of the literature, see J.E. Lane and S.O. Ersson, *Politics and Society in Western Europe* (London, Thousand Oaks and New Delhi: Sage, 3rd edn 1994), pp.176–91; also K. Janda, 'Comparative Political Parties: Research and Theory', in A.W. Finifter (ed.), *Political Science: The State of the Discipline II* (Washington, DC: American Political Science Association, 1993), pp.163–91.
2. M. Duverger, *Political Parties: Their Organization and Activity in the Modern State* (London: Methuen, 1954).
3. L.C. Mayer, 'A Note on the Aggregation of Party Systems', in P. Merkl (ed.), *Western European Party Systems: Trends and Prospects* (New York: Free Press, 1980), pp.515–20.
4. R.J. Dalton, S.C. Flanagan and P.A. Beck, 'Conclusion', in Dalton, Flanagan and Beck, *Electoral Change in Advanced Industrial Democracies; Realignment or Dealignment* (Princeton, NJ: Princeton University Press, 1984), p.451.
5. M. Pedersen, 'Changing Patterns of Electoral Volatility in European Party Systems, 1948–1977: Explorations in Explanation', in H. Daalder and P. Mair (eds.), *Western European Party Systems: Continuity and Change* (London: Sage, 1983), pp.29–66.
6. S. Wolinetz (ed.), *Parties and Party Systems in Western Democracies* (London: Routledge, 1988).
7. K. Strøm, 'A Behavioural Theory of Competitive Political Parties', *American Journal of Political Science*, 34, 2 (1990), pp.565–98.
8. G. Sartori, *Parties and Party Systems: A Framework for Analysis*, Vol. 1 (Cambridge: Cambridge University Press, 1976), pp.282–93; J.C. Thomas, 'Ideological Change in Competitive Labour Parties: A Test of Downsian Theory', *Comparative Political Studies*, 15, 2 (1982).
9. R. Inglehart, *Culture Shift* (Princeton, NJ: Princeton University Press, 1990), pp.296–8.
10. H. Kitschelt, *The Transformation of European Social Democracy* (Cambridge: Cambridge University Press, 1994), p.27.
11. A. Downs, *An Economic Theory of Democracy* (New York: Harper and Bros, 1957).
12. A. Przeworski and J. Sprague, *Paper Stones: A History of Electoral Socialism* (Chicago, IL and London: University of Chicago Press, 1986), pp.45–57.
13. W.E. Wright, 'Comparative Party Models. Rational Efficient and Party Democracy', in W.E. Wright (ed.), *A Comparative Study of Party Organization* (Columbus, OH: Merrill, 1971), pp.17–54.
14. M. Laver and N. Schofield, *Multiparty Government: The Politics of Coalition in Multi-Party Europe* (Oxford: Oxford University Press, 1990), p.96; see also I. Budge and H. Keman, *Parties and Democracy; Coalition Formation and Government Functioning in Twenty States* (Oxford: Oxford University Press, 1990), pp.17–19.
15. R.J. Dalton, 'A Divided Electorate?', in G. Smith, W.E. Paterson and S.A. Padgett (eds.), *Development in German Politics 2* (Basingstoke: Macmillan, 1996), pp.35–54.
16. Forschungsgruppe Wahlen Mannheim (FGWM), *Bundestagswahl 1998; eine Analyse der Wahl vom 27 September 1998* (Mannheim: Forschungsgruppe Wahlen, 1998), p.73.
17. See R.J. Dalton and R. Rohrschneider 'Wählerwandel und die Aufschwachung der

Parteineigungen von 1972 bis 1987', in M. Kaase und H.D. Klingemann (eds.), *Wahlen and Wähler* (Opladen: Westdeutscher Verlag, 1990); H.J. Veen and P. Gluchowski, 'Die Anhängerschaft der Parteien vor und nach der Einheit – Eine Langfristbetrachtung von 1953 bis 1993', *Zeitschrift für Parlamentsfragen*, 2 (1994).
18. FGWM, *Bundestagswahl 1998*, pp.22–3.
19. Ibid., p.29.
20. Forschungsgruppe Wahlen Mannheim (FGWM), *Bundestagswahl 1994: eine Analyse der Wahl zum 13 Deutschen Bundestag am 16 Oktober 1994* (Mannheim: Forschungsgruppe Wahlen, 1998), p.24; FGWM, *Bundestagswahl 1998*, p.24.
21. FGWM, *Bundestagswahl 1994*, p.18; FGWM, *Bundestagswahl 1998*, pp.19–20.
22. FGWM, *Bundestagswahl 1994*, p.22; FGWM, *Bundestagswahl 1998*, pp.22.
23. FGWM, *Bundestagswahl 1998*, pp.16–18.
24. Forschungsgruppe Wahlen Mannheim, *Daten zur Bundestagswahl am 27.09.1998* (Mannheim, 1998).
25. *Der Spiegel*, 41, 5 Oct. 1998, p.22.
26. F.G. Castles and P. Mair, 'Left–Right Political Scales: Some Expert Judgements', *European Journal of Political Research*, 12 (1984), pp.73–88; J. Huber and R. Inglehart, 'Expert Interpretations of Party Space and Party Locations in 42 Societies', *Party Politics*, 1 (1995), pp.73–111.
27. H.D. Klingemann, *Do Political Parties Offer a Choice? An Analysis of Election Programmes*, Election Seminar; Presse-und Informationsamt der Bundersregierung, Bonn 25 Sept. 1998 (unpublished).
28. SPD Presseservice, *Schröder; Wahlergebnis ist Verplichtung für unsere Politik* (Bonn: SPD, 27 Sept. 1998).
29. *Der Spiegel*, 40, 28 Sept. 1998.
30. SPD, *Arbeit Innovation und Gerechtigkeit: SPD Wahlprogramm für die Bundestagswah 1998* (Bonn 1998); CDU/CSU *1998–2002; Wahlplattform von CDU und CSU* (Bonn 1998).
31. FGWM, *Bundestagswahl 1998*, p.A9.
32. PDS, *Für den politischen Richtungswechsel; Sozial und solidarisch – für eine gerechte Republik; Programme der PDS zur Bundestagswahl 1998* (Berlin, 1998).
33. Alliance '90/Greens, *Grün ist der Wechsel; Programm zur Bundestagswahl 98* (Bonn, 1998).
34. Forschungsgruppe Wahlen Mannheim, *Wahl in Sachsen-Anhalt; Eine Anaylse der Landtagswahl vom 26 April 1998* (Mannheim: Forschungsgruppe Wahlen, 1998).
35. SPD, Election briefing; campaign headquarters (Bonn, 24 Sept. 1998).
36. FDP, *Es ist Ihre Wahl; Das Wahlprogramm der Liberalen zur Bundestagswahl 1998* (Bonn, 1998).
37. H.-J. Veen 'Stabilisierung auf dünnem Eis; Entwicklungstendenzen des Parteiensystems nach der zweiten gesamtdeutsche Wahl', in H. Oberreuter (ed.), *Parteiensystem am Wendepunkt? Wahlen in der Fernsehdemokratie* (München and Landsberg am Lech: Olzog Verlag, 1996, p.189.
38. S.A. Padgett, 'The German Social Democratic Party: Between Old and New Left', in D. Bell and E. Shaw (eds.), *Conflict and Cohesion in Western European Social Democratic Parties* (London: Pinter, 1994).
39. Veen, 'Stabilisierung auf dünnem Eis', pp.190–92.
40. FGWM, *Daten zur Bundestagswahl*.

Changing Party Organisations in Germany: How to Deal with Uncertainty and Organised Anarchy

ELMAR WIESENDAHL

MISLEADING IMAGES OF PARTY ORGANISATION

During elections parties are inevitably the focus of electoral and party research since they constitute the main representatives of the democratic struggle for votes and are highly visible in the campaign. Once the elections are over, it is interesting to analyse the possible reasons and explanations for their victory or defeat in retrospect. Since the parties' election campaigns and rankings during elections can hardly be separated from their strategies, tactics and operational manoeuvres, it has always seemed reasonable to analyse electoral contests in terms of rational competition between strategic protagonists.[1] Starting with the classics of party research, from Ostrogorski, Michels and Weber up to Duverger, there has been a long-standing and influential tradition[2] of examining parties as united, rationalised and powerful instruments in the hands of a centralised and oligarchic leadership struggling for political power.

While attributing to the parties an image of purposive, carefully planned organisations, this perspective conceals a multitude of ambiguous, unfinished, unplanned, uncoordinated, pointless and coincidental issues simultaneously taking place within the parties. Moreover, based on the axiom of goal rationality, the representatives of this theory share the opinion that parties can be optimally organised in a perfect unity of purpose, structure, leadership, tactics and action. This approach, however, neglects the fact that internal party life is often characterised by inertia and ritualism on the one hand and a purposeless expenditure of time, energy and motivation on the other.

Nevertheless, the followers of the rational-choice theory in party research continue to see parties as unified organisations[3] run by and for power-ambitious teams of politicians in pursuit of vote-maximising, office-seeking strategies. From this point of view the party leaders are

Elmar Wiesendahl, University of the Federal Armed Forces, Munich supposed to possess enough rationality and cognitive capabilities to be able to achieve their goals by means of strategic calculation. This construction vastly overrates the knowledge and intellectual capacity of allegedly omni-competent, rational actors, neglecting intrinsically human features of decision making like thoughtlessness, spontaneity, habit, helplessness and error. The imperturbable axiom of rationality overestimates the extent of control over the consequences of individual decisions and the ability of actors to perceive the intended and unintended consequences of their strategic moves. Rational-actor theory is bound to treat parties as unitary actors displaying consistent behaviour, because only then can it be assumed that the acquisition of power is the explicit objective of any activity. However, this can only be achieved if the analysis abstracts from the reality of group heterogeneity and interest diversity in internal party life.

Party leaders, for whom the rational-actor perspective is tailor-made, might very well agree with the characterisation, but the glossy image of parties which it projects is far removed from real life. It is extremely questionable whether parties and their front men are actually capable of grasping and influencing their surroundings by deliberate strategic manoeuvre in pursuit of clearly defined electoral objectives. The perspective grossly exaggerates the ability of party leaders to predict the effects of strategic alternatives on electoral outcomes and to select optimal campaign strategies. This school of electoral research (which includes the entire professional community of opinion pollsters, consultants and spin doctors) can do little more than postulate retrospective explanations for shifting electoral outcomes, which, whilst they might appear reasonable within their own frame of reference, are actually incapable of explaining the complex reality of relations between parties and voters. This article eschews the rational-actor model in favour of a model of organisational anarchy which is more attuned to the way parties function and develop under difficult circumstances.

INDIVIDUALISATION, AMBIGUITY AND THE AGE OF UNCERTAINTY

In the past, parties had a stable position as long as they dominated certain social groups and possessed the loyalty of reliable contingents of voters. This assumed, however, that the milieu structures demarcated as 'hunting grounds' remained sufficiently powerful to ensure that social bonds were maintained over several generations. With the decline of socially rooted partisanship, however, the traditional parties are no longer able to influence the collective mind structures of their client groups as they did in former times. While the socio-structural foundations of partisanship are not disintegrating altogether,[4] the major parties' core of loyal voters is subject to a process of permanent decline. In the 1994 Bundestag election, just 13 per cent of SPD voters consisted of workers organised in trade unions, and just 18 per cent of the voters for the CDU/CSU were strongly affiliated Roman Catholics.[5] This negative trend continued in 1998 with the figures declining to 11 and 15 per cent respectively.[6] Simultaneously, traditional homogeneous social groups such as workers, independent businessmen or farmers are becoming increasingly diverse and heterogeneous. Class variables are losing their former importance as determinants of voting behaviour.[7] Traditional social and cultural milieus are not just being eroded, but fragmentation and the loss of cohesion are now dividing previously homogeneous camps. This is aggravated by the fact that partisan identification has grown weaker over the past 25 years.[8] In 1994 only three out of ten voters claimed to identify strongly with a party.[9]

All existing empirical evidence indicates that social variables 'are increasingly losing their importance'[10] for the choice of a party, depriving the parties of contact with voters via their social situation, diminishing the predictability[11] of how to appeal to the voter and reducing the calculability of electoral contests. The bonds between the two major parties and the milieus and organisational networks of their loyal voters have weakened considerably over the years.[12] Subjective milieu research[13] indicates numerous and heterogeneous life-style groups in a fragmented German electorate. However, the research offers the party few useful hints as to how to relate to these fragmented groups.

In this context of 'dislocation and uncertainty'[14] the parties can no longer count on any group or social class outside their decreasing loyal-voter milieus. Changeability is exemplified by the defeat of the SPD and Greens in the Hesse Landtag election of February 1999 less than six months after their victory in the Bundestag election. This defeat was produced by a populist propaganda campaign of the Christian Democrats directed against the Bonn government's immigration policy and was not forecast by any of the professional observers.[15]

The parties feel instinctively that there is something going on that does not benefit them and could even turn into a threat. The only thing they know for sure is that they have lost the 'society of standard groups',[16] whose distribution had determined their former hunting grounds. A fragmented and individualised society, however, constitutes a serious problem for them. On the one hand, the decreasing support of their voters and the dwindling numbers of party members confront the parties with their increasing vulnerability;[17] on the other hand, they are unable to grasp the correlations, let alone draw strategically safe conclusions about how to reduce their vulnerability. The only certainty is that a changing society goes hand in hand with a loss of predictability. At the same time, conventions and rules that used to serve as a basis for orientation are vanishing. In contrast to the mass party model, parties today are losing their significance for people's lives to a striking extent. Simultaneously, they have lost their ability to interpret and influence the citizens' minds.

After their defeat in the 1998 election, the Christian Democrats, under their new Secretary-General Angela Merkel, have embarked upon a reconsideration of the values underpinning the cohesion of society.[18] However, the attempt to identify a value system serving as means of communication between parties and citizens is unlikely to be successful, since the electorate contains such a large variety of contradictory convictions and ideological elements. Swamped with 'all kinds of offers for making sense to one's life', the electorate's needs are already met.[19] Integration via values or programmes has little chance of success given the disintegration of social bonds and loyalty.[20]

For catch-all parties, in particular, the problems of adaptation are aggravated by the fact that there is no consistent, comprehensive and homogeneous process of social change against which to reorient their strategy. Change and conflict between the modern, the pre-modern and the post-modern ages do not occur at the same time or in the same direction. The paradoxes and contradictions of the modern age have left the parties behind. Each new trend the social sciences discover increases the burden of integration resting on the major parties even more. Because of the growing social individualisation they are, at the same time, confronted with 'multiplying and increasingly unstable needs and situations'.[21] Increasing social individualisation goes hand in hand with multiplying expectations that are difficult to grasp and even more difficult to aggregate in a pluralistic society prone to segmentation and polarisation.[22] The same applies to the pluralised co-existence of contrasting sets of values.[23]

For the parties this means that they have to survive in an increasingly confusing, contradictory and unfriendly environment. Unable to make reliable predictions about future expectations, they face an increasing degree of uncertainty and an excess of expectations. This situation is compounded by the difficulty of interpreting change, identifying the consequences and formulating the response, with an ever-present risk of misinterpreting situations and reacting wrongly.

The uncertainty and unpredictability of this volatile environment increases the parties' dependency on information, but this need remains unsatisfied. The proliferation of opinion survey data in electoral years leads to an oversupply of information, making it difficult to draw definitive conclusions. On the whole, the electorate is far too amorphous, heterogeneous and unpredictable for a reliable assessment of how voters are going to react to developments. Thus, the allegedly rationalised competition between the parties via personalities, programmes, issues, campaigns and marketing technologies are in fact based on nothing but imponderables and uncertainties, lacking the preconditions of accurate prediction and strategic orientation.[24] Even retrospective analysis of electoral results provides only an incomplete and unreliable profile of voters' preferences.[25] Given the confused, ambiguous, contradictory and changeable expectations and demands of voters articulated through the media and evaluated by an array of opinion pollsters, the rational-actor interpretation of electoral strategy lacks credibility. In the same way, internal party life is equally resistant to rational logic, and it is to this that we now turn.

ACTOR MULTIPLICITY AND THE LIMITATIONS OF CO-ORDINATED COLLECTIVE ACTION

Action is not taken by the parties, but by its organised members. For this reason, the party members are absolutely fundamental for any organisational action in a party. To be precise, it is merely the acting members that make the parties become a reality.[26] In fact, it would be quite surprising if the parties were composed of members with similar backgrounds, minds, emotions and ways of acting, while the social surroundings are becoming increasingly pluralised, fragmented and individualised. The contrary applies: parties are the organisers of actor multiplicity. 'Political parties are made up of many different types of actors with different and potentially conflicting interests.'[27] Consequently, party members do not only differ in their social backgrounds, but also in the degree of involvement, motivation and expectations concerning their actions as party members.

Party members can be divided into five groups according to their motivation and logic of action. The largest and at the same time least important group for the party's internal matters is constituted by the *sponsoring members*. These are registered due-paying members, who are in fact permanently non-active and not integrated into the party's organisational affairs. Although they are not involved in electoral activities, the financial contributions the parties receive from these 'sleeping members' must not be underestimated.

Between the non-active sponsoring members and the party activists is a second group, the *occasional activists*. From time to time, this group can be mobilised for organisational activities. Its members participate periodically in party-internal general meetings and elections. A third group is composed of *permanent activists* and supporters of the party's organisation. Activists are driven by different motivations. They are primarily motivated by political ideas and principles, and they are committed to a community they feel strongly and expressively attached to. Many of them consider the party as their political home. Activists are policy seekers who, hand in hand with like-minded people, stand up and fight for an important joint objective. For them, the party represents a movement taking up principles and trying to realise them by means of electoral success and the control of public office. Activists provide the numerous honorary members of local boards and delegates to party conventions. They can easily get frustrated and lose their loyalty to the fourth group, the careerists (see below), if their ideals or objectives are betrayed. It should not be forgotten that this group carries the main burden of party work without ever being sure of the willingness of the careerists (who have access to public offices and public resources by means of their voluntary support) to take into account grass-roots demands without compromising when taking political decisions.

A fourth group of party members consists of *careerists* who become party members and commit themselves in order to build up a salaried political career. In Germany, this group of office seekers first needs to climb the career ladder within the party in order to become public-office holders. Once they are established, the careerists often take the top positions both within the party's organisation and in parliaments at the federal, Land and European level. Further influential and profitable positions are those of the mayor and the head of a Landkreis administration. The occupants of these offices comprise what has become known as the political class.[28] What they have in common is the logic of individual ambition to acquire a permanent position in public office and thus to make a living as professional politicians. For careerists, party organisations mainly constitute a springboard or pool of resources for the pursuit of private office-seeking interests in their personal professional careers. Thus they try to use the organisation for vote-getting purposes corresponding to their private office-seeking interests.

A fifth group, which is not very large but still worth mentioning, is that of the *lobbyists*, who invest time, money and effort in party work in order to gain personal advantages concerning their jobs or businesses. Sometimes they are representatives of associations attempting to bring external collective interests to the party. They pursue party and public offices as long as these serve their personal interests. Lobbyists sympathise with careerists, since their fixation on power facilitates their access to public resources that can be exploited for personal aims.

Each of these groups of actors has its own particular reasons for party membership, each with its own ideas concerning the direction the party is supposed to take, its values, the employment of scarce organisational resources and the ordering of internal party life. There is considerable potential for conflict between the differing motivations and aims of these groups of actors, undermining group coherence and identity and inundating party-internal processes with demands for conflict resolution.

This 'polymorphic nature of party membership'[29] is entirely at variance with the idea of homogeneity and coherence among party members and the premise of a membership of like-minded men and women. Activists, lobbyists and office seekers actually display a heterogeneous composition and rarely share the same convictions.[30] Party members do not share a perception of a single objective reality but hold different subjective perceptions united only very partially by common horizons. A wide variety of actors with entirely different social experiences and backgrounds is reflected in a diversity of realities, world views and convictions among the party activists, militating against the formation of a common knowledge structure, and the unity of thought, emotion and action underlying party unity.[31] With the environment perceived in a variety of different ways, party members differ in their 'actional logic' depending upon their position in the party structure. Parties thus lack a commonly accepted set of organisational rules of interpretation that could facilitate a homogeneous perception of reality. Instead, there is a very fragile and only temporary consensus as to the definition of reality. Particularly in times of radical social changes it can be expected that conflicting realities will generate party infighting.

ORGANISATIONAL PROBLEMS OF POLITICAL PARTIES

As far as their organisation is concerned, parties can by no means be equated with enterprises, authorities or armies. On the contrary, the constant struggle to solve unresolvable organisational problems prevents them from coming close to the ideal of a purposeful and rational actor. The voluntary membership constitutes a main source of problems. The parties have to cope with the consequences of the 'informal, personal, voluntaristic nature of political activism',[32] which implies that voluntary members act on their own motivation and mostly with self-determination. A healthy membership base is essential for the functioning of parties which depend on financial contributions and voluntary labour, but increasingly experience difficulties in finding voluntary members for organisational duties. Unlike other formal organisations, parties are not entitled to obligate their members to action contrary to their personal motivation for signing up and participating. Another problem arises out of the maintenance of 'boundary fluidity'.[33] Since parties are open organisations with permeable boundaries, they are unable to exercise control over membership access. The parties are open to anyone, regardless of their ideological and personal convictions, interests and motivation for joining. It is not the parties but the prospective members who decide if and which party they join. In the absence of an admission check, the parties face extensive difficulties in stabilising their boundaries.

The voluntary nature of participation and unscreened accessibility of the parties cause large-scale fluctuation problems, since anyone can obtain or cancel his/her party membership at any point in time. 'Party membership is surprisingly volatile',[34] with a continuous coming and going of members. Sudden floods of spontaneous applications for membership are difficult to cope with on the organisational level. This is aggravated by the rise and fall of member participation. Hence, the parties are subject to the unpredictable availability of human resources, the regeneration of which is beyond the parties' control.

The effects of membership volatility are compounded by instability in internal party life, arising out of the insistent clamour of incompatible expectations. The parties' objectives are neither dictated externally nor defined by a central authority, but are subject to internal dissent and conflict between competing group interests. Thus, questions of the party's overall purpose, its political aims and priorities recur with each change in the composition of membership, and becomes a never-ending, more or less open tug-of-war for the party's direction or course. The logical consequence is that the official organisational objectives are mere compromises framed in such vague and stereotyped terms that they lack any binding or obligatory force over party actors. Even if the parties had binding and consistent objectives, other organisational problems arise, since the *realisation* of these objectives transcends party boundaries, taking place in a public-office environment subject to a wide variety of external influences. In this environment, the public office holders encounter a complex field of forces formed by competing policy actors, parliamentary and governmental majorities and minorities, legal limitations, resource limitations, a critical public opinion, organised interests, socio-economic conditions and national and international dependencies. All these factors influence the political agenda and the outcome of political decisions.[35] In the end, party members as well as the party's supporters and voters frequently experience the frustrating reality that they do not benefit either directly or indirectly from the party's objectives.

In the face of these severe organisational problems it becomes evident that the parties are not 'real' organisations at all, but are rather the objects of exhaustive but often futile organisation. Their capacity for rational action falls far short of most other organisational actors. From a rational point of view, it may be absurd, but political parties are primarily concerned with organising inconsistencies and contradictions instead of unity. Faced with such a wide variety of contradictory motivations and expectations, they must be considered as little more than organised anarchies.

PARTIES AS ORGANISED ANARCHIES

In the parties one can observe actions, events and processes taking place simultaneously, at diverse locations and with a varying mix of people without there ever being any plan or co-ordination to impart a common structure to the course of events. Instead, the observer is confronted with an anarchy of movement lacking any sense of direction so that the overall impression is one of inconsistency, contradiction, disconnection, immobility and disorder, falling well short of conventional standards of organisation. In contrast to other, more rational organisations, they appear unable to co-ordinate the actions and activities taking place within them.[36] The reasons are to be found in their organisational structure, which corresponds closely to the concept of organisational anarchy.

In March and Olsen's conception,[37] organised anarchies are the product of inconsistent and poorly defined objectives, permeable boundaries, an obscure technology and operational mode and the fluctuating participation of the membership.[38] Secondary characteristics are control deficiencies, an unclear differentiation of tasks, roles and responsibilities, communication deficits and co-ordination failure. Organisational studies of the Social Democratic Party (SPD) conform closely to this model. They point towards the confusion resulting from the co-existence within the party of two incompatible structural elements: formalism on the one hand and freedom from control on the other. These contradictory elements are manifested in fluctuations between efficient task management and time-consuming idleness, participation and apathy, professional management and improvisation, the single-minded pursuit of career goals and the self-sufficient maintenance of the *status quo*, strategic action and helplessness, a super-abundance of information for some and the exclusion from communication for others. These are compounded by the coexistence of quarrels and conspiracies on the one hand and harmony and well-being on the other, along with the selfishness of egoistical actors contrasting sharply with the selfless devotion of others.[39]

Since its inception, the CDU has always appeared 'unfinished', the antithesis of a 'homogeneous, well-structured party'.[40] The apotheosis of an organised anarchy,[41] its organisation of contradictions has always been its recipe for success, which made it the melting pot for contrasting movements and groups.[42] After German unification, the party's diversity has increased even further, and the party more than ever appears to be an unconnected conglomeration of organisational cultures varying from one Land to another.[43]

MANAGING PARTIES AS ORGANISED ANARCHIES

Parties organise multiple actors and conflicting expectations. Their organisational rationale consists of the coexistence of contradictions and inconsistencies that can be neither resolved nor harmonised. Thus, party management has to satisfy conflicting aims. On the one hand, it needs to reduce the scope for serious intra-organisational conflict by providing enough organisational room for the co-existence of contradictory demands, expectations and action rationales. On the other hand, the potentially damaging consequences of uncoordinated and incompatible action must be limited in order to avoid clashing rationales of action and goals which could impair, paralyse or even break up the party's organisation as a whole.

As organised anarchies, parties manage their elementary functional problems by the deliberate use of vagueness, fragmentation, loose coupling and hypocrisy.[44] The parties' principal response to intra-organisational conflict is often vagueness and ambiguity. Conflicts that cannot be resolved (for example, questions relating to the definition of aims, the allocation of tasks or the use of resources and distribution of power), are settled by the use of ambiguous compromise formulae. Vaguely defined aims go hand in hand with limited commitment to specific courses of action as well as the use of symbolic politics. This strategy allows different actors within the organisation to pursue conflicting goals without necessarily paralysing or breaking it. Because party goals are often defined in such ambiguous terms, intra-party groups can even act against decisions taken by party conferences or committees. The drawback of ambiguity is that decisions taken by organisational sub-units often seem to be out of step with the party's aims. This makes it virtually impossible to see how such decisions relate to the organisation's overall aims and in what respect they contribute to the achievement of collective goals.

Parties often do not resolve contentious issues, but separate issue areas that might cause functional problems. They form a colourful conglomerate of autonomous sub-units and organisational entities,[45] which do not reflect a thought-through structure with respect to functional tasks. Party members are grouped into units of varying size and degrees of organisational activity resulting in a highly decentralised party structure. The formal term 'Ortsverein' (local party association) covers a multifarious and at the same time maze-like variety of organisational sub-structures[46] which may lead different lives depending on their social environment and organisational culture.[47]

Loose coupling[48] ensures that decisions in different and isolated 'spheres of action' do not block each other, and there is no intention to create any sort of meshing.[49] In other words, the links between different organisational sub-units are weak. Feedback between them either does not take place or has little effect. As a result, a large number of conflicts are managed and decisions made at different levels of the organisation without any of the other organisational elements taking notice of it. Under these circumstances, neither the party officials at the top nor the activists at the grass-roots can check one another. Nevertheless, there are also zones of strong coupling where harmonised and closely co-ordinated collective action does take place.

It is of particular importance to the parties that the things they talk and decide about and the things that lead to real action be kept as far apart as possible. Parties are talking shops. They produce a broad stream of messages – from verbal statements to resolutions and programmes – in which they communicate their own ideas and views about other parties and social groups. The result – if only for the variety of actors – is a dissonant choir of numerous voices that want to be heard. Obviously, this hypocrisy can hardly be the basis for real action. Thus, talk and actions must be regarded as decoupled elements.[50]

It can be assumed that the issues the parties talk about, debate and discuss in public, and the decisions that important party officials and holders of public office actually take are worlds apart. Party leaders will rarely act the way they talk and will rather often talk 'with forked tongues', simply because this is what the rules of party competition demand. Many heterogeneous reference groups have to be reached, and the media want to be supplied with a constant flow of messages and images. Since those who dominate intra-party decision making are in most cases not those who are to put these ideas into practice as elected politicians, public office holders tend to eschew strong reliance on party manifestos and resolutions in their policies. In this respect, the new German Chancellor, Gerhard Schröder, even goes so far as to claim for himself the 'possibility of checking whether decisions taken by the party are feasible in reality and of sounding out whether they can be implemented in day-to-day politics'.[51] However, since there are totally different interpretations of reality, the Chancellor implicitly claims to have the right to decide which of the party's decisions are reality and to what extent party talk is realistic and can be converted into action.

PLANNED AND UNPLANNED CHANGE OF PARTIES AS ORGANISED ANARCHIES

From the viewpoint of the leading groups at the top of the party, organised anarchies cannot be put to much use. The voluntary, obstinate activists at the grass-roots are strongly committed to party programmes and ideology and are too 'undisciplined' and 'stubborn' to be led into election campaigns as an efficient army advancing in close formation. Thus, party leaders and party organisers will probably, like the former executive chairman of the British Conservative Party, Norman Tebbit, feel like a general whose troops could desert any time without him being able to do anything about it.[52] Conversely, the leading groups at the top of the party are confronted with the expectations of the grass-roots activists, holders of honorary offices and delegates, who want their party to pursue an expressive policy-maximising rationale and thus to uphold the primacy of the membership party over the vote-getting party. Office seekers and public office holders, however, would prefer the party to be much more oriented towards a pragmatic vote-maximising rationale. These two objectives are very difficult to harmonise.

Against this background, strategic modernisers in German party headquarters have successfully attempted to turn the voluntary organisations at the Land and electoral district levels into permanent professional offices. This development[53] began in the 1960s and was accompanied by a rise in the number of staff at the parties' headquarters. The employment of expensive new campaign and communication technologies further contributed to the development of electoral-professional parties,[54] with the party leaders and officials controlling this process. The resulting explosion of costs was initially covered by increasing public party subsidies.[55] By the early 1970s, however, the personnel costs exceeded the parties' capacities to such an extent that they began to strengthen the parliamentary parties' offices and to allocate more and more personnel to the public office holders. These staff members could be employed indirectly for party work. In addition, public financing led to the establishment of private party foundations which made it possible to shift the individual costs for qualification and further education of the parties' office seekers from the parties' internal budget to external institutions.[56]

The increasing emphasis on a professional party machinery and modern campaign techniques made some of the people involved in the process[57] hope that it would be possible to rationalise the entire party including its membership organisation by means of central management and top-down control,[58] thus converting the parties into efficient vote-maximising organisations. This, however, turned out to be an illusion. The plans were thwarted by the volunteers at the grass-roots level[59] who failed to live up to such expectations and adopted an attitude of defiance. The traditional grass-root units continue with their outdated routines of meetings and conferences reflecting an organisational culture which emerged 100 years ago when mass parties first developed.[60]

One of the reasons why the party leaders and modernisers in the party headquarters did not succeed in penetrating the surface of their respective parties was that, despite all modern communications technology, no satisfactory communication links could be established with the membership at the grass-roots level.[61] Conversely, the activists were unable to hamper the electoral modernisation strategy pursued by those at the top of the old membership parties, because the majority of the party members (about 85 per cent) have only limited influence on the grass-roots organisations, which are isolated from each other. It would not even have helped to interrupt the bottom-to-top flow of membership fees or donations, because there has never been a substantial flow of money from the grass-roots to the top.[62] Over the years, the holders of public office have found ways to make public resources available to the central offices at the federal and Land levels.[63] This is where loose coupling proves detrimental since it makes it impossible for the party leaders to check the grass-roots as well as for the latter to check the party leaders efficiently. If one interprets parties as organised anarchies, this means that today they comprise two incompatible organisational spheres, each with their independent rationales, resources and routines, which are prevented from clashing by loose coupling.

The ideas put forward by CDU official Peter Radunski[64] are entirely consistent with these developments and had considerable influence. He wanted to get rid of the voluntaristic elements and transform the outdated membership party into a purely electoral-professional party. This aim could not be realised since the German Political Parties Act stands in its way. In addition, the electoral value of the activists as soldiers in the campaign is still too high to forego this human capital.[65] Furthermore, party leaders and office holders find it convenient to legitimise the parties they come from by referring to them as membership parties.[66]

However, decoupling of the pre-modern membership party at the ground and the modernised electoral-professional service party at the top have come at a price. For example, German parties have suffered a decline in membership[67] for some time now, with the SPD's membership falling from 1,022,191 to 777,036 from its peak membership year in 1976 to the end of 1998. The CDU did not fare any better: Between their peak year in 1983 and the end of 1998, their membership dropped from 734,555 to 626,342. At the same time, the parties' memberships are 'ageing' as they fail to attract an adequate number of new, younger members. Also, the parties' often dull internal life dries up as a result of apathy.[68] This is aggravated by the problem that in the past a new generation of educated members from the middle classes demanded a well-developed participants' culture inside their party. They were increasingly disappointed as it became more and more obvious to them that their commitment was limited to activities within the organisational constraints.[69] With the permanent party organisations changing into vote-maximising electoral-professional parties, many of the active policy seekers felt robbed of the fruits of their work through which they had hoped to achieve political goals and change the world. This may be the reason why party members have turned from what was formerly believed to be a guaranteed pool of voters[70] into unreliable customers. One-third of them admits to having voted for another party once.[71] This points to a rapidly growing 'decline of organisational loyalty'.[72] The gradual loss of internal cohesion within the parties alienates their members from each other.[73] At the same time, the distance between politically interested active circles in the population and the organisation has grown, and there has been an increasing alienation, because the parties' modernisation made them unattractive for those potential members who would have been prepared to participate in party work without being interested in a political career.

In spite of these anticipated and unanticipated changes in German party organisations, the structural changes are not so far-reaching as to justify the term 'transformation' or even 'metamorphosis' of the mass-membership parties or catch-all parties into a new type of party as claimed by Klaus von Beyme,[74] who uses the term 'party of professional politicians'. Modernisation and increasing emphasis on the party machinery has caused the membership parties' internal structures to shift towards the organisational rationale of the electoral-professional party. The resulting type of party is a hybrid, full of tensions and contradictions, with the uncoupled membership party at the grass-roots, the office-holder party at the top and the professional party management drifting ever further apart mentally and in the different 'logics of action' followed by careerists, lobbyists and activists. In the future, further alienation between the pre-modern membership and the modern electoral party must be expected.[75]

NOTES

1. For a recent example, see E. Noelle-Neumann, 'Wahlkampf seit November 1995', *Frankfurter Allgemeine Zeitung*, 30 Sept. 1998, p.5.
2. Concerning the classic theory of party research, see E. Wiesendahl, *Parteien in Perspektive. Theoretische Ansichten der Organisationswirklichkeit politischer Parteien* (Opladen and Wiesbaden: Westdeutscher Verlag, 1998), pp.33–51.
3. Ibid., pp.96–108.
4. W. Müller, 'Sozialstruktur und Wahlverhalten. Eine Widerrede gegen die Individualisierungsthese', *Kölner Zeitschrift für Soziologie und Sozialpsychologie*, 49 (1997), pp.750–51; H.-J. Veen and P. Gluchowski, 'Die Anhängerschaften der Parteien vor und nach der Einheit – eine Langfristbetrachtung von 1953 bis 1993', *Zeitschrift für Parlamentsfragen*, 24 (1994), p.183.
5. M. Jung and D. Roth, 'Kohls knappster Sieg. Eine Analyse der Bundestagswahl 1994', *Aus Politik und Zeitgeschichte*, 51–2 (1994), p.12.
6. M. Jung and D. Roth, 'Wer zu spät kommt, den bestraft der Wähler. Eine Analyse der Bundestagswahl 1998', *Aus Politik und Zeitgeschichte*, 52 (1998), pp.17–18.
7. R. Schnell and U. Kohler, 'Empirische Untersuchung einer Individualisierungshypothese am

Beispiel der Parteipräferenz von 1952–1992', *Kölner Zeitschrift für Soziologie und Sozialpsychologie*, 47 (1995), pp.647–8.

8. P. Gluchowski and U. von Wilamowitz-Moellendorf, 'Sozialstrukturelle Grundlagen des Parteienwettbewerbs in der Bundesrepublik Deutschland', in O.W. Gabriel, O. Niedermayer and R. Stöss (eds.), *Parteiendemokratie in Deutschland* (Opladen and Wiesbaden: Westdeutscher Verlag, 1997), p.191.

9. J.W. Falter and H. Rattinger, 'Die deutschen Parteien im Urteil der öffentlichen Meinung 1977–1994', in Gabriel *et al.* (eds.), *Parteiendemokratie in Deutschland*, p.505.

10. Veen and Gluchowski, 'Die Anhängerschaften der deutschen Parteien', p.184.

11. W. Jagodzinski and M. Quandt, 'Wahlverhalten und Religion im Licht der Individualisierungsthese', *Kölner Zeitschrift für Soziologie und Sozialpsychologie*, 49 (1997), p.762.

12. Concerning the Christian Democrats (CDU), see F. Walter and F. Bösch, 'Das Ende des christdemokratischen Zeitalters? Zur Zukunft eines Erfolgsmodells', in T. Dürr and R. Soldt (eds.), *Die CDU nach Kohl* (Frankfurt a. M.: Fischer Verlag, 1998), p.52.

13. Cf M. Schmidt, 'Der gesellschaftliche Wandel oder die Herausforderung der Politik', in M. Schmidt (ed.), *Politikversagen? Parteienverschleiß? Bürgerverdruß?* (Regensburg: Universitätsverlag, 1996), pp.54–5.

14. A. Giddens, 'Brave New World: The New Context of Politics', in D. Miliband (ed.), *Reinventing the Left* (Cambridge: Polity Press, 1994), p.23.

15. F. Walter, 'Ein Sieg der deutschen Mitte', *Die Woche*, 12 Feb. 1999, p.7.

16. U. Beck and E. Beck-Gernsheim, 'Individualisierung in modernen Gesellschaften – Perspektiven und Kontroversen einer subjektorientierten Soziologie', in U. Beck and E. Beck-Gernsheim (eds.), *Riskante Freiheiten* (Frankfurt a. M.: Suhrkamp, 1994), p.32.

17. P. Mair, 'Continuity, Change and the Vulnerability of Party', in P. Mair and G. Smith (eds.), *Understanding Party System Change in Western Europe* (London: Frank Cass, 1990), pp.180–83.

18. *Hamburger Abendblatt*, 11 Dec. 1998, p.8.

19. R. Hitzler and A. Honer, 'Bastelexistenz. Über subjektive Konsequenzen der Individualisierung', in Beck and Beck-Gernsheim (eds.), *Riskante Freiheiten*, p.308.

20. See F. Walter, 'Partei der ewigen 70er: Zur Krise der SPD in der Ära Scharping', *Politische Vierteljahresschrift*, 36 (1995), pp.712–13.

21. Beck and Beck-Gernsheim, 'Individualisierung in modernen Gesellschaften', p.33.

22. K.P. Strohmeier, 'Pluralisierung und Polarisierung der Lebensformen in Deutschland', *Aus Politik und Zeitgeschichte*, 17 (1993), pp.11–23.

23. Cf. E.H. Witte, 'Wertewandel in der Bundesrepublik Deutschland (West) zwischen 1973 und 1992', *Kölner Zeitschrift für Soziologie und Sozialpsychologie*, 48 (1996), p.540.

24. R. Rose, *Influencing Voters: A Study in Campaign Rationality* (New York: St. Martin's Press, 1967); R. Rose and I. McAllister, *The Loyalties of Voters: A Lifetime Learning Model* (London, Newbury Park and New Delhi: SAGE Publications, 1990), p.2; S. Bowler and D.M. Farrell, 'The Study of Election Campaigning', in S. Bowler and D.M. Farrell (eds.), *Electoral Strategies and Political Marketing* (Oxford: St. Martin's Press, 1992), pp.1–23; J.J. Coleman, 'Party Organizational Strength and Public Support for Parties', *American Journal of Political Science*, 40 (1996), pp.806–7.

25. G. Pomper, *Passions and Interests. Political Party Concepts of American Democracy* (Lawrence, KS: University Press of Kansas, 1992), pp.41–2.

26. W.R. Schonfield, 'Political Parties: The Functional Approach and the Structural Alternative', *Comparative Politics*, 15 (1983), p.483.

27. M. Laver and N. Schofield, *Multiparty Government* (Oxford: Oxford University Press, 1990), p.10.

28. Cf. K. von Beyme, *Die politische Klasse im Parteienstaat* (Frankfurt a. M.: Suhrkamp, 1993), p.30.

29. K. Heidar, 'The Polymorphic Nature of Party Membership', *European Journal of Political Research*, 25 (1994), p.61.

30. R. Roth and E. Wiesendahl, *Das Handlungs-und Orientierungssystem politischer Parteien. Eine empirische Fallstudie* (Bremen: Forschungsgruppe Parteien demokratie, 1986), pp.104–9; R. Meyenberg, *SPD in der Provinz* (Frankfurt a. M.: Rita G. Fischer, 1978),

pp.108–20, 189–99; H. Schmitt, *Neue Politik in alten Parteien* (Opladen: Westdeutscher Verlag, 1987); B. Zeuner and J. Wischermann, *Rot–Grün in den Kommunen. Konfliktpotentiale und Reformperspektiven* (Opladen: Leske + Budrich, 1995), also see T.A. Koelble, *The Left Unraveled* (Durnham and London: Duke University Press, 1991), pp.32–5.
31. Cf. E. Wiesendahl, 'Identitätsauflösung. Anschlußsuche der Großparteien an die postindustrielle Gesellschaft', in R. Hettlage and L. Vogt (eds.), *Identitäten im Umbruch* (Opladen and Wiesbaden: Westdeutscher Verlag, in press, 1999).
32. W.E. Miller and K.M. Jennings, *Parties in Transition* (New York: Russell Sage Foundation, 1986), p.7.
33. K. Lawson, 'Conclusion: Toward a Theory of How Parties Work', in K. Lawson (ed.), *How Political Parties Work: Perspectives from within* (Westport, CT and London: Greenwood Publ. Group, 1994), p.295.
34. L. Svasand, 'Change and Adaption in Norwegian Party Organization', in R.S. Katz and P. Mair (eds.), *How Parties Organize* (London, Thousand Oaks and New Delhi: SAGE Publications, 1994), p.317.
35. Concerning the complicated and diffuse political decision making process in Germany, see M.G. Schmidt, 'Germany. The Grand Coalition State', in J.M. Colomer (ed.), *Political Institutions in Europe* (London and New York: Routledge, 1996), pp.73–93.
36. To become aware of such inconsistencies, one has to transcend the analysis of party statutes and go into the real internal functioning of parties. In contrast, see the purely formal approach of T. Poguntke, 'Party Organizations', in J.W. van Deth (ed.), *Comparative Politics: The problem of equivalence* (London and New York: Routledge, 1998), pp.156–79.
37. M.D. Cohen, J.G. March and J.P. Olsen, 'A Garbage Can Model of Organizational Choice', *Administrative Science Quarterly*, 17 (1972), pp.1–25.
38. E. Wiesendahl, 'Wie politisch sind politische Parteien?', in J.W. Falter, C. Fenner and M.Th. Greven (eds.), *Politische Willensbildung und Interessenvermittlung* (Opladen: Westdeutscher Verlag, 1984), pp.81–2.
39. P. Lösche and F. Walter, *Die SPD. Klassenpartei – Volkspartei – Quotenpartei* (Darmstadt: Wissenschaftliche Buchgesellschaft, 1992), pp.174, 194–200; P. Lösche, '"Lose verkoppelte Anarchie." Zur aktuellen Situation der Volksparteien am Beispiel der SPD', *Aus Politik und Zeitgeschichte*, 43 (1993), pp.39–40; P. Lösche, 'Haben die Volksparteien noch eine Chance? – Die SPD als lose verkoppelte Anarchie', *Politische Bildung*, 3 (1994), pp.42–4; also see S.J. Silvia, 'Loosely Coupled Anarchy: the Fragmentation of the Left', in S. Padgett (ed.), *Parties and Party Systems in the New Germany* (Dartmouth: Ashgate, 1993), pp.172–5; R. Roth and E. Wiesendahl, *Strukturbesonderheiten politischer Parteien. Zur Soziologie der Organisationswirklichkeit politischer Parteien* (Bremen: Forschungsgruppe Parteien-demokratie, 1985); A. Mintzel, 'Großparteien im Parteienstaat der Bundesrepublik Deutschland', *Aus Politik und Zeitgeschichte*, 11 (1989), pp.3–14.
40. C. Leggewie, *Die Republikaner. Phantombild der Neuen Rechten* (Berlin: Wagenbach, 1989), pp.44–5.
41. J. Schmid, *Die CDU. Organisationsstrukturen, Politiken und Funktionsweise einer Partei im Föderalismus* (Opladen: Leske + Budrich, 1990), pp.276–81; also see also J. Schmid, 'Die Volksparteien unter Anpassungsdruck', in G. Simonis (ed.), *Deutschland nach der Wende* (Opladen: Leske + Budrich, 1998), p.98; W. Schönbohm, *Die CDU wird moderne Volkspartei. Selbstverständnis, Mitglieder, Organisation und Apparat 1950–1980* (Stuttgart: Klett-Cotta, 1985), pp.218–19, 229–32.
42. P. Lösche, 'Kanzlerwahlverein? Zur Organisationskultur der CDU', in Dürr and Soldt (eds.), *Die CDU nach Kohl*, pp.70–71.
43. For further information, particularly on east Germany, see U. Schmidt, *Von der Blockpartei zur Volkspartei? Die Ost-CDU im Umbruch 1989–1994* (Opladen: Westdeutscher Verlag, 1997); U. Birsl aund P. Lösche, 'Parteien in West- und Ostdeutschland', *Zeitschrift für Parlamentsfragen*, 29 (1998), pp.7–24.
44. Wiesendahl, *Parteien in Perspektive*, pp.219–41
45. K. Lawson, 'Introduction', in Lawson (ed.), *How Political Parties Work*, pp.17–19.
46. Cf H. Kaack, *Geschichte und Struktur des deutschen Parteiensystems* (Opladen: Westdeutscher Verlag, 1971), pp.24–46.

47. K.-H. Naßmacher, *Parteien im Abstieg* (Opladen: Westdeutscher Verlag, 1988), p.267.
48. K.E. Weick, 'Educational Organizations as Loosely Coupled Systems', *Administrative Science Quarterly*, 17 (1976), pp.3–5.
49. M.A. Schwartz, *The Party Network: The Robust Organization of Illinois Republican* (Madison, WI: University of Wisconsin Press, 1990), p.260.
50. For basic information, see N. Brunsson, *The Organization of Hypocrisy: Talk, Decision and Actions in Organizations* (Chichester: John Wiley and Sons Inc., 1989).
51. *Frankfurter Rundschau*, 7 April 1998 *(Translator's note: the original quote is in German)*.
52. D. Kavanagh, *Election Campaigning: The New Marketing of Politics* (Oxford: Blackwell Publishers, 1995), p.35.
53. A. Mintzel, *Die CSU in Bayern* (Opladen: Westdeutscher Verlag, 1972); A. Mintzel, 'Auf der Suche nach der Wirklichkeit der Großparteien in der Bundesrepublik Deutschland', in H.-D. Klingemann uand W. Luthardt (eds.), *Wohlfahrtsstaat, Sozialstruktur und Verfassungsanalyse* (Opladen: Westdeutscher Verlag, 1993), pp 66–104.
54. A. Panebianco, *Political Parties: Organization and Power* (Cambridge: Cambridge University Press, 1988), p.264.
55. For information on the enormous increase in public financing for political parties, see C. Landfried, *Parteifinanzen und politische Macht* (Baden-Baden: Nomos, 2nd edn 1994), pp.114f., 271; R. Ebbighausen *et al.*, *Die Kosten der Parteiendemokratie. Studien und Materialien zu einer Bilanz staatlicher Parteienfinanzierung in der Bundesrepublik Deutschland* (Opladen: Westdeutscher Verlag, 1996), pp.437–45; H.H. von Arnim, *Die Partei, der Abgeordnete und das Geld. Parteienfinanzierung in Deutschland*, Neuausgabe (München: Knaur, 1996), pp.119–30.
56. T. Drysch, *Die staatliche Finanzierung der Parteien in Österreich, in der Schweiz und in der Bundesrepublik Deutschland* (Opladen: Leske + Budrich, 1998), pp.198–9.
57. Cf Schönbohm, *Die CDU wird moderne Volkspartei*, pp.295–300
58. H.-J. Lange, *Responsivität und Organization. Eine Studie über die Modernisierung der CDU von 1973–1989* (Marburg and Berlin: Schüren, 1994), p.16.
59. P. Haungs, 'Die CDU: Prototyp einer Volkspartei', in A. Mintzel and H. Oberreuter (eds.), *Parteien in der Bundesrepublik Deutschland* (Opladen: Leske + Budrich, 1992), pp.198–9; P. Haungs; 'Die CDU im Parteiensystem des vereinigten Deutschland', in P. Eisenmann and G. Hirscher (eds.), *Die Entwicklung der Volksparteien im vereinigten Deutschland* (München: Siedler, 1992), pp.15–17.
60. E. Wiesendahl, 'Der Marsch aus den Institutionen. Zur Organisationsschwäche politischer Parteien in den achtziger Jahren', *Aus Politik und Zeitgeschichte*, 21 (1990), pp.10–14.
61. S.E. Scarrow, *Parties and their Members, Organizing for Victory in Great Britain and Germany* (Oxford: Oxford University Press, 1996), p.61; E. Wiesendahl, 'Parteienkommunikation', in O. Jarren, U. Sarcinelli and U. Saxer (eds.), *Politische Kommunikation in der demokratischen Gesellschaft* (Wiesbaden and Opladen: Westdeutscher Verlag, 1998), pp.444–5.
62. Lösche, 'Lose verkoppelte Anarchie', p.42.
63. Landfried, *Parteifinanzen und politische Macht*, pp.94–95, 280–81; Ebbighausen *et al.*, *Die Kosten der Parteiendemokratie*, pp.167–8, 440–41; H. von Arnim, *Fetter Bauch reagiert nicht gern. Die politische Klasse – selbstbezogen und abgehoben* (München: Knaur, 1997), p.327; for European development, see P. Mair, 'Party Organizations: From Civil Society to the State', in Katz and Mair (eds.), *How Parties Organize*, p.4.
64. P. Radunski, 'Fit für die Zukunft? Die Volksparteien vor dem Superwahljahr 1994', *Sonde*, 4 (1991), pp.3–8.
65. Scarrow, *Parties and Their Members*, pp.40–48.
66. S. Immerfall, 'Strukturwandel und Strukturschwächen der deutschen Mitglieder parteien', *Aus Politik und Zeitgeschichte*, 1–2 (1998), p.7; for information on the characteristics of membership parties, see Scarrow, *Parties and Their Members*, pp.19–20; E. Wiesendahl, *Parteien in Perspektive*, pp.14–15.
67. For information on the development of membership, see Scarrow, *Parties and Their Members*, pp.57–8; E. Wiesendahl, 'Noch Zukunft für die Mitgliederparteien? Erstarrung und Revitalisierung innerparteilicher Partizipation', in A. Klein and R. Schmalz-Bruns

(eds.), *Politische Beteiligung und Bürgerschaftsengagement in Deutschland – Möglichkeiten und Grenzen* (Baden-Baden: Nomos, 1997), pp.350–56.

68. Wiesendahl, 'Noch Zukunft für die Mitgliederparteien?', pp.357–63; for the CDU, see C. Wagner, 'Bis zum Bauch im Wasser. Die Kehrseite der CDU– Erfolgsgeschichte', *Blätter für deutsche und internationale Politik* (1996), pp.194–9.

69. For further information, see recent studies on member surveys conducted by the SPD executive (ed.), *Aus Erfahrung lernen. Die wichtigsten Ergebnisse aus der Befragung von Mitgliedern und Funktionsträgern* (Bonn, 1992); SPD executive (ed.), *Junge Frauen in der SPD* (Bonn, 1994); H.-J. Veen and V. Neu, *Politische Beteiligung in der Volkspartei* (Konrad-Adenauer-Stiftung, Interne Studien no. 113, Sankt Augustin, 1995).

70. See R.S. Katz, 'Party as a Linkage: A Vestigal Function?', *European Journal of Political Research*, 18 (1990), p.15.

71. See M.Th. Greven, *Parteimitglieder* (Opladen: Westdeutscher Verlag, 1987), pp.136–39.

72. W. Streeck, 'Vielfalt und Interdependenz. Probleme intermediärer Organisationen in sich ändernden Umwelten', *Kölner Zeitschrift für Soziologie und Sozialpsychologie*, 39 (1987), p.475.

73. For information on the mistrust of the SPD grass roots towards the party leaders, see F. Walter, 'Die SPD nach der Vereinigung – Partei in der Krise oder bereit zur Regierungsübernahme?', *Zeitschrift für Parlamentsfragen*, 26 (1995), pp.88–9.

74. K. von Beyme, 'Funktionswandel der Parteien in der Entwicklung von der Massenmitgliederpartei zur Partei der Berufspolitiker', in Gabriel *et al.* (eds.), *Parteiendemokratie in Deutschland* (Opladen and Wiesbaden: Westdeutscher Verlag, 1997), pp.272–3.

75. See U. Sarcinelli, 'Parteien und Politikvermittlung: Von der Parteien- zur Mediendemokratie?' in U. Sarcinelli (ed.), *Politikvermittlung und Demokratie in der Mediengesellschaft* (Opladen and Wiesbaden: Westdeutscher Verlag, 1998), pp.293–6.

Luck and Good Management: Helmut Kohl as Parliamentary and Electoral Strategist

PETER PULZER

On 28 September 1998, a day after German electors had voted to defeat his government, Helmut Kohl declared that he would step down not only as Chancellor, a post he had held for 16 years, but also as chairman of the CDU, a post he had held for 25 years. This was an unprecedented reaction to a German electoral outcome, even taking into account that it was a reaction to an unprecedented electoral verdict. According to the Basic Law (Art. 23), it is the Bundestag, not the people, who elect the head of government. In the 45 years since the Basic Law was adopted, only one change of Chancellor has taken place as a result of a Bundestag election: the change from Kiesinger to Brandt in 1969. All others – from Adenauer to Erhard (1963), from Erhard to Kiesinger (1966), from Brandt to Schmidt (1974) and from Schmidt to Kohl (1982) had happened in mid-term, as a result either of a revolt by the Chancellor's party or of a coalition crisis. Even the post-election change of 1969 was not a foregone conclusion. The grand coalition of CDU and SPD was not defeated by the voters and could have continued in power had the two parties wished it. The change, which was bitterly resented by the incumbent Chancellor and the CDU, happened because the SPD and FDP, with the blessing of President Heinemann, had agreed on it.[1] In fact, in 1998 the Basic Law had, as always, the last word. Kohl remained in office until the Bundestag assembled on 27 October and cast its votes in favour of Gerhard Schröder. But, however unprecedented the events of 27 September may have been, there was nothing predetermined about Kohl's reaction to them. There is no convention in Germany that a head of government should offer to resign immediately upon electoral defeat, analogous to the convention that has existed in Britain since 1868, when Disraeli resigned on learning of the Liberal victory at the polls, instead of waiting to be defeated in the House of Commons. Kohl therefore set a precedent, not merely by losing an election, but by drawing conclusions from the defeat as if Germany possessed a parliamentary

Peter Pulzer, All Souls' College, Oxford

constitution on the Westminster model. He set another precedent, by automatically associating the chancellorship with the leadership of the dominant party, again in accordance with Westminster conventions. Other Chancellors, including Adenauer and Brandt, have combined the two posts, but did not see the necessity of giving up the party leadership on ceasing to be Chancellor. Having targeted the party ladder as the way to the chancellorship for most of his early career, Kohl had less difficulty in seeing the connection between government and party offices than any of his predecessors or, initially at least, his immediate successor.

KOHL CLIMBS THE LADDER

To illustrate this point, it may be as well to summarise Kohl's party career, in both his native Land of Rhineland-Palatinate and in federal politics. He is unusual for a Christian Democrat of his generation in having been a professional politician for almost the whole of his adult life – a career path more usual in a bureaucratised mass-integration party like the SPD. In 1959, before he was 30 years old, he had become a city councillor and chairman of the CDU in Ludwigshafen, the biggest city in Rhineland-Palatinate, as well as a member of the Landtag. Even before that he had been active in the CDU's youth organisation, the Junge Union, which he had joined in 1947 while still at school, becoming chairman of the Junge Union's Land branch in 1954, at the age of 24. This position was a stepping stone to the Land executive (*Landesvorstand*) a year later.[2] Once in the Landtag, he advanced even faster. Within two years – at the age of 31 – he was deputy leader of the CDU *Fraktion*, within four years, in 1963, its leader, and within five years chairman of the Land organisation, which entitled him to membership of the CDU's federal executive (*Bundesvorstand*). He was re-elected to the Land chairmanship four times, in 1966, 1968, 1970 and 1972, each time overwhelmimgly. Leadership of the Land party was a prerequisite for realising the ambition of succeeding the veteran Peter Altmeier as Prime Minister. An informal agreement between the two men left Altmeier free to seek a further term in 1967, provided he stepped down in mid-term to hand the succession to Kohl. This duly happened, enabling Kohl to acquire his first executive office without a contest. He was re-elected in 1971 at the head of a CDU that won 50 per cent of the vote, its highest share in seven Landtag elections, and improved on this figure in 1975 with 53.9 per cent, an all-time record.

   Though Rhineland-Palatinate is one of the smaller (and at that time was one of the poorer) Länder, with a marginal role in federal politics and not an obvious springboard for a national political career, Kohl was now established as a formidable vote winner, ready for a move onto the national political scene. His first 14 years in politics were marked by that combination of factors that are essential for success in public life: luck and good management.[3] The luck consisted in the retirement of the founder-generation of West German politicians, personified in Rhineland-Palatinate by Altmeier, and in a favourable climate for the CDU. The 1971 Landtag election was marked by the decline of the neo-Nazi NPD, which had entered the Landtag in 1967, and the crisis in the FDP following its entry into the 'social-liberal' coalition of Willy Brandt. Though the SDP actually gained slightly more from this trend to the major parties (3.7 per cent, compared with the CDU's 3.4 per cent), it was the CDU's absolute majority that caught the headlines. Moreover, the crowning victory of 1975, in which the CDU's lead over the SPD widened from 9.5 per cent to 15.4 per cent, was a much less ambiguous endorsement of Kohl.

The good management consisted in Kohl's understanding of the role of party in the maturing West German political system. Unlike the SPD, which had risen from the ashes of the Third Reich to assume its highly structured mass-membership organisation within three or four years, the CDU was a party of local and regional notables, with a small and largely inactive membership base. It owed its strength to its voter appeal, not the enthusiasm of militant activists. Of the first three CDU Chancellors none had risen through the ranks; indeed they became party leaders as a result of becoming Chancellor, not the other way round. Konrad Adenauer had indeed been an established politician in the old Zentrum party before 1933 and chairman of the British zone CDU before becoming Chancellor, but he did not become chairman of the federal CDU until 1950, a year after being elected Chancellor. His successor, Ludwig Erhard, entered politics at the top, first as Minister for the Economy in Bavaria, then as economic director of the Anglo-American bi-zone from 1947 to 1949 and finally as Adenauer's Minister for the Economy. He was elected party chairman in March 1966, only eight months before he ceased to be Chancellor, and held the office for only 14 months. The third, Kurt-Georg Kiesinger, had a slightly more conventional party career, beginning as a member of the first Bundestag in 1949, but was within nine years, in 1958, Prime Minister of Baden-Württemberg, an altogether shorter and easier rise than Kohl's systematic march through the ranks. He succeeded Erhard as chairman in May 1967, having already been Chancellor for nearly six months.

Parallel to his steady, even if not effortless, advance in his Land party, Kohl made sure of his base in the federal party organisation. In 1969, the year he became Prime Minister of Rhineland-Palatinate, he was elected one of the vice-chairmen of the federal CDU. In 1971, still only 41 years old, he stood for the national chairmanship, but was defeated by the more senior Rainer Barzel. Yet the combination of luck and good management once more came to his aid. Barzel's sun set almost as soon as it had risen. In 1972, with the Bundestag evenly balanced between government and opposition deputies, he attempted to topple Brandt from the chancellorship by means of the constructive vote of no confidence and failed. Later that year, after the dissolution of the Bundestag, he led the CDU to its worst result since 1949. He was constrained to resign in 1973, enabling Kohl to embark on his 25-year national leadership of the party.

Once he was chairman, he drew the lesson for the national party that he had drawn locally: that personal political success and long-term electoral success depended on command of a sound party structure. As long as the CDU was the natural majority party of the Federal Republic, the need to modernise the organisation could be neglected. The change of government in 1969 was attributed by many in the CDU to a conspiracy rather than a clear electoral verdict: the CDU had, after all, still emerged as the strongest single party. After 1972 that consolation was no longer available. Moreover, the CDU's grip on politics in the Länder was weakening, Kohl's triumphs in Rhineland-Palatinate notwithstanding. The CDU lost control of the largest Land, North Rhine-Westphalia, in 1966 – never, as it turned out, to regain it. This trend threatened not only the CDU's control of the Bundesrat, but its implantation in a level of government that was the main source of new blood.

Kohl's record as party moderniser in Rhineland-Palatinate provided ambiguous guidelines. In two respects his leadership was unquestionably successful. In eight years party membership almost doubled, from 33,000 in 1966 to 60,000 in 1974. He also introduced new talent to the party's representation in Bonn, including two future Federal Presidents, Richard von Weizsäcker and Roman Herzog.[4] In other respects he had acted as a young man on the make. Having entered the party organisation through the Junge Union, he demanded rejuvenation of the leadership and even presented himself as advocate of the party's left wing. He also adopted the classic device of the party rebel, that of demanding the sovereignty of the *Fraktion*, which was his power-base in the early 1960s, over the government, even on nominations to ministerial posts. Once he was national party leader these sins of his youth were conveniently forgotten. The lessons he remembered were the necessity of building up a membership base and of appealing to the centre ground of politics.

KOHL AS PARTY LEADER

In the question of membership recruitment the success of the newly installed national leadership is easily documented, though Kohl needs to share the credit with the CDU's general secretaries, Bruno Heck (1967–73),

Kurt Biedenkopf (1973–77) and Heiner Geißler (1977–89). As long as the CDU was the governing party, grass-roots membership had not counted for much. Elections were predominantly plebiscites on behalf of first Adenauer and then Erhard. It was only with the loss of power in 1969 that the organisational deficit became glaring and the resulting recruitment drive was already well under way by the time Kohl became party chairman. From 304,000 in 1969, membership had gone up to 457,000 in 1973. By 1982, the year in which Kohl became Chancellor, it was 719,000.[5] Indeed, in the early 1980s the combined memberships of the CDU and CSU almost equalled that of the SPD. Equally important for the future of the party was the rejuvenation of the Junge Union, where the proportion of under-25s rose from 25 per cent in the early 1970s to over 50 per cent in 1983.

The appeal to the centre ground meant that Kohl was committed to coalition government. In contrast with elections under the Westminster model, which are almost invariably zero-sum games, Kohl appreciated that in Germany the opportunity of governing without a coalition partner was likely to be the exception rather than rule. Anxious to keep the SPD out of power, he concluded at an early stage that partnership with the FDP was essential. A CDU–FDP coalition had been the rule in Rhineland-Palatinate and Kohl offered the FDP participation in his government even after securing his absolute majority in 1971. This strategy was not universally popular within the party. True, the consensus-minded wing that favoured grand coalitions with the SPD, initially strong, was gradually weakened under Adenauer's influence. At the other extreme, there were those who disliked the dependence on the FDP, particularly identified with the Bavarian CSU and its leader, Franz-Josef Strauß, who pressed the party to aim for absolute majorities. It was this wing that was to cause Kohl most trouble in the late 1970s.

Kohl's entry into federal electoral politics came in 1976. The omens for success were good, in marked contrast with the circumstances of the 1972 election. In 1972 the CDU was defeated not only by Brandt's charisma and the triumph of *Ostpolitik*, not to mention Rainer Barzel's unappealing personality, but also by poor organisation and inept campaigning. By 1976 the effects of the CDU's organisational and political renewal, over which Kohl had presided, were in evidence. Since the CDU could no longer count on the 'Chancellor bonus' that had stood it in good stead until 1969, and since it could no longer pretend to itself that its oppositional role was a temporary accident that time would put right, it needed to campaign professionally and now had the resources to do so.[6] The circumstances of Brandt's departure from office and the straitened economic situation following the oil shocks had taken much of the shine off the SPD's triumph. It is, moreover, worth remembering that election campaigning hardly ever stops in Germany. Staggered Landtag elections mean that there are few electorally latent phases. Between March 1974 and April 1976 there were ten Landtag elections – one in each Land – and in all but one of these the CDU made substantial gains. In February 1976, eight months before the Bundestag election, the CDU took power in Lower Saxony, giving it a lead of 25 votes to 16 in the Bundesrat. With their high turn-out and direct impact on federal politics, Landtag elections can be crucial in affecting the standing of parties and party leaders, as we shall see in later episodes.

As far as the circumstances of the campaign permitted, Kohl pursued the tactics that had secured his previous successes. Since the FDP was still in coalition with the SPD, he could not credibly recommend a coalition on the Rhineland-Palatinate model, but he could stress the merits of that model and his belief in government by coalition. He also presented himself as a man of the centre ground: 'Ich propagiere kein Freund-Feind-Verhältnis' ('I do not propagate a friend–enemy relationship').[7] This was a slightly disingenuous claim, as the CDU's official slogan, inspired by the CSU, was the highly polarising 'Freedom instead of Socialism'. Predictably, Helmut Schmidt, as incumbent, led Kohl in the polls, but by a much narrower margin than Brandt had enjoyed four years earlier. The outcome was a confirmation of the CDU's recovery. It received 48.6 per cent of the vote, its second-best result ever and a higher share than Kohl achieved in three of the four federal elections that he later won.

This near-victory had a twofold effect on his chances. On the one hand it convinced him that he was the coming man and that he had therefore to move his base from Mainz to Bonn. Parliament, not a provincial capital, needed to be the springboard for a future Chancellor. He therefore resigned his premiership and took up his Bundestag seat. But a near-victory is also a defeat and this gave Strauß, who had never approved of Kohl's centrist candidature, his chance for revenge. At a post-election meeting of the CSU Bundestag caucus at Wildbad Kreuth he proposed turning the CSU into a nation-wide conservative party that would compete with the CDU for the right-of-centre vote, and ending the joint *Fraktion* of the two parties in the Bundestag. This was not the first time Strauß had played with the idea of a 'fourth party'; the reasoning behind it lay, then as on this later occasion, in the question of what to do about the FDP: whether to seduce it back from the SPD, as Kohl wanted to, or to crush it, so as to secure an absolute majority for Christian Democracy. As it turned out, the Kreuth decision was a 23-day wonder. Unity of a sort was restored when it emerged that all Strauß's plan would achieve was to end the CDU's role as an integrationist *Volkspartei*, the preservation of which Kohl saw as the key to future electoral victory.

KOHL AS CHANCELLOR

This victory, however, proved to be elusive. Kohl was still only leader of the opposition; the agenda-setting intiative lay, as usual, with the Chancellor. As Schmidt's *Modell Deutschland* acquired firmer contours, the SPD improved its electoral standing. In all except one of the Landtag elections between 1976 and 1980, the CDU/CSU lost votes, an unusual experience for an opposition party. Under the leadership of Oskar Lafontaine the SPD became, for the first time, the strongest party in Saarland. These disappointing developments made Kohl a less attractive standard-bearer for the 1980 Bundestag election, and enough CDU delegates joined with the CSU to nominate Strauß. That candidature was a predictable disaster. The Christian Democrats lost 4.1 per cent; even in Bavaria Strauß did less well than Kohl had done four years earlier. The *tertius gaudens* was Strauß's arch-enemy, the FDP, which rose from 7.9 per cent to 10.6 per cent. Strauß's discomfiture marked the revival of Kohl's fortunes.

The reinforced social-liberal majority turned out to be more fragile than at first appeared. Unlike Kohl, Schmidt had neglected the management of his party, which continued to be led by Brandt as chairman even after his resignation as Chancellor. Discontent within the left wing of the SPD with Schmidt's strict budgetary policy, and, above all, his 'twin-track' decision on the deployment of NATO missiles, brought strains into the coalition, culminating in its collapse in September 1982. Once more luck enabled Kohl to show good management. Given the readiness of the FDP to leave the apparently sinking ship of the Schmidt government, Kohl was the only plausible CDU candidate for the chancellorship. He was duly elected to that post on 1 October in accordance with Art. 67(1) of the Basic Law, the first time that a constructive vote of confidence had been successfully applied. A coalition with the FDP corresponded exactly with his long-term strategy. The price for achieving this was generous treatment of his coalition partner, including the retention of Hans-Dietrich Genscher as Foreign Minister. He was quite willing to pay this price, partly as a way of disciplining his party, even more to snub the CSU, which had only one seat fewer than the FDP.

To be Chancellor was gratifying, to be Chancellor without a popular mandate was not. Although he gained office in strict accordance with the constitution, and one of the aims of the Basic Law was to prevent premature dissolutions of parliament of the kind that had been the bane of the Weimar Republic, Kohl announced that he regarded himself head of a provisional government only, for the purpose of passing the budget that the Schmidt government had failed to pass. All participants – Kohl himself, Genscher and the relevant *Fraktionen* – made it clear that thereafter they proposed to hold fresh elections.[8] The only device available for this purpose was that prescribed by Art. 68 (1) of the Basic Law, which permitted dissolution if the Chancellor lost a vote of confidence, but there was no majority for a successor. In other words, this article was not designed for the purpose to which the government now wished to put it, as a means of securing a dissolution even though the government enjoyed an adequate working majority. The constitutionality of this move therefore had to be determined by the Federal Constitutional Court. The Court sanctioned it by a majority vote, but only on the grounds that the Bundestag's confidence had been granted for a limited period and that the government's survival was therefore not assured.[9] It is, however, reasonable to say that Kohl's and Genscher's motives were rather different. Political conventions in the Federal Republic had changed since the adoption of the Basic Law. Though the Bundestag still formally elected the Chancellor, that procedure had become, to borrow Bagehot's formulation, the dignified part of the constitution; its efficient secret lay in the role of the electorate. The campaigning language of the parties had made this quite clear. In 1980 both the SPD and the FDP had stated that a vote for them was a vote for Schmidt's continued chancellorship. The evolution of the party system from 1949, when it still bore some resemblance to that of Weimar, meant that an unambiguous choice of one chancellorship candidate or another had become the norm. A Chancellor without an electoral mandate, especially one at the head of a coalition different from that endorsed at an election, therefore suffered from deficient legitimacy. In this case the deficit was rectified by the election of 6 March 1983, at which the CDU emerged with 48.8 per cent, its second highest vote ever, and only six seats short of an absolute majority.

It would be a mistake to assume from the way Kohl finally became Chancellor that his career up to that point was marked by a strategy of Napoleonic consistency for getting from the Junge Union to the Palais Schaumburg. Yet his progress and ultimate success did reflect his understanding of the West German political system. He appreciated that progress up the political ladder required command of a party structure and that the stronger the party organisation, the more effective campaigning would be. He also appreciated that the Federal Republic can be governed only from the political centre, preferably by coalition; hence his rejection of the type of confrontational politics preached by Strauß. He appreciated further that elected office needs constant re-legitimisation by voters and that all elections, whether European, federal, regional or even local, are useful to this end – hence his frequent interventions even in Land election campaigns after he became Chancellor. He appreciated above all that to be effective, executive leadership must be combined with party leadership. To that extent he had a better understanding of the degree to which the German political system has become parliamentarised than many of his contemporaries. It explains why he insisted on retaining the party chairmanship once he had become Chancellor, despite opposition to this combination of offices from within the CDU. It also explains why, following his defeat in 1998, he resigned both offices simultaneously. Just as he saw no point in being Chancellor without also being party leader, so he saw no point in being party leader without also being Chancellor.

However, from the perspective of a newly elected head of government, the relationship with party and parliament undergoes a change. From that point onwards, both these institutions are required to occupy subordinate positions. The party must be managed, if only to secure its continued usefulness as a *Kanzlerwahlverein* (an association for electing the Chancellor), but it must be prevented from imposing policies and personalities on the government. In party management Kohl retained his expertise. All those within the party who challenged his authority, whether Kurt Biedenkopf, Heiner Geißler or Lothar Späth, were marginalised. Parliament required different treatment. While his government could not survive without the support of the Bundestag majority, Kohl delegated the management of the parliamentary party to others. His parliamentary appearances were few. As far as possible he faced the Bundestag with *faits accomplis*, the outcome of decisions made not so much round the cabinet table, but in the chancellery, or in *tête-à-têtes* with individual ministers, senior civil servants or personal advisers. In so far as he had problems with parliament, these arose from the Bundesrat, especially from 1997 onwards, and these had their cause in the CDU's increasing electoral weakness at the Land level. The instruments through which he had risen had largely served their purpose. Now that he was Chancellor, he could exploit to the full the bonus that that office conferred. His real power base was the voters, who had given him unprecedented majorities in Rhineland-Palatinate and almost unprecedented support federally in 1976 and 1983. They were to confirm him in office three more times, even if less decisively.

In the early years of Kohl's chancellorship it was by no means obvious that he would be the Federal Republic's longest serving head of government. Like many modern politicians he was initially a better campaigner than policy executant. The much vaunted '*Wende*' (political turn-around), with which he embarked on government, turned out to have little substance. He secured re-election in 1987 with a vote of 44.3 per cent for the CDU/CSU, more or less average for the post-1969 years. His coalition's majority was slightly reduced, from 58 seats to 41. He owed this moderate success partly to an improved performance by the FDP, now recovering from the crisis of 1982, and even more to the continuing weakness of the SPD, which was far from recovering from its internal crisis. The course of his second term was even less promising than his first. Kohl's informal leadership style impressed neither his party nor the voters. Though he managed to retain control of his party, thanks to the combination of chairmanship and chancellorship,[10] his grip on the electorate weakened. Landtag elections resulted in some spectacular declines in the CDU vote. Though the CDU managed to capture control of normally 'red' Hesse, it lost Schleswig-Holstein and Lower Saxony to the SPD, Saarland having already gone that way in 1985. Only with some difficulty did Kohl stave off a challenge to his chancellorship candidature for 1990. But before that election could take place, events presented him with the most spectacular combination yet of luck with the chance of good management. The collapse of the GDR, coinciding with the accelerated negotiations for a Treaty of European Union, enabled Kohl to turn the defects of his leadership style into assets.

THE CHANCELLOR OF UNITY

The evolution of Kohl's chancellorship shows how little the Basic Law tells us about the powers of that office. The capacity to determine policy guidelines (*Richtlinienkompetenz*) – the wording of Article 65 hardly differs from that of Article 56 of the Weimar constitution – depends heavily on personal and macro-political factors. It was the favourable conjuncture these two that enabled Kohl to transform himself from a potential election loser to being the Chancellor of Unification, whether German or European. From both these processes the party, parliament and even the cabinet were largely excluded. In part this lay in the nature of the questions to be answered. All chancellors have had more discretion – and a clearer view of their role – in foreign affairs and *Deutschlandpolitik* than in the wear-and-tear of domestic politics. All the same, a look at the roll-call of Kohl's principal advisers and negotiating assistants shows how few of them were drawn from the regular organs of the constitution. A principal ally in both negotiations was Jacques Delors, the President of the European Commisssion, a principal domestic participant the Bundesbank. In the negotiations for European Monetary Union he relied principally on Horst Köhler, State Secretary in the Ministry of Finance, Hans Tietmeyer, a member of the Council of the Bundesbank, and, in a more informal capacity, Alfred Herrhausen, chairman of the Deutsche Bank.[11] This choice of participants caused many resentments; it also enabled Kohl to get his way on both EMU and the European Central Bank.

Procedures were not very different when it came to German unification. In Dieter Grosser's 584-page authorised history of the unification process, the Bundestag gets eight index references, the Bundesrat seven, the CDU nine. In contrast, Köhler gets 20, Johannes Ludewig, head of the economic section of the chancellery, 26 and Tietmeyer 47.[12] The fruits of these negotiations were presented to the German parliament as *faits accomplis*. They went through with little debate and less difficulty. But they were not conducted in a domestic vacuum. The SPD had declared itself in favour of monetary union; the principle was therefore not contentious. As for unification, polls throughout 1990 showed majority support, increasing as the year went on. In addition there was tangible electoral evidence. The first democratic election for the Volkskammer of the GDR on 18 March 1990 gave the CDU-led Alliance for Germany 48 per cent. Though nominally an election for an East Geman parliament, it was, in effect, a referendum on unification and a vote of confidence in Kohl. Kohl had revealed himself as something no one had taken him for before: a gambler who wins. Only two months earlier CDU strategists had assumed that the SPD enjoyed a structural advantage in the GDR, based on the historical strength of the working-class left in that part of Germany: hence the decision not to let the CDU fight on its own. In fact, the CDU won the majority of the working-class vote. In the most heavily industrialised of the GDR's 14 districts, Karl-Marx-Stadt (that is, Chemnitz), with 61 per cent employed in manufacturing, the Alliance won 60.8 per cent, its highest vote.[13]

The Bundestag election of 2 December 1990 was the first free all-German election for 58 years: its outcome was a foregone conclusion. Kohl profited not only from his own triumph as a unifier, but, as in 1987 and again in 1994, from the weakness of the opposition. His opponent Oskar Lafontaine's apparent lack of enthusiasm for unification produced the worst result for the SPD since 1961: 33.5 per cent. Yet Kohl was somewhere short of a landslide. In the area of the old Federal Republic, the CDU's share was 44.1 per cent, a fraction down on 1987. The government's majority was boosted by the Genscher effect, which gave the FDP 10.6 per cent, a gain of 1.5 per cent. In the old GDR, the CDU, this time campaigning on its own, won 41.8 per cent, slightly down on the Alliance's Volkskammer triumph. Kohl's third and fourth terms were very different from his first two, though no less difficult. On the one hand, he was now a world-class statesman: no one could any longer say he was a provincial out of his depth in Bonn. On the other hand, he had to manage a more a heterogeneous society, a more fragmented party system, more severe allocational disputes and a more complex federal structure, consisting of 16 instead of ten Länder. His management of unification enabled him to bestride German domestic politics. It would not have been difficult to predict that whoever won the first all-German election would dominate German politics for the best part of a decade, and so it turned out. Yet there was a price for this dominance. It was one thing to occupy the commanding heights, another to win on details. Kohl had underestimated – or at least had given the impression of underestimating – the burden of rehabilitating the East German economy and of meeting the expectations of

East German citizens. He had promised 'blossoming landscapes' in the former GDR, admittedly without naming a final date; rather more rashly, he had promised that no German would be worse off as a result of unification. When it turned out that the resulting budget deficit made higher interest rates unavoidable and that transfer payments, which absorbed some four per cent of the GDP of the western Länder, required tax rises, there was understandable anger among the voters. This was shown not only in opinion poll findings, but in Landtag elections and therefore the composition of the Bundesrat. The government had already lost control of the Bundesrat as a result of the Lower Saxony election in May 1990; to this was now added the loss of Rhineland-Palatinate in 1991. For the first time Kohl's home state was governed by a coalition of the SPD and FDP under Rudolf Scharping. The eastern Länder to some extent re-balanced these losses. The first elections there in October 1990 produced one CDU government (in Saxony), one SPD-dominated 'traffic light' coalition (with the FDP and Greens, in Brandenburg) and four grand coalitions in which the CDU was the senior partner (in Thuringia, Saxony-Anhalt and Mecklenburg-West Pomerania, as well as the newly constituted Land of Berlin, which voted in December). The first sign that the grip of the CDU on the eastern Länder was loosening came with the second wave of Landtag elections in 1994, when the grand coalition in Saxony-Anhalt collapsed and was replaced by a minority SPD–Green administration, relying on PDS toleration.

Yet, when it came to the Bundestag election of 1994, the Kohl factor could once again produce victory for the government, if only just. The CDU/CSU and FDP emerged with a majority of ten seats over the combined opposition – it would have been six had the CDU not obtained most of the *Überhangmandate* (surplus seats), by winning a disproportionate number of constituency seats in the eastern Länder. The 1994 election also showed more clearly than its predecessor the deepening cleavage between east and west. In the western Länder the shares of the votes scarcely differed from those of the last pre-unification election of 1987, ranging from a gain of 0.5 per cent by the SDP to a loss of 2.2 per cent by the CDU/CSU. The eastern Länder were much more volatile. The PDS nearly doubled its 1990 vote, from 13.1 per cent to 19.8 per cent. The FDP lost three-quarters of its support, from 12.9 per cent to 3.5 per cent. Of the major parties, the CDU lost 3.3 per cent compared with 1.9 per cent in the west, while the SPD gained 7.1 per cent, compared with 1.7 per cent in the west.[14]

AN ELECTION TOO FAR

Though the SPD had stopped the rot, it still did not look like a winning party. Its Chancellor candidate, Rudolf Scharping, had looked unconvincing. Once more the CDU had won thanks to its opponent's weakness as much as its own merits. For the following two years the CDU's re-confirmed dominance continued. Kohl and the CDU stayed ahead in the opinion polls and the CDU improved its share of the vote in five out of eight Landtag elections, without, however, depriving the SPD of its majority in the Bundesrat. When, therefore, Kohl announced in April 1997 that, contrary to his previous declared intentions, he would seek his party's nomination for another four-year term, it looked as though he had stolen a march yet again on his opponents. Despite some murmurings from the CDU's 'young Turks' – as well as some old Turks, such as Kurt Biedenkopf – he could be certain of the nomination. He could be equally certain of the FDP's support. The SPD had no nominee for the chancellorship and was not planning to have one for another year. Yet beneath the surface there were less favourable developments. At the 1995 SPD congress, in a ruthlesslessly planned operation, Oskar Lafontaine seized the party chairmanship from the lacklustre Scharping and set about renewing the party's organisation and morale. In addition, Lafontaine's main rival, Gerhard Schröder was planning his re-election as Prime Minister of Lower Saxony to ensure his claim to the SPD nomination as Chancellor candidate. He succeeded triumphantly on 1 March 1998, after which the SPD lead in the polls, already in evidence since 1997, widened dramatically. Even more ominously, Schröder led Kohl by more than 2:1 as the preferred Chancellor.

Personalities were not the only reason for the change of fortune. Unemployment had remained stubbornly high at over ten per cent overall and nearly twice that in the eastern Länder. Above all, the government was beginning to pay the price for its electoral failures at the Land level. These were underlined by further CDU losses in Saxony-Anhalt in April 1998, which confirmed the PDS-supported SPD administration in office. In the first post-unification legislative period it had been possible to secure consensus between Bundestag and Bundesrat on major measures, in particular the Solidarity Pact of 1993. Now, in anticipation of a change of government, the SPD was determined to use its blocking majority in the Bundesrat, with the result that nothing came of Kohl's much heralded 'reform of the century' in taxation and social security.

The election of 27 September 1998 confirmed these anticipations. The CDU/CSU dropped 6.3 per cent to 35.1 per cent, its FDP partner 0.7 per cent to 6.2 per cent The SPD gained 4.5 per cent to reach 40.9 per cent and became the strongest party for only the second time since the Second World War. The difference between east and west was further accentuated. In the eastern Länder the CDU lost 11.2 per cent to 27.3 per cent, in the western 5.0 per cent to 37.1 per cent. The SPD gained 4.8 per cent in the west to reach 42.3 per cent, but only 3.1 per cent to 35.6 per cent in the east, where it had to share the protest vote with an improved PDS (+1.8 per cent) and extreme right (+3.0 per cent).

For only the second time in his long career Kohl, now aged 68, discovered what it was like to lose an election. Was the cause bad luck or bad management? Overwhelmingly the latter. Kohl and his government suffered not only from office fatigue, but from the wrong choice of issue. He campaigned predominantly on his past achievements over German and European unity, yet European Monetary Union, arguably one of the major revolutions of the twentieth century, aroused scarcely any interest during the campaign. Germans were worried about jobs and pensions; their criterion was future competence, not historical triumphs. There was a special irony in Kohl's defeat, in that he failed to learn the lessons of his own career. He had risen through his ability to turn his party into an effective electoral machine and using parliament, first in Mainz and then in Bonn, as his campaigning base. Once elected Chancellor he was determined, unlike his predecessor, Helmut Schmidt, to see the party leadership as an essential supporting tool. Events confirmed this assumption since, more often than not, Kohl fared less well than the CDU in popularity. This differential was strikingly in evidence in the months up to the election, when the popularity gap between Kohl and the CDU steadily widened, and since even the CDU had now fallen behind the SPD, its greater appeal could not save him.[15] In many ways the old methods worked less well in the more heterogeneous party landscape after unification, as illustrated by the CDU's failure in Landtag elections. The frequent purges demotivated sections of the party, as the circle of Kohl's trusted advisers grew narrower. Above all, he never learnt to use some of the main organs of the constitution to his advantage, in particular the cabinet and the Bundestag; instead, he worked by circumventing them.

In Kohl's first federal election the CDU won nearly half the total vote, in his last, 22 years later, little more than one-third. Yet in important respects the comparison is misleading. In the intervening period the party system has changed and the GDR has become part of the Federal Republic. Had Kohl retired from the political scene in 1998, he would have gone down in history as Adenauer's equal as an election winner, one of Max Weber's 'dictators of the electoral battlefield'.[16] Over the whole period, the CDU's ability to retain its constituency has been remarkable. It remains the most successful Christian Democratic party in Europe, even though the social structure has moved against it. The number of observant Christians has declined; even the old Catholic milieu is not what it was. Farmers now make up no more than five per cent of the economically active population. The advantage that the CDU possessed among women voters disappeared in the early 1970s. Given these conditions, it has done remarkably well. Success, it has been said, has many fathers, but one of the claimants to paternity must be Helmut Kohl, who helped to oversee the party's organisational revival after the 1969 defeat.

NOTES

1. A. Baring, *Machtwechsel. Die Ära Brandt-Scheel* (Stuttgart: Deutsche Verlag-Anstalt, 1982), pp.173–85.
2. W. Hackel, *Die Auswahl des politischen Nachwuchses in der Bundesrepublik Deutschland. Die Junge Union als Sprungbrett für politische Karriere in der CDU* (Stuttgart: Verlag Bonn Aktuell, 1978), pp.243–4, 252; cf. C. Huneeus, 'How to Build a Modern Party: Helmut Kohl's Leadership and the Transformation of the CDU', *German Politics*, 5, 3 (Dec. 1996), pp.439, 442.
3 For details on Kohl's career, see W. Filmer and H. Schwan (eds.), *Helmut Kohl* (Düsseldorf: Econ Verlag, 2nd edn., 1990), and P. Hintze and G. Langguth (eds.), *Der Kurs der CDU. Reden und Beiträge des Bundesvorsitzenden 1973–1993* (Stuttgart: Deutsche-Verlags Anstalt, 1993).
4. Huneeus, 'How to Build a Modern Party', pp.443, 445.
5. A. Mintzel and H. Oberreuter (eds.), *Parteien in der Bundesrepublik Deutschland* (Bonn: Bundeszentrale für politische Bildung, 1990), p.432.
6. G. Pridham, *Christian Democracy in Western Germany* (London: Croom Helm, 1977), pp.342–6.
7. H. Kohl, 'Ich bin ein Mann der Mitte', *Die Zeit*, 16 July 1976, p.3. For the campaign in general, see W. Kaltefleiter, *Vorspiel zum Wechsel. Eine Analyse der Bundestagswahl 1976* (Berlin: Duncker und Humblot, 177), chapter II.4, 'Zwischen Sympathiewerbung und Konfrontation', pp.168–75.
8. Verhandlungen des Deutschen Bundestages, Vol.122, 17 Sept. 1982, 7078A (Kohl), 7082C (Genscher), 13 Oct. 1982, 7215 A-B (Kohl), 7254A (Genscher).
9. Entscheidungen des Bundesverfassungsgerichts, 2BvE I/8, 16 Feb. 1983, Vol.62, pp.1–63, especially, pp.22–5, 56–9.
10. R. Sturm, 'The Chancellor and the Executive', in S. Padgett (ed.), *The Development of the German Chancellorship: Adenauer to Kohl* (London: Hurst and Co., 1994), pp.93–4.
11. K. Dyson, 'Chancellor Kohl as Strategic Leader: The Case of Economic and Monetary Union', *German Politics*, 7, 1 (April 1998), pp.37–62.
12. D. Grosser, *Das Wagnis der Währungs-, Wirtschafts- und Sozialunion. Politische Zwänge und Konflikt mit ökonomischen Regeln* (Stuttgart: Deutsche Verlags-Anstalt, 1998), pp.573–84.
13. G.A. Ritter and M.A. Niehuss, *Wahlen in Deutschland 1946–1991. Ein Handbuch* (Munich: C.H. Beck, 1991), pp.191–8.
14. P. Pulzer, 'Pointing the Way. The Electoral Transition from the Bonn Republic to the Berlin Republic', *German Politics*, 4, 2 (Aug. 1995), pp.149–50.
15. O.W. Gabriel and F. Brettschneider, 'Die Bundestagswahl 1998. Ein Plebiszit gegen Kohl?' *Aus Politik und Zeitgeschichte*, B52/98, 18 Dec. 1998, pp.24–6.
16. M. Weber, 'Politics as Vocation', in H.H. Gerth and R. Bendix (eds.), *From Max Weber: Essays in Sociology* (London: Routledge and Kegan Paul, 1948), p.106.

Coalition Politics and Management in the Kohl Era, 1982–98

THOMAS SAALFELD

The coalition between the Christian-Democratic CDU/CSU and the liberal FDP under Chancellor Helmut Kohl lasted for approximately 16 years. It followed the FDP's withdrawal from its coalition with the Social Democrats (SPD) on 17 September 1982[1] and a constructive vote of no confidence against Chancellor Helmut Schmidt's (SPD) minority government. With the votes of the CDU/CSU and most FDP members of the Bundestag, Helmut Schmidt was dismissed and Helmut Kohl elected Federal Chancellor on 1 October 1982 in the first and so far only successful constructive vote of no confidence against a German Federal Chancellor. Kohl's coalition government lasted until the elections of 27 September 1998, when it was voted out of office. It was the longest serving democratic coalition government in German parliamentary history. There is little doubt that it would have been continued had the voters renewed its mandate in 1998. The aim of this article is to shed some light on important factors contributing to the stability of the CDU/CSU–FDP coalition. Its longevity was by no means inevitable. There were serious policy differences between the FDP and the CDU/CSU. For example, there were tensions between the FDP and the conservative wing of the Christian Democrats over foreign policy, internal security, civil liberties or citizenship throughout Helmut Kohl's chancellorship. The present article seeks to offer explanations for this high degree of coalition stability. Although it is informed by various aspects of formal coalition theory, it is largely an analytical narrative aiming to shed some light on the structural features and dynamics of coalition governance in the 'Kohl era' including issues of coalition management.

INSTEAD OF A MODEL: ANALYTICAL PERSPECTIVES

Formal coalition theory, the dominant theoretical approach in the field of coalition studies, is based on the assumption that collective outcomes (such as coalition stability) can only be explained meaningfully as the result of

Thomas Saalfeld, University of Kent at Canterbury

aggregated individual choices (methodological individualism). Such individuals may be single politicians or political parties, which are often treated as if they were 'unitary actors'. On the whole, individual choices are assumed to be based on purposive action in pursuit of specified goals. Models in this tradition do not claim that politicians were omniscient actors with perfect information or there was certainty about the outcomes of different strategies, although some models deliberately assume perfect information in order to simplify complex bargaining situations for analytical purposes. In most cases, however, uncertainty about outcomes as well as the extent and costs of information are built into models of coalition bargaining. It is the very purpose of such models (especially of the neo-institutional variety) to study rigorously the genesis and effects of institutions as means of reducing uncertainty by imposing constraints on actors' choices and facilitating co-operation. The axioms on which rational-choice models are based are never entirely realistic (indeed, they are not intended to be), but as many of the phenomena we are interested in occur 'behind closed doors', theoretical models and assumptions are inevitable in order to bridge the gap between the observable and the unobservable.

What are the assumed goals of politicians in such models? The first generation of formal models of coalition formation and stability were 'office-seeking models', assuming 'that political parties or political factions … aimed exclusively at a maximal share of the spoils of office'.[2] The maximal share of the spoils of office could only be gained in so-called 'minimal-winning coalitions', a coalition that loses its majority by the subtraction of any of its members.[3] Minimal-winning coalitions were predicted (a) to be more likely to be formed and (b) to be more likely to remain in office than both minority governments (because in parliamentary democracies they are always in danger of being defeated in a vote of no confidence) and 'oversized' coalitions (because certain parties are 'dispensable', if their withdrawal does not threaten the government's overall majority).

The predictive power of 'office-seeking' models remained relatively modest. Therefore, a second generation of game-theoretic models attempted to combine assumptions about 'office-seeking' goals with assumptions about 'policy-seeking' motivations. This family of models assumes that politicians choose allies primarily because they help them attain particular policy goals. Most formal coalition theories in this tradition have been spatial models resting on 'some conception of party policy as a particular location within a policy space, and of policy differences between parties as related to the distance separating these locations'.[4] The smaller the ideological or policy differences between a set of parties in a policy space of one or more dimensions, the more likely is a coalition between such parties, and the more likely is the resulting coalition government to be stable. The larger the number of relevant policy dimensions, the more difficult it is to form coalitions and sustain them over a whole legislative period, because there is a greater chance that coalition parties are seriously divided on one or more of those dimensions. Based on this reasoning, theorists are able to make predictions about policy in one- or two-dimensional policy spaces. The party occupying the core (or 'median') position 'is able to move the policy of any coalition of which it is a member towards its own preferences', because 'it has a greater choice of coalitions to participate in than any other party', and 'it can bargain for concessions up to a point where policy closely approaches or even coincides with its own position'.[5]

Both schools, office-seeking and policy-seeking, have one characteristic in common. They focus on certain, relatively stable 'structural attributes', which are believed to influence the formation and stability of coalitions. Models based on office-seeking assumptions emphasise the size of a coalition. Models based on policy-pursuit assumptions, by contrast, focus on the parties' proximity in a one-dimensional or multi-dimensional ideological space. The literature refers to a large number of further structural attributes which are believed to influence coalition stability, such as certain properties of the constitution, the party system and the cabinet. Such attributes are treated as constraints on the coalition parties' choices, determining, amongst other things, their incentives to continue the coalition. A number of important structural attributes and their effects on coalition stability under Helmut Kohl will be discussed in the following section of this article.

Explanations of coalition stability focusing on structural attributes were criticised for their static nature. They (unrealistically) 'reference government or parliamentary attributes whose values are fixed or set at the time a government takes office; none takes account of the (subsequent) events that actually bring governments down'.[6] The most radical challenge against the structural-attributes approach was levelled by scholars who argued that most coalitions were brought down by 'random events' such as political scandals, international crises, illnesses or deaths of heads of government. Such events occurred independently of any parliamentary or government characteristics and therefore could not be explained by them.[7] Empirical studies revealed, however, that structural attributes do serve as 'filters', influencing the impact of random events. Moreover, events are often not independent of actors, but used by them to achieve strategic goals.[8] Pure 'random-events models' therefore proved to be empirically unsatisfactory. Recent 'unified models' have attempted to account for the complex interaction between exogenous events and structural attributes using cross-national quantitative data.[9] The fourth section of this article will provide a brief narrative of the nature and impact of such events in the Kohl era.

Other studies have attempted to go beyond structural-attributes and random-events perspectives by focusing on the logic and dynamics of coalition bargaining between formation and termination of a coalition.[10] This article attempts to capture some of these institutions and dynamic processes. For example, coalition governance will be taken to involve continuous intra-party as well as inter-party bargaining.[11] Internal dissent within coalition parties will not be assumed away, as is the case in many of the earlier game-theoretic studies of coalition stability. Empirical studies of coalition government in Germany and elsewhere show that *intra*-party dissent is often more important than inter-party differences as the main cause of coalition terminations.[12] The article will emphasise Helmut Kohl's abilities as a party manager as one of the explanations for coalition stability between 1982 and 1998.

Michael Laver and Kenneth Shepsle have developed their 'portfolio-allocation model', in which they assume that every cabinet that forms does so as a result of equilibrium processes.

> An equilibrium cabinet, once it is formed, stays formed because no political actor with the ability to act in such a way as to bring down the cabinet and replace it with some alternative has the incentive to do so. Conversely, no actor with the incentive to replace the cabinet with some alternative has the ability to do so. Thus we expect an equilibrium cabinet to be stable, remaining in place until a change in the external environment transforms either the incentives of some pivotal actor or the "pivotalness" of some actor already possessing the appropriate incentives.[13]

What are the conditions for such an equilibrium? Amongst other factors, cabinets are assumed to be in equilibrium 'if the government portfolio with jurisdiction over each relevant policy dimension is allocated to the party with the median legislator on that dimension'.[14] The forecast policy output of this cabinet is the 'dimension-by-dimension median' (DDM) in the policy space. Such a 'DDM cabinet' is taken to be in equilibrium if there is no alternative government in the winset, that is, the area delineated by the overlapping indifference curves of the relevant parties. Another stable equilibrium solution is the existence of what Laver and Shepsle call a 'strong party'. Where such a party exists, it is able to govern even as a one-party minority.[15] This latter condition is empirically less relevant in the German context, while the former is highly relevant.

In their model, Laver and Shepsle relax the unitary-actor assumption without giving up the aim of providing a rigorous, deductive and parsimonious theory of coalition formation and stability. They emphasise the relative political autonomy of ministries in cabinet systems and predict 'that jurisdiction-specific policy outputs will tend toward those preferred by the party of the relevant minister'.[16] This seems to be particularly relevant in the German case, given the relatively high degree of ministerial autonomy in a 'sectorised' executive. This would also seem to suggest that 'negative co-ordination' is the typical logic of policy making. According to Fritz Scharpf's definition:

> positive coordination is an attempt to maximize the overall effectiveness and efficiency of government policy by exploring and utilizing the joint strategy options of several ministerial portfolios. ... Negative coordination, by contrast, is associated with more limited aspirations. Its goal is to assure that any new policy initiative designed by a specialized subunit within the ministerial organization will not interfere with the established policies and the interests of other ministerial units. ... Procedurally, positive coordination is associated with multilateral negotiations in intra- or interministerial task forces ... By contrast, negative coordination is more likely to take the form of bilateral "clearance" negotiations between the initiating department and other units whose portfolios might be affected – but whose own policy options are not actively considered.[17]

Negative co-ordination has a number of disadvantages, especially a reduction in the scope for innovation.[18] Recent work on coalition governance,[19] however, suggests that specific forms of coalition governance may enhance coalition stability and avoid an excessive reliance on negative co-ordination between government departments. Coalition participants achieve a degree of positive co-ordination through coalition agreements, conflict management devices as well as monitoring and contract enforcement mechanisms. The present article will deal with mechanisms such as coalition committees, coalition 'round tables' and other formal and informal devices of conflict containment and management in the CDU/CSU–FDP coalition of 1982–98 in the penultimate section. In doing so, coalition government is treated 'as an on-going bargaining process in which there is much still to be played for',[20] even after its formation.

Finally, unified models of cabinet duration have attempted to overcome the static nature of earlier game-theoretic studies of coalition politics in a further sense. Classical game-theoretic models analysed coalitions essentially as 'one-shot games'. From this perspective, potential coalition partners bargain in order to gain instant gratification. Yet coalitions have a history. Bargaining is more appropriately compared to repeated games in which tit-for-tat strategies are effective in securing co-operation even in prisoners' dilemma-type situations.[21] Traditional game-theoretic models of coalition stability give too little weight to the parties' memories of past co-operation.[22] Coalitions are sequential exchanges between parties often based on 'deferred reciprocal compensation'.[23] Party leaders may choose to forgo short-term benefits for the sake of long-term co-operation and compensation. They are also aware of the fact that reputation for sincerity and credibility 'are the currency with which politicians and parties hope to procure executive power'.[24] It will be shown that Kohl's ability to negotiate compromises within his own party increased his credibility *vis-à-vis* the FDP as coalition partner, and that the Chancellor took a long-term view of the co-operation between Christian Democrats and Liberals. This explains why he did not exploit the opportunities for short-term gains at the liberal coalition partner's expense. This, in turn, stabilised the coalition.

STRUCTURAL ATTRIBUTES AND COALITION STABILITY

The stability of the coalition cabinets under Helmut Kohl (1982–98) was extraordinary by both international and historical standards. Table 1 provides data on average coalition duration, volatility and various party-system indicators for the 14 Bundestag terms since 1949 compared to the eight legislative terms of the Weimar Republic (1919–33). Constitutional changes (see below) and historical learning on the part of Germany's political elites may have contributed to the fact that the average cabinet in the Federal Republic between 1949 and 1998 lasted approximately 700 days, more than three times as long as the average cabinet duration in the Weimar Republic (232 days).[25] Three out of five coalition cabinets under Kohl lasted the entire legislative term (between 1,368 and 1,412 days). The cabinet formed after the constructive vote of no confidence against Helmut Schmidt (1982–83) lasted only for a few months until the early elections of March 1983. Its termination was voluntary. The average duration for the 1987–90 parliamentary term (681 days) is depressed by the fact that, after 1,329 days in office, the CDU/CSU–FDP coalition was voluntarily enlarged to include the (East German) German Social Union (DSU), which held eight Bundestag seats between October and December 1990. This cabinet lasted for 33 days until the Bundestag was dissolved for the first all-German elections. If these two Kohl cabinets are counted as one single cabinet lasting for 1,362 days, the average Kohl cabinet between 1983 and 1998 lasted for 1,385 days – approximately twice as long as the average for the Federal Republic overall and approximately six times as long as the average Weimar cabinet. The other data in Table 1 will be referred to below.

A number of 'structural attributes' of a political system are believed to influence coalition durability.[26] General regime attributes such as

TABLE 1

CABINET AND PARTY SYSTEM CHARACTERISTICS FOR THE WEIMAR REPUBLIC
(1919–32) AND THE FEDERAL REPUBLIC OF GERMANY (1949–98)

Election	Average cabinet duration in days in the parliament following election	Aggregate volatility (Pedersen Index)	Number of parties in parlament	Share of anti-system parties	Effective number of parties in parliament (Laakso and Taagepera Index)	Fractionalisation of parliament (Rae Index)
			Weimar Republic			
1919	160	—	8	0.0	4.10	0.76
1920	205	32.1	10	0.9	6.41	0.84
1924 (May)	195	27.0	11	19.9	7.10	0.86
1924 (Dec.)	288	9.8	11	11.9	6.21	0.84
1928	319	13.2	14	13.4	6.13	0.84
1930	390	22.1	14	31.8	7.10	0.86
1932 (July)	169	21.2	14	52.4	4.30	0.77
1932 (Nov.)	57	6.2	13	50.7	4.79	0.79
			Federal Republic			
1949	1,452	—	9	4.9	3.99	0.75
1953	479	19.3	5	0.0	2.77	0.64
1957	713	9.2	4	0.0	2.39	0.58
1961	353	14.3	3	0.0	2.51	0.60
1965	480	7.7	3	0.0	2.38	0.58
1969	1,125	6.7	3	0.0	2.24	0.55
1972	708	6.0	3	0.0	2.34	0.57
1976	1,390	4.1	3	0.0	2.31	0.57
1980	284	4.6	3	0.0	2.44	0.59
1983	1,398	8.4	4	0.0	2.51	0.60
1987	681 (1,362)[1]	6.0	4	0.0	2.80	0.64
1990	1,368	9.1	5	0.0	2.65	0.62
1994	1,412	8.9	5	0.0	2.91	0.66
1998	—	8.4	5	0.0	2.90	0.66

Notes: The small category 'others' in Mackie and Rose's data on the Weimar Republic was treated as a party for the calculation of the Pedersen Index, the Rae Index and the effective number of parties in parliament (Laakso and Taagepera), but not for the number of parties. The PDS was counted as a party in parliament although they were not recognised as a full parliamentary party according to the Bundestag's rules of procedure in 1990 and 1994. The same is true for the group of the 'National Right' in the first Bundestag.

1. It is contentious in the German debate whether the PDS should be considered an anti-system party opposed to liberal democracy. Since the Constitutional Court has not banned it, it is not treated as such a party, whereas the 'National Right' – including members of the Socialist Reich Party (SRP) – and the Communist Party (KPD) in the first Bundestag (1949–53) are treated as anti-system parties, because they were banned in 1952 and 1956 respectively. As for the Weimar Republic, only the KPD and NSDAP were counted as anti-system parties, although the constitutionality of a number of other parties such as the DNVP was questionable.

Sources: Data for the Weimar Republic calculated from T.T. Mackie and R. Rose, *The International Almanac of Electoral History* (Basingstoke: Macmillan, 1974), p.159; cabinet duration data were kindly provided by Ekkart Zimmermann. Data for the Federal Republic of Germany calculated from P. Schindler, *Datenhandbuch zur Geschichte des Deutschen Bundestages 1949 bis 1983* (Bonn: Presse- und Informationszentrum des Deutschen Bundestages, 1983), pp.34–39; *Datenhandbuch zur Geschichte des Deutschen Bundestages 1983 bis 1991* (Baden-Baden: Nomos, 1994), pp.80–82; Kürschners Volkshandbuch, Deutscher Bundestag 13. Wahlperiode (Darmstadt: Neue Darmstädter Verlagsanstalt, 1995), p.37; Presse- und Informationsamt der Bundesregierung: *Bulletin* No. 69 (21 Oct. 1998), p.859; T. Saalfeld, 'Deutschland: Auswanderung der Politik aus der Verfassung?' in W.C. Müller and K. Strøm (eds.), *Koalitionsregierungen in Westeuropa: Bildung, Arbeitsweise und Beendigung* (Wien: Signum, 1997), p.68.

constitutional rules about investiture votes, parliamentary votes of no confidence, the government head's dissolution powers, electoral terms or opposition rights are powerful constraints influencing a coalition's political survival chances. For example, a formal investiture requirement such as the election of the federal Chancellor according to Article 63 of the Basic Law rules out governments without sufficient parliamentary support *a priori*. Cabinets that form under such 'positive' investiture requirements tend to have better survival chances than coalitions that are formed in constitutional contexts lacking such requirements, that is, where governments simply stay in office as long as they do not suffer a defeat in a vote of confidence ('negative' investiture requirements).[27] The constructive vote of no confidence according to Article 67 of the Basic Law protects governments against 'negative majorities' and makes it very difficult for a parliament to depose a cabinet. It can do so only if it simultaneously elects an alternative head of government with an absolute majority of its members. This high barrier against 'negative majorities' tends to strengthen the incumbent government.[28] Coalition stability in Germany is also enhanced by the fact that the federal Chancellor is greatly restricted in his powers to dissolve the Bundestag, and that the Bundestag cannot dissolve itself.[29] Coalitions are therefore usually formed to last at least for an entire parliamentary term.

General regime attributes also include properties of the party system. The number of parties in the system, for example, is believed to be of great importance. The more parties represented in a parliament, the more difficult coalition formation and survival are believed to be. The presence of anti-system or other extreme parties is taken to have a destabilising effect, as is the degree of ideological polarisation in a parliament. Despite the advent of the Green Party (1983) and the Party of Democratic Socialism (PDS, 1990), the German party system has remained characterised by 'moderate pluralism',[30] with a relatively low degree of fractionalisation and no representation of anti-system parties[31] after 1953. Table 1 shows that anti-system parties were represented in the first Bundestag (1949–53) only, whereas the Communists and National Socialists obtained almost one-third of the seats in the 1930–32 Weimar Reichstag and more than half of the seats in both elections of 1932. As a result, the Federal Republic did not experience the need to form ideologically heterogeneous (minority) coalitions of pro-system parties, as did the Weimar Republic. From 1953 onwards the number of parliamentary parties and groups represented in the Bundestag was much lower than in the Weimar Reichstag. Although the number of parties increased from three to five between 1980 and 1998, the 'effective number of parties',[32] which makes adjustments for the relative size of parties, increased only from 2.44 to 2.91 between 1980 and 1994.

The Rae Index of fractionalisation gives a similar picture. This index expresses 'the probability that two members drawn at random from the universe belong to different parties' and 'varies from zero (maximal concentration – there is only one party) to a maximum of one (in practice, as many parties as there are seats)'.[33] Only the first Bundestag (with the *highest* degree of fractionalisation in the post-war period) had almost as many 'effective parties' as the *least* fractionalised Reichstags of 1919 and 1932 (the reduction of the 'effective number of parties' in the Reichtags elected in 1932 was largely due to the growing strength of Communists and National Socialists). Between 1958 and 1998, Rae's index of fractionalisation varied between 0.55 and 0.66. Even the most fractionalised Bundestag of 1949–53 had a slightly lower Rae Index (0.75) than the least fractionalised Weimar Reichstag (1919–20, with an index score of 0.76). Thus, as far as the party system is concerned, the conditions for stable coalitions were favourable throughout the Federal Republic's history, including Kohl's chancellorship. The modest re-fractionalisation of the party system since 1983 has not reached destabilising proportions (if compared to the situation in the Weimar Republic).

A further important set of structural attributes that are believed to be related to the durability of governments are properties of the cabinet. Two main groups of structural cabinet attributes are thought to be of particular importance: (a) attributes referring to the size of the cabinet's parliamentary majority and (b) attributes referring to its ideological diversity. According to most existing coalition theories focusing on structural cabinet attributes, (west) Germany could have been expected to produce stable coalition governments during the Kohl era, because voters regularly endowed the CDU/CSU and FDP with stable majorities at Bundestag elections. Minority governments – which can generally be expected to be less stable than majority governments – have never been necessary. In addition, the CDU/CSU–FDP coalitions between 1982 and 1998 fulfilled the minimal winning criterion.[34] Such coalitions are usually predicted to be more stable than those that are not.

A second set of structural cabinet attributes is often held to be the ideological compatibility of coalition parties. Warwick's[35] comparative work, in particular, represents powerful evidence concerning the importance of ideological diversity in parliament and cabinet. Ideologically compact or 'connected' coalitions are more likely to form than ideologically diverse ones, because the members find it easier to reach agreement over policy. They are also more likely to be stable as they 'will be better able to withstand the strains imposed by the need to make unanticipated policy decisions during the lifetime of a government'.[36] Assuming a one-dimensional ideological space, authors have predicted 'that minimal

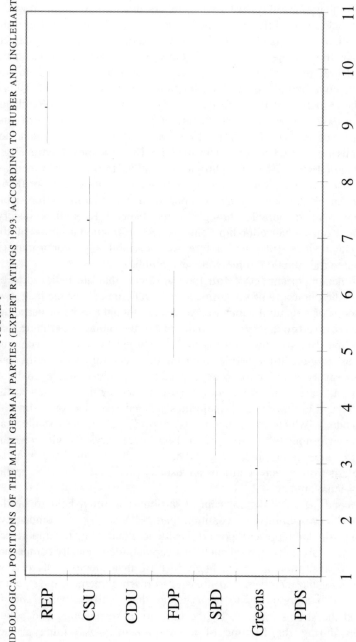

FIGURE 1

IDEOLOGICAL POSITIONS OF THE MAIN GERMAN PARTIES (EXPERT RATINGS 1993, ACCORDING TO HUBER AND INGLEHART)

Ideological Position (1 = extreme left, 11 = extreme right, range of 1 standard deviation)

connected winning coalitions will form. It can be extended to predict that minimal winning coalitions will also be more likely to stay formed'.[37]

The ideological positions of the parties strongly favoured a coalition between the CDU/CSU and the FDP. Figure 1 provides estimates of the ideological positions of seven German parties on a one-dimensional, general left–right scale ranging from '1' (extreme left) to '11' (extreme right) in 1993. It is based on data provided by John Huber and Ronald Inglehart, who estimated the policy positions of parties using expert ratings.[38] The data points in Figure 1 show each party's ideological position as the arithmetic mean of the experts' placements of the parties on a one-dimensional left–right scale. The lines represent the range of one standard deviation of the expert ratings below ('left' of) and above ('right' of) the mean value on the scale from 1 to 11. Based on the parties' ideological placement, there are only two closely connected coalition options with overlapping 'ranges' of one standard deviation: a 'red–green' coalition between the SPD and Greens and the CDU/CSU–FDP coalition. The ideological positions of the CDU, CSU and FDP are relatively close and the overlapping ranges of one standard deviation suggest that there was a great deal of common ground between the parties. The same is true for the SPD and Greens, a coalition that was numerically unfeasible between 1983 and 1998, as was a coalition between the SPD and FDP. Based on these estimates, a coalition of the SPD and CDU/CSU or a 'traffic-light coalition' of the SPD, Greens and FDP would have been ideologically too heterogeneous. The parties would have been too distant from each other in terms of their overall left–right placement. The FDP controlled the overall 'median legislator' (a measure combining the parties' position in the ideological space with their 'weight' [number of seats]) in a one-dimensional policy space for the entire period between 1982 and 1998, and its coalition with the CDU/CSU was the only connected minimal-winning coalition.

Yet, the ideological space of German politics is not one-dimensional. The picture could change considerably, if two or more dimensions are distinguished. The data on which Figures 2 and 3 are based are estimates provided by Hans-Dieter Klingemann and Andrea Volkens, who carried out quantitative content analyses of the parties' election manifestos.[39] Klingemann and Volkens used the coding categories of the Manifesto Research Group of the European Consortium for Political Research and counted the number of statements within each category appearing in the parties' election manifestos. We have selected the following categories to estimate the parties left–right placement on three dimensions:

(a) Social policy: the lower the percentage of statements demanding an expansion of the welfare state, the more 'right-wing' a party's position on this dimension.

(b) Constitutional liberalism: the lower the percentage of statements propagating more democracy and democratisation, the more 'right-wing' a party's position on this dimension.

(c) Foreign and defence policy: the higher the percentage of statements in favour of military strength, the more 'right-wing' a party's position on this dimension.

The data in Figures 2 and 3 represent averages for the period 1949–94. Although these averages may gloss over some variations across time, they can be taken as generally accurate estimates. Figures 2 and 3 represent two-dimensional policy spaces where economic and social policy ('expansion of the welfare state') represents the horizontal axis. The vertical axis measures the parties' position on the foreign policy dimension ('military strength', Figure 2) and constitutional liberalism ('democracy and democratisation', Figure 3). The figures demonstrate that the CDU/CSU–FDP coalitions of 1982–98 were ideologically connected minimum-winning coalitions in terms of the coalition parties' economic and social policy positions. In both parties' election manifestos (1949–94), the percentage of statements advocating an expansion of the welfare state was much lower than for the other parties (5.9 per cent for the CDU/CSU and 5.7 per cent for the FDP, see Figure 3). Unlike Huber and Inglehart's general left–right placement, the FDP is slightly 'right' of the CDU/CSU on this dimension, although the differences are minimal. As a result, the CDU/CSU controlled the median legislator on this dimension. There were, however, considerable differences between the CDU/CSU and the FDP over foreign policy and constitutional issues (including democratisation and civil liberties). On these two dimensions, the CDU/CSU and the FDP are not ideologically connected.

As for the parties' positions on the foreign policy dimension (measured as statements advocating 'military strength'), the SPD and the CDU/CSU are ideologically closer to each other than the CDU/CSU and the FDP (Figure 2). It was the SPD that controlled the median legislator on this dimension between 1983 and 1998, although the differences between the SPD and FDP are minimal, and Laver and Hunt's scales, based on expert interviews, have the FDP in the median-legislator position.[40] If Laver and Hunt's scales are correct, the CDU/CSU–FDP cabinet controlled the dimension-by-dimension median legislator on the two policy dimensions that were generally seen to be the most important ones: economic policy and foreign policy. This structure is taken to make for particularly stable coalitions (see above). At any rate, the continued relative proximity of the SPD and FDP on this dimension remained a potential source of tension between the CDU/CSU and the FDP throughout Kohl's chancellorship, especially when the CDU/CSU moved to the right.

FIGURE 2

IDEOLOGICAL DISTANCES IN A TWO-DIMENSIONAL POLICY SPACE
(EXPANSION OF WALFARE STATE AND MILITARY STRENGTH, AVERAGES 1949-94)

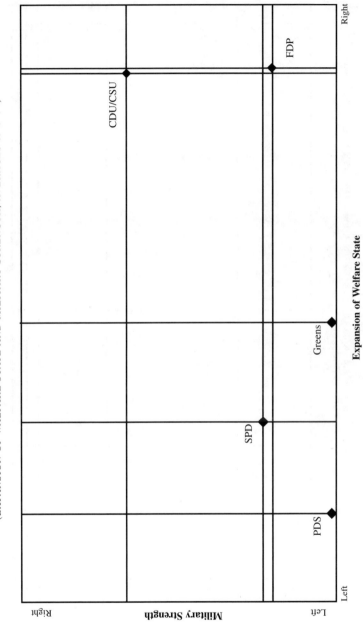

FIGURE 3

IDEOLOGICAL DISTANCES IN THE GERMAN PARTY SYSTEM IN A TWO-DIMENSIONAL POLICY SPACE
(EXPANSION OF WELFARE STATE AND DEMOCRACY AND DEMOCRATISATION, AVERAGES 1949–94)

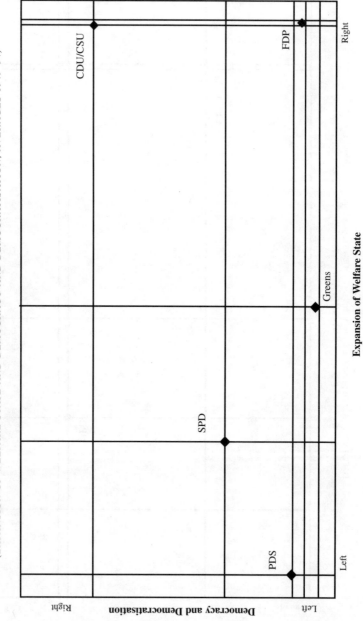

In terms of constitutional liberalism, the FDP's position is closer to the positions of the PDS and Green Party, with the SPD in an intermediate position between the CDU/CSU on the right and the PDS, Greens and FDP on the left (Figure 3). On this dimension, the CDU/CSU–FDP coalition clearly did not control the dimension-by-dimension median legislator. Kohl's coalition was in danger, therefore, when constitutional liberalism (measured as the frequency of statements mentioning 'democracy and democratisation') or other civil-liberties issues replaced either economic or foreign policy as one of the dominant issue dimensions.

Looking at the entire post-war period, the far-reaching consensus between the CDU/CSU and FDP in questions of economic and social policy was never matched by a similar consensus in questions of foreign and defence policy and constitutional issues including civil liberties or the acceptance of a multicultural society (see below).[41] These differences will also become evident when we briefly refer to coalition 'crises' during the Kohl era in the following section on 'critical events'.

A set of structural attributes that has been neglected so far are attributes of the individual coalition parties. In recent studies, Laver and Moshe Maor have paid more systematic attention to the influence of (intra-) party structures on coalition bargaining and stability. The organisational characteristics of the CDU, CSU and FDP seem to lend support to Maor's thesis that party centralisation and coalition stability are inversely related. The CDU is a relatively decentralised party. Much internal power is located in the federal-state party organisations and elites (for example, state premiers). The party's interest-based associations (*Vereinigungen*) and policy committees (*Bundesfachausschüsse*) have an important role in the formulation of party policy.[42] One of Kohl's main strengths was his skill as leader of this decentralised party. Unlike his Social Democratic predecessor, Helmut Schmidt (1974–82), who never led his party, Kohl was and remained the leader of the CDU's extra-parliamentary organisation throughout his chancellorship. He was very effective in forming and maintaining alliances of key players within the CDU. His personal networks and 'finely filtered personal early-warning system'[43] on the lower levels of the CDU's organisational structure as well as his abilities as a shrewd tactician helped him to secure his own position and contributed to a relatively unified party within the coalition.

Kohl's emphasis on co-ordination in networks was the appropriate answer to the organisational complexity and decentralised nature of modern German political parties, which can be described as loosely coupled organisations or, indeed, 'organised anarchies' (see Elmar Wiesendahl's contribution to this volume). Under such conditions, hierarchical co-ordination is almost certainly doomed to failure given the scope for 'opportunistic behaviour' at the lower levels of the organisation, and the information problems ('hidden action') faced by organisational leaders. Networks, by contrast, are not primarily based on hierarchichal control, but on mutual trust between actors. This trust develops in repeated interactions and is based on the participants' reputation and credibility. According to Fritz Scharpf, networks based on generalised trust can reduce the high transaction costs of hierarchical co-ordination and 'will enable rational actors to enter into vulnerable positions, and to engage in high-risk (and potentially high-gain) mixed-motive transactions under conditions of incomplete information'.[44] We shall return to Kohl's emphasis on personal networks in the penultimate section on coalition management.

In addition to the decentralised structure of his own party, Kohl was never in a position to impose discipline on the CSU. The CDU/CSU has always been an alliance of two Christian-Democratic parties. Outside the Bundestag, the CDU and its Bavarian 'sister party', the CSU, have operated as separate organisations (without competing against each other in elections: the CSU competes in Bavaria only, the CDU in the rest of the Federal Republic). Inside the Bundestag, however, they have formed a common parliamentary party since 1949. This close co-operation has been formally renewed after each election. Within this union, the smaller CSU has usually acted as a particularly cohesive block. Co-operation has not always been free of tensions. Especially from the early 1960s onwards, the two parties' relationship has often been characterised by differences over policy and strategy.[45] Nevertheless, the cohesion of the union (and its reliability as a coalition partner) could be maintained due to the use of 'consociational' structures in the parliamentary party. Since 1972, the smaller CSU has formally enjoyed the right to veto decisions of the common parliamentary party in case of disagreement between the two parties. That is to say, its members, who are in a minority within the common parliamentary party, cannot be outvoted by the majority of CDU members. The nature of the CSU as a partner with equal rights was strengthened in the inter-party treaty of 1976. Henceforth, the CDU/CSU leadership has had to negotiate a common position before it entered negotiations with a coalition partner or the opposition.[46] The veto rights for the smaller CSU are effective even in the face of serious policy disputes. Together with Kohl's informal networks within his own party and informal coalition committees (see below), this seems to have helped the CDU/CSU to commit itself sufficiently credibly to coalition pacts with the FDP.

In the FDP, the situation was very different. With its rapidly decreasing strength at the regional and local levels, its reliance on access to the spoils of government office at the national level increased. Throughout the Kohl era, the party was heavily dominated by the Bundestag parliamentary party and its leaders – Hans-Dietrich Genscher, Martin Bangemann (1984–88), Otto Count Lambsdorff (1988–93), Klaus Kinkel (1993–95) and Wolfgang Gerhardt (1995–) – who enjoyed considerable freedom to define the party's strategy and make binding commitments on its behalf in coalition negotiations. The homogeneity of the parliamentary party was enhanced by the exodus (for example, Günther Verheugen, Ingrid Matthäus-Maier, Helga Schuchardt or Andreas von Schoeler) and marginalisation (for example, Gerhart-Rudolf Baum, Hildegard Hamm-Brücher or Burkhard Hirsch) of 'left-liberal' supporters of the former SPD–FDP coalition after 1982.[47] The homogeneity of the FDP's parliamentary party and its dominance *vis-à-vis* the extra-parliamentary organisation facilitated the management of the CDU/CSU–FDP coalitions between 1982 and 1998. The relationship between party centralisation and coalition stability may, therefore, be more complex than Maor suggests. In Germany during the Kohl era, highly decentralised (CDU) and highly centralised (CSU, at least at the national level) parties provided favourable conditions for coalition stability as did parties characterised by a high degree of autonomy of the parliamentary party *vis-à-vis* the extra-parliamentary party organisation (FDP). Although Maor is right to emphasise organisational features of coalition parties as key variables, his account remains problematic from the position of methodological individualism as structures as such do not 'determine' outcomes (such as coalition stability). Yet Maor's variables need to be incorporated into formal models of coalition bargaining.

CRITICAL EVENTS AND COALITION STABILITY

Structural regime, cabinet, party system and party attributes of a coalition are important, but cannot 'determine' a coalition's fate. Laver and Shepsle argue that every cabinet that forms does so as a result of equilibrium processes. Yet after its formation a cabinet exists in a stream of events outside the control of the parties involved, some of which might lead to its termination. Some events can be anticipated. They will have influenced coalition bargaining between actors with 'rational foresight' before a cabinet is formed and may have been addressed in a coalition agreement. Other events are unanticipated and can destabilise an equilibrium cabinet. 'Shocks may destabilize a cabinet that was previously in equilibrium by shifting key parameters of the government formation environment in ways that were not taken into account when the government was put together.'[48] Laver and Shepsle give examples such as party splits (changing the relative 'weights' of the parties), the emergence of new issues (changing the main policy dimensions), changes in the parties' perceptions of each other and their ability to win stand-offs against each other.

The most pressing policy problems facing the CDU/CSU–FDP coalition at its inception in 1982 were to be found in the areas of economic and defence policy. The government had to deal with the economic crisis that had affected Germany since 1981 and to reduce the budget deficit left by the Schmidt government. Privatisation, deregulation and lower taxes for business and industry were also high on the new government's agenda. Outside the realm of economics, NATO's decision to deploy US Intermediate Nuclear Forces in Germany and other European NATO countries as a response to the Soviet deployment of SS20 missiles was the dominant issue. This decision had been strongly supported by Chancellor Schmidt, whose party, the SPD, was divided over the issue: Schmidt was one of the main proponents of the policy, Willy Brandt, the SPD's leader, was extremely sceptical, as were large sections of the SPD's rank and file. On both issues, the leaderships of CDU/CSU and FDP had no fundamental disagreement. More importantly from Laver and Shepsle's perspective, the CDU/CSU–FDP coalitions controlled the dimension-by-dimension median legislators on these dimensions (if Laver and Hunt's data are correct, see above).

Nevertheless, there were also disturbances. From the mid-1980s onwards, the public perception of the most important policy issues changed. The issue of immigration and political asylum came increasingly to the fore. Dietrich Thränhardt argues that this was not so much a result of dramatically increasing numbers of immigrants and asylum seekers (that is, an 'external shock'), but at least partly a result of the CDU/CSU's campaign strategy, which emphasised immigration in the late 1970s and early 1980s, creating expectations that decisive changes in immigration policy would take place

FIGURE 4:

SUPPORT FOR MULTICULTURALISM IN ELECTION MANIFESTOS (1949–94)

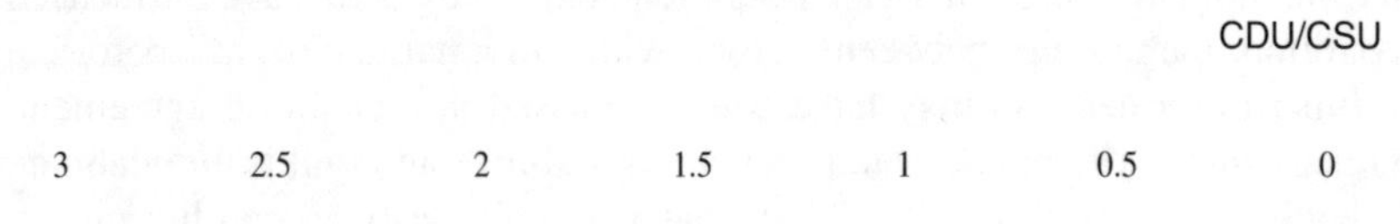

CDU/CSU

| 3 | 2.5 | 2 | 1.5 | 1 | 0.5 | 0 |

Based on content analyses of election manifestos.

Source: H.-D. Klingemann and A. Volkens, 'Struktur und Entwicklung von Wahlprogrammen in der Bundesrepublik Deutschland 1949–1994', in O.W. Gabriel *et al.* (eds.), *Parteiendemokratie in Deutschland* (Bonn: Bundeszentrale für politische Bildung, 1997), p.526.

under a government led by the Christian Democrats. During the 1980s, Thränhardt argues, it became increasingly clear that the CDU/CSU–FDP government was not able or willing to deliver the solutions the CDU/CSU had promised in opposition.[49] The increasing importance of the immigration and asylum issues had implications for the CDU/CSU's coalition with the FDP. Both issues involve questions of civil liberties and multiculturalism, which form a policy dimension dividing the CDU/CSU and FDP (especially the CSU and FDP). The SPD controlled the median legislator on this position. This is illustrated by Figure 4, which is also based on Klingemann and Volkens' analyses of election manifestos of 1949–94. Especially with the successes of the Republikaner Party between 1986 and 1992, the CDU/CSU began to sharpen its profile on the political right in order to re-integrate voters who were attracted by the Republikaner Party and other extreme right-wing parties and groups.[50] Nevertheless, the issues of immigration and asylum never gained sufficient importance to replace the two main axes of party conflict (economic and foreign policy) permanently.

Other events accentuated differences between the CDU/CSU and FDP, too. The United States Strategic Defense Initiative led to a confrontation between the FDP and CSU in 1985. The question of the German–Polish border led to repeated clashes between the FDP on the one hand and the right of the CDU and, in particular, the CSU on the other (January 1985, November 1989). Apart from these internal disagreements over defence policy, the coalition faced the rise of environmental policy on the issue agenda. This development benefited the Green Party and, to some extent, the SPD, which had begun to address these issues in the context of its programme review under Oskar Lafontaine. A 'red–green' majority at the national level at the 1990 general elections increasingly became a serious possibility, with a chance for the SPD to control the median legislator on the environmental dimension. Yet in 1989/90 the issue agenda was transformed radically in the coalition's favour. Unification was an external event that greatly stabilised the coalition. It reaffirmed Chancellor Kohl's authority within his own party (see below). Similarly, FDP leader and Foreign Secretary Genscher's popularity surged. Initially, both the CDU and FDP benefited in electoral terms. In addition, the dominance of economic and foreign policy as dominant policy dimensions of party competition was re-established. 'German unification brought the socio-economic dimension even more to the forefront than was true for the 1980s when environmental issues challenged the priority of the socio-economic policy of the first Kohl governments.'[51] The clear electoral losers of German unification were, at least between 1990 and 1994, the opposition parties, the SPD and the Greens. The CSU, too, could be considered a loser in this process, as its inability to expand to the 'new Länder' reduced its relative weight in national politics. The relative weakening of the CSU may have reduced the conflict potential between the Christian Democrats and the Free Democrats.

In Germany, 'public opinion shocks' occur not only in the form of opinion polls, but also in the shape of federal-state election (*Landtagswahl*) results. The parties treat them as hard behavioural indicators of their popularity as national and regional level are often inseparable. Landtag elections have a significant impact on policy making at the national level: the composition of Länder governments determines the composition of the Bundesrat, the upper house of the legislature. A series of losses at the Länder level may precipitate a coalition crisis. There is little doubt, for example, that the termination of the 'social-liberal' coalition was triggered by the SPD's poor showing in federal-state elections between 1980 and 1982. The FDP began to fear it might be pulled below the five per cent threshold by its association with the Social Democrats.[52] Tables 2 and 3 list the absolute gains and losses for the coalition parties in all Landtag elections between the constructive vote of no confidence against Schmidt in 1982 and the Bundestag elections of 1998. They illustrate that the FDP was exposed to a series of severe 'public opinion shocks' in the form of defeats in Landtag elections. After a number of poor Landtag election results following the FDP's changeover to the CDU/CSU (1982–84, see Table 2), the party managed to stabilise itself in electoral terms in the federal states. It benefited from unification at the federal level as well as at the level of the Länder. Between 1993 and 1995, however, the FDP experienced another traumatic erosion of its support in the Länder. It suffered losses in 12 out of 13 elections in that period and failed to overcome the five per cent threshold in all nine federal-state elections of 1993 and 1994. It also failed to straddle the five per cent hurdle for the European Parliament elections in 1994. Especially in the five 'new' Länder, the party's support dropped dramatically after good results in 1990. At the time of the 1998 federal elections, the FDP was only represented in four out of 16 federal-state parliaments (Landtage). Its electoral base at the regional level was seriously eroded, although the party defended its position as a pivotal 'functional party' (*Funktionspartei*) at the national level. These electoral shocks at the sub-national level contributed to the replacement of Klaus Kinkel as party leader by Wolfgang Gerhardt in 1995 and the FDP's attempt to gain a stronger profile *vis-à-vis* the CDU/CSU – especially in the question of taxation. The party increasingly attempted to present itself as a neo-liberal corrective against the *de facto* 'grand coalition' of the two major parties and powerful interest groups. Its attempt to gain more profile as a tax-lowering party supporting privatisation, deregulation and flexibility in state and economy led to clashes with the Christian Democrats, especially with Finance Minister Theo Waigel (CSU), who had to find the funds to cover the spiralling costs of unification.

TABLE 2

ABSOLUTE CDU AND CSU GAINS AND LOSSES IN FEDERAL STATE
(LANDTAG) ELECTIONS BETWEEN 1 OCTOBER 1982 AND 27 SEPTEMBER 1998

	1982	1983	1984	1985	1986	1987	1988	1989	1990	1991	1992	1993	1994	1995	1996	1997	1998
Baden-Württemberg			-1.5				-2.9				-9.4				+1.8		
Bayern (CSU)	-0.8				-2.5				-0.9				-2.1				+0.1
Berlin				-1.6				-8.7						-3.5			
Brandenburg									+3.2 (29.4)				-10.7				
Bremen		+1.4				-9.9				+7.3				+1.9			
Hamburg	-4.6				+3.3	-1.4				-5.4		-10.0			+5.6		
Hesse	-0.4	-6.2				+2.7				-1.9				-1.0			
Mecklenburg-West Pomerania									(38.3)				-0.6				-7.5
Lower Saxony					-6.4				-2.3				-5.6				-0.5
North Rhine-Westphalia				-6.7					+0.2					-0.3			
Rhineland-Palatinate		+1.8				-6.8				-6.4							
Saarland				-6.7					-3.9				+5.2				
Saxony									(53.8)				+4.3				
Saxony-Anhalt									(39.0)				-4.6				-12.4
Schleswig-Holstein		+0.7				-6.4	-9.3				+0.5				+3.4		
Thuringia									(45.4)				-2.8				

Notes: No gains/losses could be calculated for the 'new' Länder in 1990. The figures in italics and brackets refer to the percentage of second votes gained by the party.

Sources: A. Mintzel and H. Oberreuter (eds.), *Parteien in der Bundesrepublik Deutschland* (Opladen: Westdeutscher Verlag, 2nd edn 1992); U. Andersen and W. Woyke, *Wahl '98. Zur Bundestagswahl 1998* (Opladen: Leske+Budrich, 1998); *Zeitschrift für Parlamentsfragen*, various issues.

TABLE 3

ABSOLUTE FDP GAINS AND LOSSES IN FEDERAL STATE (LANDTAG) ELECTIONS BETWEEN 1 OCTOBER 1982 AND 27 SEPTEMBER 1998

	1982	1983	1984	1985	1986	1987	1988	1989	1990	1991	1992	1993	1994	1995	1996	1997	1998
Baden-Württemberg			-1.1				-1.3				±0.0				+3.7		
Bayern	-2.7				+0.3				+1.4				-2.4				-1.1
Berlin				+2.9				-4.6	+2.5					-3.9			
Brandenburg									*(6.6)*				-4.4				
Bremen		-6.1				+5.4				-0.5				-6.1			
Hamburg	-2.2				+2.2	+1.7				-1.1		-1.2				-0.7	
Hesse	-3.5	+4.5				+0.2				-0.4				+0.1			
Mecklenburg-West Pomerania									*(5.5)*				-1.7				-2.2
Lower Saxony					+0.1				±0.0				-1.6				+0.5
North Rhine-Westphalia				+1.0					-0.2					-1.8			
Rhineland-Palatinate		-2.9				+3.8				-0.4					+2.0		
Saarland				+3.1					-4.4				-3.5				
Saxony									*(5.2)*				-3.5				
Saxony-Anhalt									*(13.5)*				-9.9				+0.6
Schleswig-Holstein		-3.5				+3.0	-0.8				+1.2				+0.1		
Thuringia									*(9.3)*				-6.1				

Notes: No gains/losses could be calculated for the 'new' Länder in 1990. The figures in italics and brackets refer to the percentage of second votes gained by the party.

Sources: A. Mintzel and H. Oberreuter (eds.), *Parteien in der Bundesrepublik Deutschland.* (Opladen: Westdeutscher Verlag, 2nd edn. 1992); U. Andersen and W. Woyke, *Wahl '98. Zur Bundestagswahl 1998* (Opladen: Leske+Budrich, 1998); *Zeitschrift für Parlamentsfragen*, various issues.

Similarly, the CDU went through a series of severe defeats in Landtag elections between 1984 and 1989 (see Table 3). These defeats eroded the government's majority in the Bundesrat, undermined Kohl's authority as party leader and drove him to the brink of resignation. In the run-up to the Bremen Annual Conference of 1989, Kohl's leadership was directly threatened by an attempt of the CDU's General Secretary, Heiner Geißler, the premier of Baden-Württemberg, Lothar Späth, and the premier of Lower Saxony, Ernst Albrecht, to persuade Kohl to renounce the party leadership. Späth was to succeed Kohl as party leader. The attack on his chancellorship was to commence after a possible severe defeat in the European elections of 1989. In the summer of 1989, Kohl apparently considered his resignation as Chancellor. Yet, due to his excellent personal networks within the CDU and his ability to forge and maintain coalitions with key allies in his party, he managed to fend off the challenge to his leadership. The Bremen Annual Conference was a triumph for Kohl, as he was re-elected as party leader.[53] This episode bears witness not only to Kohl's qualities as a party leader, but also to his sheer luck. The Chancellor was helped by unanticipated events: at the very moment he had to fend off the most serious challenge to his leadership, the Hungarian government announced its decision to allow large numbers of East German citizens to leave Hungary via Austria. This development put the whole process of unification in motion, or at least it greatly accelerated it. It was crucial for Kohl to consolidate his position as a party leader and federal Chancellor.[54] The coalition won the Bundestag elections of 1990 almost certainly because of unification.[55]

In sum, the CDU/CSU–FDP coalition under Helmut Kohl's chancellorship experienced a number of unanticipated 'external shocks': the increasing importance of immigration as a potentially divisive issue, heavy losses in elections at the Länder level resulting in a constant leadership crisis in the FDP (the party had five leaders between 1982 and 1998) and a serious challenge to Kohl's leadership in the CDU in 1989. Yet there were also events that seemed to have helped to stabilise the coalition: German unification or, to give another example, the change in the CSU leadership from Strauß, who passed away in 1988, to Waigel (see Table 1).

COALITION MANAGEMENT AND COALITION STABILITY

In the absence of effective hierarchical co-ordination, mutual trust is one of the key ingredients of rational co-operation without excessive transaction costs. Chancellor Kohl recognised that a long-term coalition with the FDP required mutual trust. He recognised the smaller party's sensitivities in the face of the five per cent threshold and its fears of being marginalised by its senior coalition partner. These fears had been a constant source of tension in the CDU/CSU's earlier coalitions with the FDP during the second half of the 1950s. Although the FDP was in an extremely unfavourable bargaining position in the early years of Kohl's chancellorship, the Chancellor avoided exploiting the Liberals' weak position in an attempt to build a long-term coalition. He clearly withstood the temptation of short-term benefits from 'defection' in the co-operation game with the FDP in the expectation of long-term mutual benefits. There are two important examples of that: the issue of early elections in 1982 and co-operation with the SPD Bundesrat majority from 1990 onwards.

One could argue that allowing Chancellor Schmidt to call the shots in the formal termination of the SPD–FDP coalition in 1982[56] weakened the FDP's bargaining position vis-à-vis the CDU/CSU tremendously, and that the CDU/CSU did exploit this situation. Lösche and Walter, for example, maintain that the FDP was left with no alternative but to seek a coalition with the Christian Democrats. Its walk-away value (in the terminology of bargaining theory) in the negotiations with the Christian Democrats was so low that the CDU/CSU was able to humiliate the Liberals by excluding former Minister of the Interior, the 'social-liberal' Gerhart Rudolf Baum, from the Cabinet and, indeed, the coalition negotiations. The CSU gained the Ministry of the Interior for Friedrich Zimmermann, whose preferences in the field of law and order were almost impossible to accept for the FDP's civil-liberties wing.[57] This is only one example of a number of concessions the weakened FDP had to make.

Yet Kohl and the CDU leadership did not opt for early elections in 1982, which could have eliminated the FDP as a party represented in parliament. The CSU leader Strauß pressed for early elections in 1982, at a time when the FDP was in an existential crisis. The 'Wende' had shaken the FDP to its foundations. The party had lost a number of prominent parliamentary spokespersons and a significant share of its mid-level elite. In the years following the 'Wende' its membership declined by more than one-quarter from approximately 87,000 in the last year before the collapse of the Social-Liberal coalition (1981) to 64,000 in 1986 and recovered only as a result of the party's unification with its eastern German counterpart, LDPD, in 1990.[58] Finally, it suffered a number of severe electoral defeats at the federal-state level as the former Chancellor Schmidt and the SPD successfully launched a highly emotional campaign against the FDP and portrayed its leaders as 'traitors'.[59]

Given the results of opinion polls and the state elections of Hesse in 1982, it seemed possible, or even likely, that the FDP would have failed to straddle the five per cent threshold at the national level in 1982. In this situation, Strauß believed that the CDU/CSU had a real chance to achieve an overall majority.[60] Kohl, by contrast, opted for a compromise that saved the long-term co-operation with the FDP: he recognised the need to obtain a democratic mandate for his government and agreed to early elections, but only in March 1983. This gave the FDP enough breathing space to recover from the shock of 1982. Kohl clearly preferred long-term co-operation with the FDP to the short-term chance of an overall majority, possibly for one legislative term only. Kaltefleiter argues that Kohl continued to treat the FDP with consideration whenever it seemed to be in a crisis and believes this to be a key explanation for Kohl's long chancellorship. He clearly did not go for Adenauer's 1950s strategy of absorbing the smaller right-wing parties in the early years of the Federal Republic. Kaltefleiter also argues that Kohl's leadership style contrasted with that of Helmut Schmidt, who used the strategic weaknesses of the FDP much more to his own advantage and employed an authoritarian leadership style *vis-à-vis* the liberal members of his cabinet.[61]

Kohl also had to find a fine balance between loyalty to the coalition partner and short-term policy gains in the necessary negotiations with the SPD Länder governments in the Bundesrat. The CDU/CSU–FDP coalition lacked a majority in the Bundesrat from May to October 1990 and between early 1991 and its election defeat in 1998. Given the fact that the SPD governed in various coalitions with the Greens, the CDU and the FDP in a number of federal states, it cannot be said the SPD 'controlled' the Bundesrat.[62] Nevertheless, important SPD Länder governments had to be persuaded, if the Kohl government wanted its legislation to be passed by the Bundesrat (especially so-called 'consent laws', that is, laws for which Bundesrat consent is mandatory according to the Basic Law). Many of the decisive negotiations had to be conducted not only within the coalition and the coalition parties, but also between the federal government and the state governments controlled by the SPD. The Conference Committee (*Vermittlungsausschuß*) of the Bundestag and Bundesrat became a very important body.[63] The dependence on SPD support in the Bundesrat increased the CDU/CSU's leverage *vis-à-vis* its liberal coalition partner in a number of policy areas such as social or immigration policy. In some of these areas the SPD was closer to the Christian Democrats' position than the FDP. Yet Kohl generally withstood the temptation to operate with 'changing majorities', that is, to pass legislation with SPD support against the will of the FDP (for example, in the context of asylum, immigration and data protection).

Beyond Kohl's long-term coalition strategy, the CDU/CSU–FDP coalition employed a number of important institutional devices to deal with inevitable policy conflicts and avoid exclusive reliance on 'negative co-ordination'. Kohl's coalition cabinets were able to employ 'positive co-ordination' in the vast majority of *important* issues. The Federal

Chancellor's Office, for example, was an effective instrument of positive co-ordination. Its sections mirror the government's departmental structure and enhance the Chancellor's monitoring capacity *vis-à-vis* individual departments. The 'mirror sections' maintain close communications with the appropriate departments. From 1984 onwards, the Chancellor's Office was headed by politicians with considerable authority in the CDU/CSU parliamentary party. Wolfgang Schäuble (1984–89) and his successors Rudolf Seiters (1989–91) and Friedrich Bohl (1991–98) had been chief whips (*Erster Parlamentarischer Geschäftsführer*) of the CDU/CSU parliamentary party before they were appointed to head the Chancellor's Office. All three retained close links with the parliamentary party and helped the Chancellor to retain, or, where necessary, rebuild support amongst Christian Democratic backbenchers. As a result of his strong support in the CDU/CSU parliamentary party, Kohl was able to commit himself more credibly to agreements with the FDP. On the whole, therefore, the role of the Chancellor's Office facilitated interdepartmental co-ordination and stabilised the coalition.

It was already mentioned that coalition governance is as much a matter of constant intra-party bargaining as bargaining between parties. Coalition compromises negotiated at the leadership level need to gain support from the parliamentary and extra-parliamentary parties involved. Compared to Schmidt, Kohl was particularly successful in addressing the intra-party dimension of coalition governance. Apart from his close links with the CDU/CSU parliamentary party, Kohl placed considerable emphasis on maintaining the support of influential politicians in the CDU outside the Bundestag. The CDU's National Executive Committee (*Bundesvorstand*) and its Presidium were important instruments of co-ordination within the CDU. During his chancellorship, the emphasis of intra-party co-ordination outside the Bundestag increasingly shifted towards the Presidium, which included the CDU state premiers. In addition, Kohl maintained a close network of informal personal contacts with party officials at all levels of the CDU organisation. In his case study on west–east German relations under Kohl, Karl-Rudolf Korte appropriately speaks of Kohl's 'political family' as a group of persons who were loyal to the Chancellor and advised him independent of their formal rank in the functional hierarchy of government.[64] Kohl's informal contacts served as an information system for the Chancellor to give him early warning about dissatisfaction amongst the party rank and file. It also helped him to target his communications to the party. Compared to his predecessor as Chancellor, Helmut Schmidt, Kohl preferred co-ordination in personal networks to 'rational-bureaucratic hierarchy' and thereby managed to maintain a better understanding of, and grip on, his party. It was, therefore, easier for Kohl to convince his own party about the necessity of compromises with his coalition partner, the FDP.

The cornerstone of coalition government in Germany, however, is regular, informal meetings of coalition leaders, that is, so-called 'coalition talks', 'coalition working groups' and coalition 'round tables' with varying degrees of formalisation.[65] Under Kohl, the overall direction of policy, important policy decisions and questions of coalition governance were dealt with flexibly in such informal bodies. The Cabinet and the parliamentary majority parties were often left with the task of implementing the decisions made by these bodies. Close observers argue that routine matters were dealt with in Cabinet, important policy changes were regularly prepared in coalition talks.[66] This shift of the locus of policy making was criticised by some authors as a process undermining the authority of constitutional bodies such as the Cabinet, but also the Bundestag.[67]

The rationale behind coalition government in informal bodies is straightforward: coalition agreements require the support of all coalition partners' parliamentary parties and, depending on the power structure of the respective party, may also need the support of the extra-parliamentary party organisation. Purely governmental or parliamentary structures such as the Cabinet are insufficient to generate the necessary consensus within the parties as a whole. Furthermore, the federal nature of the German polity and the fact that the federal states implement the bulk of domestic policies, make consultation beyond the Cabinet table a must. Often, state (prime) ministers and officials are important actors in the process of federal coalition governance, although they are not formally members of the Cabinet or the Bundestag. Finally, sensitive issues (for example, in foreign policy) or difficult negotiations in which all sides have to make hard choices and compromise require a high degree of confidentiality. Cabinet is too large and heterogeneous a body to guarantee confidentiality. It is known that Kohl never believed in the complete confidentiality of Cabinet meetings.[68] The informal bodies Kohl relied on usually comprised the Federal Chancellor, some Cabinet ministers and representatives of the extra-parliamentary party leadership as well as the leadership of the parliamentary parties. The smaller coalition partners were usually particularly interested in establishing formal committees, which were to ensure regular consultation. There is evidence to suggest that the increasing importance of coalition rounds and the increasing formalisation of their proceedings from the mid-1980s onwards was a result of FDP pressure against the original intentions of Kohl[69] – informal meetings of party leaders or party experts have a tendency to increase the relative weight of the junior coalition partner(s) vis-à-vis a dominant senior partner.[70]

Coalition governance under Helmut Kohl was based on a complicated web of institutional arrangements that took account of the sensitivities of

CSU and FDP, the inter-party as well as the intra-party dimensions of coalition conflicts. Together with a number of favourable structural conditions and fortunate events, these informal structures contributed to the longevity of the CDU/CSU–FDP coalition. It also allowed a degree of 'positive co-ordination'. Despite its adverse effect on the authority of the Cabinet as a decision-making body, governing in informal bodies (as well as the role of the Chancellor's Office) can be thought of as a means of avoiding the disadvantages of purely negative co-ordination.[71]

CONCLUSIONS

The CDU/CSU–FDP coalition under Helmut Kohl's chancellorship was extremely stable. After nearly 16 years in office it was deposed by the electorate. Paradoxically, one of the main reasons for its defeat at the polls may have been its very longevity. Many voters believed it was 'time for a change', especially with respect to the person of the Chancellor.[72] The stability of this coalition is remarkable both in cross-national and diachronic comparison. Although the 1969–82 coalition between the SPD and FDP was also very durable and lasted for approximately 13 years, its termination was to be expected from the late 1970s onwards. The coalition was arguably saved by Franz Josef Strauß's nomination as CDU/CSU Chancellor candidate for the 1980 elections.

The extraordinary stability of the CDU/CSU–FDP coalition of 1982–98 was to some extent a result of structural features. After the experience of government instability in the Weimar Republic, the Basic Law was deliberately constructed to ensure such stability. The German Federal President, for example, has no constitutional powers to intervene actively in the process of government formation or termination. This was clearly a lesson the authors of the Basic Law learned from the fateful construction of the office of Reich President in the Weimar Republic. Unlike the Weimar Reichstag, the Bundestag is not allowed to dissolve itself. The Federal Chancellor is protected from 'negative majorities' by the constructive vote of no confidence. The five per cent threshold of the Federal Elections Act (*Bundeswahlgesetz*) has been effective to prevent a fragmentation of the party system at the parliamentary level. The Federal Constitutional Court was given powers to ban extremist parties on the grounds of unconstitutionality, thus reducing the risk of 'polarised pluralism'[73] and its centrifugal impact on party competition so characteristic of the Weimar party system with its strong political extremes.

Apart from constitutional and statutory safeguards, coalition stability has also been enhanced by political and sociological factors. Unlike their Weimar predecessors, the two major parties, the CDU/CSU and the SPD, became pragmatic and inclusive 'catch-all parties'. Their further development to 'loosely coupled systems', which is analysed by Elmar Wiesendahl in this volume, has had no negative effect on coalition stability. The social and economic changes of the late 1960s and 1970s (for example, post-materialism and the rise of the Green Party) and German unification led only to a moderate increase in party-system fractionalisation. The main political cleavages in Germany remained relatively stable, the rise of the 'post-materialist' Green Party and the East German PDS notwithstanding. The main dimensions of political conflict and co-operation in Germany have remained remarkably stable even after unification. Franz Urban Pappi and Gabriele Eckstein show empirically that 'parties compete within the same frame of reference' in both parts of Germany, although the party preferences 'of the East Germans are more left-leaning than those of the West Germans'.[74] Yet structural features do not guarantee stable coalition government. Coalitions were less stable prior to 1969, although many if not all of the structural features have remained constant. Furthermore, not all of the structural features would have led to the expection of such a long-lasting co-operation between the Christian Democrats and Liberals under Helmut Kohl. The policy differences between the parties in areas such as foreign policy and civil liberties were considerable and caused a number of serious controversies, which were exacerbated by Franz-Josef Strauß's deep-seated dislike for the FDP.

The impact of external events, too, is ambivalent. The government experienced a number of 'public opinion shocks'. The FDP, for example, went through two phases of extremely adverse public opinion. This was expressed in severe election defeats at the federal-state level, between 1982 and 1984 and between 1993 and 1995. The government's public standing in the late 1980s and before the elections of 1994 was also poor. Survey researchers predicted election defeats at the national level in 1989 (for 1990) and 1993 (for 1994). Nevertheless, such events failed to destroy the coalition. In fact, some unexpected external events helped it to survive. The classic example in this context is German unification, which boosted Helmut Kohl's authority at a time when he needed it most. It also helped to narrow the gap between the CDU/CSU and the FDP in foreign policy matters and reinforced economic policy as the main dimension of party competition – a policy area in which Christian Democrats and Liberals fundamentally agreed. This seems to suggest that the ability of external events to stabilise rather than destabilise a coalition may have been underrated in the study of coalitions from an event-oriented perspective and may have to be included more explicitly in such models.

It would be impossible to explain the stability of the CDU/CSU–FDP coalition of 1982–98 adequately without referring to the various mechanisms of coalition governance and Kohl's leadership. Kohl was acutely aware of the precarious situation of the FDP at the brink of the five per cent threshold of Germany's electoral laws. He made credible commitments to a long-term partnership with the FDP and withstood the temptation of short-term benefits from 'defection' on a number of important occasions. He also created an institutional framework that allowed long-term co-operation without merely resorting to 'negative co-ordination'. The Chancellor's Office under Kohl was an effective instrument of inter-ministerial co-ordination. Kohl's ability to mobilise support for the coalition's policies within his own party contrasted starkly with Schmidt's failure in this respect. The conditions within the FDP were also favourable, although they were favourable for different reasons. The exodus of many 'social-liberal' critics of the CDU/CSU–FDP coalition in the early 1980s had created a much more homogeneous party. The relative autonomy of the predominantly 'market-liberal' parliamentary party and its leadership *vis-à-vis* the extra-parliamentary organisation allowed the FDP leaders sufficient room for manoeuvre. Last, but not least, the coalition used a flexible and highly effective system of informal coalition talks, round tables, expert working groups and committees in which conflicts could be ironed out. Governing in these bodies, which were flexible enough to include both representatives of the parliamentary and extra-parliamentary parties, may be considered as the 'efficient secret' of coalition governance under Kohl, although some observers cricitise the cost of governing in informal bodies: a loss of authority of constitutional bodies such as the cabinet and parliament.

NOTES

I am grateful to Stephen Padgett for his helpful comments on an earlier draft of this article. Needless to say, any error or opacity remaining is my responsibility alone.

 1. For a summary of the events, see D.L. Bark and D.R. Gress, *A History of West Germany, Volume 2: Democracy and its Discontents 1963–1991* (Oxford: Blackwell, 2nd edn 1993), pp.376–9.
 2. I. Budge and H. Keman, *Parties and Democracy: Coalition Formation and Government Functioning in Twenty States* (Oxford: Oxford University Press, 1990), p.11.
 3. W. Riker, *The Theory of Political Coalitions* (New Haven, CT: Yale University Press, 1960), pp.32–3.
 4. Budge and Keman, *Parties and Democracy*, pp.19–20.
 5. Ibid., p.21.
 6. P.V. Warwick, *Government Stability in Parliamentary Democracies* (Cambridge: Cambridge University Press, 1994), p.8.
 7. J.P. Frendreis, D.W. Gleiber and E.C. Browne, 'The Study of Cabinet Dissolutions in Parliamentary Democracies', *Legislative Studies Quarterly*, 11 (1986), pp.619–28.
 8. E.C. Browne, J.P. Frendreis and D.W. Gleiber, 'The Process of Cabinet Dissolution: An Exponential Model of Duration and Stability in Western Democracies', *American Journal of Political Science*, 30 (1986), pp.628–50; K. Strøm, Contribution to 'Contending Models of Cabinet Stability', *American Political Science Review*, 82 (1988), pp.923–30.
 9. G. King *et al.*, 'A Unified Model of Cabinet Dissolution in Parliamentary Democracies', *American Journal of Political Science*, 34 (1990), pp.846–71; Warwick, *Government Stability*.

10. Cf. M. Laver and K. Shepsle, *Making and Breaking Governments: Cabinets and Legislatures in Parliamentary Democracies* (Cambridge: Cambridge University Press, 1996); A. Lupia and K. Strøm, 'Coalition Termination and the Strategic Timing of Parliamentary Elections', *American Political Science Review*, 89 (1995), pp.648–65; see also the contributions to W.C. Müller and K. Strøm, *Koalitionsregierungen in Westeuropa: Bildung, Arbeitsweise und Beendigung* (Wien: Signum, 1997); P. Mitchell, 'The Life and Times of Coalition Governments: Coalition Maintenance by Event Management' (unpublished Ph.D. thesis, European University Institute, Florence, 1996); A. Timmermans, 'High Politics in the Low Countries: Functions and Effectos of Coalition Policy Agreements in Belgium and the Netherlands' (unpublished Ph.D. thesis, European University Institute, Florence, 1996).
11. Cf. M. Laver, 'Divided Parties, Divided Government', *Legislative Studies Quarterly*, 24 (1999), pp.5–30; with an emphasis on party organisation, see M. Maor, *Parties, Conflicts and Coalitions in Western Europe: Organisational Determinants of Coalition Bargaining* (London: Routledge, 1998).
12. See W.C. Müller and K. Strøm, 'Schluß: Koalitionsregierungen und die Praxis des Regierens in Westeuropa', in Müller and Strøm (eds.), *Koalitionsregierungen in Westeuropa*, p.740; for Germany, see T. Saalfeld, 'Deutschland: Auswanderung der Politik aus der Verfassung?' in Müller and Strøm (eds.), *Koalitionsregierungen in Westeuropa*, pp.93–9.
13. Laver and Shepsle, *Making and Breaking Governments*, p.61.
14. Ibid., p.66.
15. Ibid, pp.70–76.
16. M. Laver and K.A. Shepsle, 'Coalitions and Cabinet Government', *American Political Science Review*, 84 (1990), pp.873–90.
17. F.W. Scharpf, 'Coordination in Hierarchies and Networks', in F.W. Scharpf (ed.), *Games in Hierarchies and Networks: Analytical and Empirical Approaches to the Study of Governance Institutions* (Frankfurt am Main: Campus and Boulder, CO: Westview, 1993), pp.143–4.
18. Ibid., p.144.
19. For first results, see Müller and Strøm (eds.), *Koalitionsregierungen in Westeuropa*. (A revised and updated volume is forthcoming in English language.)
20. P. Mitchell, 'Coalition Discipline, Enforcement Mechanisms, and Intraparty Politics', in S. Bowler, D.M. Farrell and R.S. Katz (eds.), *Party Discipline and Parliamentary Government* (Columbus, OH: Ohio State University Press, 1999), p.270.
21. Cf. R. Axelrod, *The Evolution of Cooperation* (New York: Basic Books, 1984).
22. M.N. Franklin and T.T. Mackie, 'Familiarity and Inertia in the Formation of Governing Coalitions in Parliamentary Democracies', *British Journal of Political Science*, 13 (1983), pp.275–98.
23. G. Sartori, *The Theory of Democracy Revisited. Part One: The Contemporary Debate* (Chatham, NJ: Chatham House, 1987), p.229.
24. Mitchell, 'Coalition Discipline', p.270.
25. A cabinet begins with its investiture in parliament and ends with (a) a change in the person of Kanzler, (b) a change in the party composition of the coalition or (c) a general election.
26. M. Laver and N. Schofield, *Multiparty Government: The Politics of Coalition in Europe* (Oxford: Oxford University Press, 1990), pp.147–58.
27. T. Bergman, 'Formation Rules and Minority Governments', *European Journal of Political Research*, 23 (1993), pp.55–66.
28. For example, it saved the SPD–FDP coalition under Chancellor Willy Brandt in 1972.
29. The early dissolution of 1983 was highly contentious and justified by exceptional circumstances: the FDP had campaigned for the continuation of its coalition with the Social Democrats for a whole legislative term in 1980. In 1982, it decided to withdraw from the coalition and form a new government coalition with the CDU/CSU. The informal 'pre-electoral pact' with the SPD cast doubt about the democratic legitimacy of the first Kohl cabinet.
30. See G. Sartori, *Parties and Party Systems: A Framework for Analysis* (Cambridge: Cambridge University Press, 1976), pp.173–85.
31. It is contentious in the German debate whether or not the PDS should be considered an anti-system party opposed to liberal democracy. Since the Federal Constitutional Court has not banned it, it is not treated as such a party in this context, whereas the German Right Party

(DKP/DRP) – which included later members of the Socialist Reich Party (SRP) – and the Communist Party (KPD) in the first Bundestag (1949–53) are treated as anti-system party, because they were banned by the Federal Constitutional Court in 1952 and 1956 respectively. For the Weimar Republic, only the KPD and NSDAP were counted as anti-system parties in Table 1, although the constitutionality of a number of other parties such as the DNVP was highly questionable.

32. M. Laakso and R. Taagepera, '"Effective" Number of Parties: A Measure with Application to West Europe', *Comparative Political Studies*, 12 (1979), pp.3–27.
33. Sartori, *Parties and Party Systems*, p.307; the calculation of the index is explained there.
34. Cf. Saalfeld, 'Deutschland', p.63.
35. Ibid.
36. Laver and Schofield, *Multiparty Government*, pp.150–51.
37. Ibid., pp.150–51.
38. J. Huber and R. Inglehart, 'Expert Interpretations of Party Space and Party Locations in 42 Societies', *Party Politics*, 1 (1995), pp.73–111.
39. The raw data can be found in H.-D. Klingemann and A. Volkens, 'Struktur und Entwicklung von Wahlprogrammen in der Bundesrepublik Deutschland 1949–1994', in O.W. Gabriel, O. Niedermayer and R. Stöss (eds.), *Parteiendemokratie in Deutschland* (Opladen: Westdeutscher Verlag, 1997), p.526.
40. M. Laver and W.B. Hunt, *Policy and Party Competition* (London: Routledge, 1992), p.108.
41. For further data, see Klingemann and Volkens, 'Struktur und Entwicklung', p.526; see also F.U. Pappi, 'The West German Party System', *West European Politics*, 7 (1984), pp.7–26.
42. See J. Schmid, *Die CDU: Organisationsstrukturen, Politiken und Funktionsweisen einer Partei im Föderalismus* (Opladen: Leske+Budrich, 1990).
43. K.-R. Korte, *Deutschlandpolitik in Helmut Kohls Kanzlerschaft: Regierungsstil und Entscheidungen 1982–1989* (Stuttgart: Deutsche Verlags-Anstalt, 1998), p.465 (my translation).
44. Scharpf, 'Coordination in Hierarchies and Networks', pp.147–55, *verbatim* quote pp.153–4.
45. A. Mintzel, *Geschichte der CSU: Ein Überblick* (Opladen: Westdeutscher Verlag, 1977), pp.345–7.
46. Ibid., pp.345–63, 400, 409–12.
47. For an analysis of the FDP's organisational problems, see P. Lösche and F. Walter, *Die FDP: Richtungsstreit und Zukunftszweifel* (Darmstadt: Wissenschaftliche Buchgesellschaft, 1996).
48. Laver and Shepsle, *Making and Breaking Governments*, pp.196–7.
49. D. Thränhardt, 'The Political Uses of Xenophobia in England, France and Germany', *Party Politics*, 1, 3 (1995), pp.323–45.
50. For a brief analytical account, see T. Saalfeld, 'Up and Down with the Extreme Right in Germany, 1949–96', *Politics*, 17 (1997), pp.1–8.
51. F.-U. Pappi and G. Eckstein, 'Voters' Party Preferences in Multiparty Systems and their Coalitional and Spatial Implications: Germany after Unification', *Public Choice*, 97 (1998), p.246.
52. See, for example, Lösche and Walter, *Die FDP*, p.107.
53. The episode is summarised (with further references) by Korte, *Deutschlandpolitik in Helmut Kohls Kanzlerschaft*, pp.463–8.
54. Ibid., pp.467–8.
55. M. Jung and D. Roth, 'Wer zu spät geht, den bestraft der Wähler: Eine Analyse der Bundestagswahl 1998', *Aus Politik und Zeitgeschichte* B52 (1998), p.4.
56. Schmidt played a much more active part in the 'dramaturgy' of the termination than the folk wisdom of FDP 'treason' usually suggests. Undoubtedly, the FDP leadership – the Economics Minister, Count Lambsdorff, in particular – had begun to work for a change from the second half of the 1970s onwards. But in 1981/82 Schmidt appears to have deemed a termination inevitable and 'orchestrated' the termination skilfully with a view to maximise the electoral payoff for the SPD and, arguably, to enhance his own reputation. See W. Jäger and W. Link, *Geschichte der Bundesrepublik Deutschland, Volume 5/II: Republik im Wandel 1974–1982: Die Ära Schmidt* (Stuttgart: Deutsche Verlags-Anstalt, 1987), pp.201–63.
57. Lösche and Walter, *Die FDP*, p.109.
58. In fact, as a result of German unification and the absorption of the East German LDPD, the

party's membership increased from 65,485 to 178,625 in 1990. All data from P. Lösche, *Kleine Geschichte der deutschen Parteien* (Stuttgart: Kohlhammer, 1993), p.205.

59. See Jäger and Link, *Geschichte der Bundesrepublik Deutschland*, pp.251–63.
60. The relationship between Strauß and the FDP had been hostile ever since his forced resignation as Defence Minister in the Spiegel Affair (1962). Strauß's role as the CDU/CSU's Chancellor candidate in the elections of 1980 is likely to be one of the reasons why the SPD–FDP coalition was not terminated earlier. See Lösche and Walter, *Die FDP*, p.105.
61. W. Kaltefleiter, 'Die Kanzlerdemokratie des Helmut Kohl', *Zeitschrift für Parlamentsfragen*, 27, 1 (1996), p.35. Some evidence of this is presented in Jäger and Link, *Geschichte der Bundesrepublik Deutschland*, pp.201–53.
62. C. Jeffery, 'The Territorial Dimension', in G. Smith, W.E. Paterson and S. Padgett (eds.), *Developments in German Politics 2* (Basingstoke and London: Macmillan, 1996), p.89.
63. Kaltefleiter, 'Die Kanzlerdemokratie des Helmut Kohl', p.36.
64. Korte, *Deutschlandpolitik in Helmut Kohls Kanzlerschaft*, pp.25–6.
65. For a summary see Saalfeld, 'Up and Down with the Extreme Right in Germany'.
66. Cf. Waldemar Schreckenberger, Kohl's first head of the Chancellor's Office (W. Schreckenberger, 'Informelle Verfahren der Entscheidungsvorbereitung zwischen der Bundesregierung und den Mehrheitsfraktionen: Koalitionsgespräche und Koalitionsrunden', *Zeitschrift für Parlamentsfragen*, 25, 3 (1994), p.334); see also W. Rudzio, 'Informelle Entscheidungsmuster in Bonner Koalitionsregierungen', in H.-H. Hartwich and G. Wewer (eds.), *Regieren in der Bundesrepublik 2: Formale und informale Komponenten des Regierens* (Opladen: Leske+Budrich, 1991), p.137.
67. See, for example, Schreckenberger, 'Informelle Verfahren'.
68. Korte, *Deutschlandpolitik in Helmut Kohls Kanzlerschaft*, p.51.
69. Ibid., pp.58–9.
70. J. Kaarbo, 'Power and Influence in Foreign Policy Decision Making: The Role of Junior Coalition Partners in German and Israeli Foreign Policy', *International Studies Quarterly*, 40 (1996), pp.518–19.
71. Scharpf, 'Coordination in Hierarchies and Networks', p.144.
72. Cf. Jung and Roth, 'Wer zu spät geht, den bestraft der Wähler'; O.W. Gabriel and F. Brettschneider, 'Die Bundestagswahl 1998: Ein Plebiszit gegen Kanzler Kohl?' *Aus Politik und Zeitgeschichte* B52 (1998), pp.20–32.
73. Sartori, *Parties and Party Systems*, pp.131–73.
74. Cf. Pappi and Eckstein, 'Voters' Party Preferences', pp.253–4.

The Red–Green Coalition

CHARLES LEES

In a recent interview with the magazine *Stern*, Green Environment Minister Jürgen Trittin claimed that, on the basis of his experience, there was no longer much to choose between the SPD and the CDU. As a result, Trittin argued, the Greens should no longer be in thrall to the Social Democrats but should be prepared to consider the Christian Democrats as potential coalition partners, at least in the medium term.[1] Trittin's remarks were immediately condemned by politicians within his own party, as well as the SPD and – more surprisingly – the CDU itself! Few can doubt that they were at least in part the product of frustration with the red–green coalition's somewhat shaky start in office.

The coalition agreement of October 1998 identified three main themes which were to provide the core of the red–green legislative programme. First, the reduction of unemployment by up to a million over the four-year term. Second, rapid withdrawal from the use of nuclear power and a parallel programme of ecological tax reform. Third, the reform of Germany's citizenship laws, in order better to reflect the multi-cultural reality of life in the Federal Republic. Of these three themes, the first can be regarded as a traditional social democratic concern, whilst the other two are the result of 'New Left' thinking within the party and, of course, co-operation with the Greens. After only a few months in office, the government's plans in all three areas lie in tatters.

When he took over as Federal Chancellor, Gerhard Schröder re-emphasised his claim that his term in office should be judged by the government's ability to tackle Germany's chronically high rate of unemployment. This was around 10.5 per cent when he came to power, but had risen to 11.5 per cent by the second month of 1999 (up 250,000 in January alone). Schröder has put his faith in a typically corporatist solution in order to tackle this problem, the so-called 'Jobs Pact'. In theory the pact is the type of arrangement that plays to Schröder's strengths, allowing him to take on the role of facilitator between business and organised labour and hammer out some form of *modus vivendi* between the social partners.

Undoubtedly, Schröder's template for the Jobs Pact was the period of *Konzertierte Aktion* in the late 1960s and early 1970s, which provided a

Charles Lees, University of Sussex

stable corporatist framework within which the social partners addressed the economic problems associated with the end of the *Wirtschaftswunder*, the collapse of Bretton Woods and the subsequent oil shocks of the 1970s. However, any attempt to replicate such an institution in the very different social and economic conditions of the late 1990s is fraught with difficulty. Lowering expectations amongst a populace who have enjoyed more than 40 years of impressively rising living standards is a slow and painful process and, as Bodo Hombach recently observed, narrow sectional interests have the ability to impose what is effectively a veto on changes that they perceive to be against their interests. Thus, with unemployment rising, making the Jobs Pact work will need all of Schröder's powers of persuasion.

If tackling unemployment is the SPD's primary concern, the phasing out of nuclear energy is the benchmark by which the Green *Basis* – and indeed most of its senior politicians – will judge the success of the red–green coalition and, with Jürgen Trittin at the helm of the Environment Ministry, initial hopes for rapid progress on this front were high. The ability to exercise power at the highest level was, after all, what Rudi Dütschke's idea of 'the long march through the institutions' was all about. Yet within a few months of coming to power, Trittin and his supporters have had to take on board a harsh lesson in the limits of executive power.

Trittin planned, first, to revise the federal energy law and establish a legal framework for withdrawal from nuclear power. The revised law would then provide a basis for so-called 'consensus talks' with the nuclear industry in order to hammer out a timetable for such a process. However, in revising the energy law, Trittin proposed that the Federal Republic should move quickly to end the reprocessing of nuclear fuel. But this last move was a step too far. Trittin's suggestion that the Federal Republic unilaterally cancel its contracts with reprocessing plants in France and Britain led to an intergovernmental row with its European neighbours on the eve of the Federal Republic's term in the EU presidency. Moreover, the threat by British Nuclear Fuels to retaliate by returning unprocessed fuel rods to the Federal Republic raised the prospect of a re-run of the civil disturbances associated with the transportation of nuclear waste to dumps such as Gorleben and provoked a harsh response from the (SPD) Minister Presidents of Lower Saxony and North Rhine-Westphalia, who would be delegated to handle the security for such transports. At the same time, both the nuclear industry and German industrialists terrified of higher energy costs kept up a steady PR offensive against Trittin's proposals.

By the beginning of 1999, Trittin had accumulated a formidable set of political opponents both at home and abroad. Faced with international as well as domestic pressures, Schröder forced his Environment Minister to climb down. Trittin's plan to set an overall deadline for withdrawal was shelved indefinitely and, in future, the shut-down of any of the Federal Republic's 19 nuclear reactors would be decided on the merits of each case. In the short term at least, Trittin's programme has been axed and his own position has been weakened.

Up until early February 1999, the coalition's plans to reform the Federal Republic's Citizenship Law appeared to be in course. Based on the *Reichs- und Staatsangehörigkeits Gesetz* (RuStAG) of 1913, the law's emphasis upon ethnicity and cultural homogeneity has increasingly become inappropriate to the social conditions of late twentieth-century Germany.

The government's plan to replace the existing law with one allowing dual citizenship was agreed during the coalition negotiations and immediately opposed by the CDU/CSU, who launched a signature campaign against it. However, the Christian Democrats' success in tapping into the fears of 'ordinary' Germans was not fully appreciated until the defeat of the ruling red–green coalitions in Land elections in Hesse in early February.[2] At the time of writing, the Federal Republic's political classes regard this defeat as signifying the end of the new citizenship law in its present form. However, it is also a serious blow to the future of the red–green coalition itself, not least because the loss of the SPD's majority in the Bundesrat means that the coalition will suffer from the same institutional gridlock that dogged the last years of Helmut Kohl's government. Whether the SPD can regain its majority in the upper house will depend on the outcome of a series of Land elections in 1999 (especially in Berlin and Bremen), and in the meantime it will have to compromise with the CDU in order to ensure the passage of government legislation through the second chamber. Obviously, the operation of what many regard as a *de facto* grand coalition will put further pressure on the SPD's relationship with the Greens.

With the resignation of Oskar Lafontaine as Finance Minister in March 1999, the red–green coalition's fortunes appeared to have reached rock-bottom. However, it would be a mistake to underestimate the political skills of Gerhard Schröder and the events of early 1999 may prove to be a turning point. The loss of Hesse was a blow, but it was a result of declining support for the Greens. Indeed, the SPD's support actually rose slightly, which has been interpreted by those close to the Chancellor as a mandate to return to a more traditional 'social democratic' policy stance. From now on the emphasis will be on tackling unemployment rather than the more esoteric concerns of the environment. Moreover, the Greens' poor showing means that they must choose either to keep their heads down and go along with the SPD or go back into opposition. Having barely settled into office, many senior Green politicians would be reluctant to opt for the latter course. In short, the Greens' options are limited.

ARGUMENTS AND STRUCTURE

This article starts from the assumption that the Greens' options are indeed limited and goes on to assert that, whatever the political context that provoked his outburst, Trittin's comments are fundamentally wrong and arise from a flawed analysis of the Greens' strategic position. Although it would be foolhardy to rule out an alliance with the CDU at the Länder level in the medium term, this article argues that at present the only practical coalition partner for the Greens at the federal level remains the SPD. The problem for the Greens is that this reliance is not reciprocated by the Social Democrats, who retain the ability to emphasise selectively those aspects of their policy programme that are closer to the bourgeois parties (the CDU and FDP).

This article will pursue this argument sequentially. The next section develops the theoretical framework underpinning the discussion and posits the idea of an 'established' model of red–green co-operation, generated by trial and error through an analysis of the history of red–green coalitions in the Federal Republic. The following two sections go on to look at the two national parties' ideological stance and election programmes prior to the 1998 federal elections, whilst the one after that examines the composition and division of portfolios in the light of the established model of red–green co-operation. Finally, the concluding section will argue that, despite its apparent instability, the events and issues that constitute the 'political life' of the Federal Republic's first national red–green coalition can be explained and to a certain extent predicted in the light of the sub-national experience.

DEVELOPING AN 'ESTABLISHED' MODEL OF RED–GREEN POLITICAL CO-OPERATION

In order for the Greens to enter government, at least one of three conditions had to be satisfied. First, that the potential for the selective emphasis of those policy domains where the Greens and SPD were reasonably close was greater than that which existed between the SPD and any other potential coalition partner. In theoretical terms this can be classified as a question of 'ideological range', as posited by Abram de Swaan.[3] De Swaan's model predicts that the winning set will comprise the minimal connected winning coalition with the smallest ideological range, in other words a 'closed minimum range' of cabinet formation. De Swaan's theory is often referred to as the 'median legislator' (or 'median party') model because it is predicated upon the assumption that the party that controls the median legislator in any potential coalition is decisive because it blocks the axis along which any connected winning coalition must form. Similar models focus on voting games, and involve some variation upon the game-theoretical concept of the 'core' or 'barycenter',[4] which Eric Browne[5] suggests could be used to augment de Swaan's 'median legislator' model of coalition formation.

The second condition is a function of the SPD's need to keep any 'surplus majority' to a minimum in order to maximise (i) office-seeking payoffs and (ii) the relative weight of the SPD within the coalition. In other words, the SPD's choice of coalition partner is constrained by a 'minimum-winning' criterion, as associated with the work of William H. Riker.[6] The focus of Riker's model lies with the strategies adopted by the parties, who are assumed to be rational actors, as they attempt to gain admission to any coalition that may form. Each player is assigned a 'weight' within the bargaining process, which serves to differentiate between the possible coalitions. These weights are determined by the resources that the players bring to any potential coalition. Given that office seeking rather than policy is assumed to be the central formation criteria, these resources take the form of votes, parliamentary seats or power. Within this environment, Riker predicts that players will try to create coalitions that are only as large as they believe will ensure winning. In its pure theoretical form, such a 'minimal winning' coalition would be so small as to maximise the payoffs (which are assumed to be a function of each player's weight) to each coalition member. Thus, with repeated 'plays' of the bargaining game (through which irrelevant alternatives are discarded) there would be a tendency towards the smallest sub-set of potential minimal winning coalitions. However, in European party systems, parties cannot normally be disaggregated towards such a 'minimum winning' coalition of 50 per cent plus one vote, so in practical terms 'minimal winning' coalitions are the more likely outcome, even after repeated plays.

Finally, if neither of these conditions is satisfied, the article works from the assumption that the Greens' only remaining hope of gaining office would be if all other potential coalition partners either refuse the prospect of co-operation or attach unacceptable conditions to it. In practical terms, the relative weakness of the FDP meant that this last condition was a question of whether the CDU would want to enter into a grand coalition with the SPD and, if so, under what conditions? Up until the last days of the election campaign, Helmut Kohl refused to countenance such a move, although he did leave the option open as it became clear that the race was tighter than he had hoped.

This article, therefore, concentrates upon 'ideological range' and 'minimum winning' criteria and argues that the red–green coalition is the 'rational' outcome of the distribution of seats following the Bundestag elections because it is the predicted minimal winning coalition that minimises the policy distance of members from the median legislator/core. Nevertheless, as a counterweight to these theoretical assumptions, a 'party politics' approach remains central, in that it is recognised that neither party can be regarded as a 'black box'. Much has been written about the political antecedents of the red–green coalition, with emphasis upon the origins of the Green Party in the student protest movement of the late 1960s and the anti-nuclear and peace movements of the 1970s. These volatile origins have been vividly contrasted with the SPD's relatively staid political culture and record in government (with the implication that a red–green coalition at the national level will be inherently unstable, with profound political and economic implications for Germany and Europe). Yet the SPD is also notoriously fractious and difficult to lead. The party's internal institutions of power reflect the Federal Republic's multi-level structure of governance, with the party machine at the Länder level being crucial to an individual's power base and future prospects. Because of this, the SPD has more internal power centres and these constrain the strategic actions of the party leadership in a way that is not the case within, for example, the British Labour Party.[7] To sum up, the assumptions that inform this article are used heuristically, rather than in a deterministic fashion. Parties are rational agents and do act strategically, but they also – thankfully – retain the capacity to surprise us.

The knowledge which informs the two parties' strategic actions has been garnered at the sub-national level. Over 20 years ago Dodd wondered if 'provincial or state parliaments could provide the long-term setting in which party coalitions could be attempted ... with the intermediate provincial experience making national-level coalitions more possible'.[8] Nevertheless, the bulk of the literature on coalition behaviour continued to view coalition formation at a particular level of government as a discrete event. However, recent empirical work by Downs suggests that there are vertical linkages between national and sub-national governments. Downs' work suggests that these are not just of a top-down nature, but that the experience of sub-national government arrangements also constitutes a bottom-up flow of information – a 'feedback' effect – to national party elites. Moreover, key actors at both levels of government are aware of this function.[9]

If one accepts this premise, then the history of red–green co-operation at the Länder level in the Federal Republic can be regarded as a lesson-drawing process, characterised by the 'emulation of virtue'[10] and the discounting of negative experiences by party elites. Such lessons are drawn from what is undoubtedly a chequered history. Nevertheless, if one assumes that this feedback effect does exist, has it helped generate an 'established' model of red–green coalition behaviour?

Recent research into sub-national red–green coalitions in the Federal Republic[11] suggests that one can posit the outlines of an 'established' model of red–green coalition formation and maintenance. Such an established model is the result of the steep learning curve which both parties have had to negotiate in order to arrive at some form of *modus operandi* for successful political co-operation. This learning curve possesses three dimensions. The first dimension is that of intra-party conflict, of both an ideological and office-seeking nature. Since the early 1980s, the Greens have assumed a more formal and hierarchical party structure. Local Green party organisations are no longer the particularist institutions they once were. They have become more homogenised, their ideological profile more moderate and their strategic behaviour more predictable.

The second dimension is that of inter-party conflict and co-operation along the same lines. The formative years of political co-operation between the SPD and the Greens were characterised by a lack of trust and good faith on both sides. In the early 1980s many in the SPD regarded co-operation with the Greens as a necessary evil at best, whilst those politicians on the SPD's New Left who were relatively well-disposed towards the Greens were not to gain the ascendancy within the party until later in the decade. For their part, the Greens had an even longer way to travel, having to overcome substantial ideological and structural blocks to becoming a 'good' coalition partner.[12]

The third dimension is that of expertise. This goes beyond the narrow issue of staffing ministries and moves into a wider debate about the structure of German policy making. Evidence at the Länder level indicates that this dimension is crucial to the success of the Green 'project'. If the civil service is to be harnessed to the Green agenda, the structure of ministries needs to be opened up and democratised, allowing better access to the policy-making process for 'outsider' groups. This is both because the Greens' relative lack of experienced personnel and expertise puts a premium on such openness (in other words, they cannot afford to spread their talent too thinly), and also because they need to be able to demonstrate to 'their' client groups that participation in red–green coalitions has concrete benefits. Inevitably, such benefits will include access to the policy-making machine and its powers of patronage (through public procurement for experimental environmental projects and so on). However, to democratise the norms and structures of a ministry requires that one must 'own' the portfolio (unlike in Lower Saxony, where the Greens only owned the State Secretary post within the Environment Ministry) and, even then, the experience of Hesse – where such reforms have taken place – is that it is a task for a second or third term in office.[13]

Drawing upon the wealth of experience that has been acquired during the period of co-operation at the sub-national level, one can identify three sets of issues that must be resolved in order to facilitate successful coalition formation and maintenance. This 'ideal type' is drawn from the often rocky process of political co-operation between the SPD and the Greens and draws upon both positive lessons (Hesse, Lower Saxony) and negative examples (Berlin), as well as the discounting of unsuccessful alternative arrangements such as the *ad hoc* arrangements in Hamburg in 1982 and the ill-starred 'traffic light' coalitions of the early 1990s in Brandenburg and Bremen.

The first 'bundle' of issues relates to the parties' ideological stance and election programmes. For the SPD, this meant that a selective emphasis of the post-materialist and/or libertarian dimension to their ideological programme – that is, 'quality of life' issues – has been a prerequisite of successful co-operation with the Greens. For their part, the Greens have found that working with the SPD has required a moderation of the more post-materialist and/or libertarian side of their ideological profile, and in particular their ambivalence to consumer capitalism, the state's monopoly on legitimate force and its external defence arrangements. In the past the Greens have been so slow to resolve their attitude to the latter issue because, as they have only held power at the sub-national level, they have never really had to. Apart from when domestic issues were tangentially connected (such as the 'Eurofighter' row in Lower Saxony), the only time the foreign policy domain has been explicitly salient to a sub-national red–green coalition was in West Berlin in 1989, when SPD leader Walter Momper demanded – and received – the Berlin Alternative Liste's grudging acceptance of the city's 'five power' status (and by implication a *de facto* acceptance of the legitimacy of Germany's involvement in NATO). Obviously, something similar would be required before the Greens could be regarded as 'safe' coalition partners at the national level.

The second bundle of issues relates to the composition and division of portfolios, codified in a formal coalition agreement. Early attempts at red–green co-operation indicated that a formal coalition agreement was required if any degree of stability was to be established. Moreover, the lessons of the past meant that the SPD regarded ownership of the Finance, Economics and Industry ministries as the *sine qua non* of co-operation with the Greens. Moreover, they would want to 'hold on to' as many of the so-called 'sensitive' portfolios as possible (for example, Justice) during the coalition negotiations. For the Greens, the Lower Saxony experience meant that a red–green coalition would not be possible without their owning the Environment portfolio, preferably with both the Ministerial and State Secretary posts. In addition, they would want to acquire what they would regard as a 'blue-chip' portfolio (like Justice) if at all possible, whilst avoiding the creation of 'super-ministries' as part of the coalition horse-trading. This last point was vividly demonstrated in Hesse, where the creation of a Ministry for Environment, Energy, Health, Youth and the

Family exposed ministers to conflicting and irreconcilable political pressures relating to the trade-off between growth and ecology.

The third 'bundle' of issues relates to the staffing and structure of the civil service and is linked to the wider issue of expertise which, for reasons already noted, were sensitive for the Greens. Their coalition partners, the SPD, were 'expertise rich', which meant that when they took over a ministry existing staff could be replaced from in-house if so desired. This reduced the start-up costs to the SPD when taking office, leading to continuity of policy making and the retention of institutional knowledge. Moreover, it had the effect of a 'virtuous circle' in that such expertise filtered back into the party networks, informing their policy making discourse and educating future cadre. All in all, it meant that the reform of the policy-making apparatus was generally quite low down the SPD's agenda. By contrast, the Greens were 'expertise poor', with very few in-house resources to call upon when taking over a ministry and precious little experience within the party networks. Thus, for the Greens it was crucial that they open up the existing policy network to their client groups in order not only to get access to their expertise but, over time, in order to train their own personnel.

IDEOLOGICAL PROFILES AND ELECTION PROGRAMMES

Since the early 1980s, the SPD has undergone a process of programmatic renewal, in response to (i) the decline in its vote; (ii) the extraordinary personal appeal and political acumen of Helmut Kohl; (iii) the growth of the Greens, which has served to put pressure on the SPD along the post-materialist or 'new politics' dimension; (iv) the eclipse of Keynesian social democracy (as both a normative and descriptive model) and (v) the persistence of the PDS in the new Länder after 1989. This process was launched at the 1984 Party Conference in Essen and led to the approval of a new 'basic programme' in 1989. The national party continued to under-perform during the 1990s, as it struggled to reconcile itself to the conflicting pressures acting upon it. On the one hand partisan dealignment and the emergence of a post-materialist value orientation within the electorate meant that the SPD could no longer rely on a strategy of political mobilisation around traditional social cleavages,[14] whilst on the other hand the experience of the Kohl years suggested that the SPD could not afford to ignore the political centre either. This dilemma was neatly encapsulated in the personal battle for nomination as Chancellor candidate between Oskar Lafontaine and Gerhard Schröder.

Schröder's obvious popularity with the general public eventually won out and Lafontaine stood down in favour of his rival.[15] From then on the SPD's campaign strategy focused on the idea of the *Neue Mitte* (New Centre), a variation on the New Democrat/New Labour strategy of 'big tent' politics. The SPD intended to build an electoral coalition that would occupy the centre ground whilst leaving open the possibility of coalition with the Greens.

The heat may have gone out of the *realo-fundi* debate of the 1980s, but the Greens still possess the capacity to open up old wounds over fundamental ideological issues. This capacity is aggravated by the fact that, unlike most European parties of the left, the Greens still attach great importance to grass-roots democracy exercised through the party conference. For many years, senior Green Party politicians such as Joschka Fischer have expressed their misgivings about the central role of conference in drawing up a realistic policy programme that was acceptable to both the voters and potential coalition partners.

In October 1997 Jürgen Trittin (then the Greens' national spokesperson) announced the party's draft programme for the upcoming Bundestag elections, to be voted on by delegates to the Greens' national conference in March 1998. Amongst other things, it proposed a national withdrawal from the use of nuclear energy and the disbanding of NATO. As such it drew immediate criticism from both within the Green Party itself and from the SPD. Joschka Fischer took the *realo* position that 'unrealistic demands' would hamper any post-election coalition negotiations whilst the SPD flatly rejected the draft programme as a basis for negotiations. After much debate the draft programme was re-drafted and the NATO commitment was downgraded to a long-term goal for Germany and her allies rather than a unilateral act to be taken at once. This left the road clear for the SPD to praise the new draft programme, with Federal Secretary General Müntefering telling a radio talk-show that the ditching of the anti-NATO stance 'spelled good news for the Social Democrats'.[16]

Nevertheless, the ideological tussle continued. In quick succession, the March 1998 conference voted against German participation in S-FOR in Bosnia, the eventual dissolution of NATO and steep rises in the price of petrol (up 300 per cent over ten years) in order to reduce emissions, whilst the majority of the Bundestag *Fraktion* abstained or voted against NATO enlargement when it was discussed in the Bundestag in March 1998. Then, on the same day as state elections in Schleswig-Holstein, one Green MdB went on record suggesting that Germans should restrict themselves to one air journey every five years. The cumulative effect of these actions was to give the impression to both voters and potential partners that the Greens' idealist tendency was more in the ascendant and the Greens poll ratings halved from ten per cent to around six per cent.[17]

The ideological turbulence that afflicted the Greens in the early months of 1998 should not be taken at face value. It is a feature of election campaigns that parties try and profile themselves against each other in order to mobilise their core support. The problem parties face is doing this without alienating the wider electorate. This is particularly the case where two or more parties are competing for votes from within a particular social milieu. Raschke and Schmidt-Beck estimate the Greens' 'core' potential electorate to be around five per cent of total voters. In addition, they identify an additional 'fringe' potential electorate of around eight per cent of voters, of which they could count on upon about a third consistently voting Green.[18] The rest of this group is open to competition from the SPD (and, to a much lesser extent, the PDS). Given the need to reach beyond their core support and mobilise voters from with this milieu, it is no surprise to find that the substance of the Greens' electoral programme did not live up to the image of the party portrayed by the press, competing parties, or even their own spokespeople and activists. Indeed, the programme has much in common with the SPD's programme or even, in parts, the CDU and FDP. Programmatically, the Greens have become a mainstream party.

Five factors have served to bring the Greens into the political mainstream. First, the merger of the more moderate Alliance '90 and 'eastern' Greens with the Greens in the west has resulted in an overall moderation of both the Green voters' and membership's ideological profile. Second, the original generational cohort from which the movement in the west arose has got older, more established and integrated. Third, the Greens' internal structure has become more institutionalised and hierarchical (as already noted). Fourth, through the process of *Themenklau*, the agenda around which the Greens have mobilised, has been co-opted by the other parties. Fifth, with the FDP no longer able to rely on passing the five per cent barrier in the Länder and increasingly reliant at both the local and national level upon the second votes of CDU supporters, many in the Greens have identified a possible future 'king-maker' role for the party. All of these factors have served either to change the particular mix of policies put forward by the Greens or make them less controversial than was the case in the 1980s.

COMPARISON OF PARTY PROGRAMMES

If one excluded the remote possibility that the ruling CDU/CSU–FDP coalition would be returned to office – and opinion polls appeared to rule this out – then the two most probable outcomes of the 1998 Bundestag elections were a grand coalition or a red–green coalition. Either outcome obviously put the SPD in a strong position, not least because the party's policy programme spanned traditional 'bread and butter' concerns as well as a more post-materialist issue agenda. A full typology of the issues involved is set out in Figure 1.

FIGURE 1

TYPOLOGY OF GREENS, SPD AND CDU PARTY PROGRAMMES FOR
1998 *BUNDESTAG* ELECTIONS

Domain	Greens	SPD	CDU
(1) Foreign affairs	(I) Ambivalence towards Nato. (ii) Ambivalence towards 'Western values'. (iii) Ambivalence towards out-of-area operations	(i) Pro-Nato (ii) Moderate emphasis on 'Western values'. (iii) Limited acceptance of out-of-area operations	(i) Pro-Nato. (ii) Strong emphasis on 'Western values'. (iii) Pro-out-of-area operations
(2) Freedom and democracy	(i) Some ambivalence towards 'bourgeois democracy'. (ii) Emphasis on autonomy of individual	(i) Acceptance of 'bourgeois democracy'. (ii) Moderate emphasis on autonomy of individual.	(i) Acceptance of 'bourgeois democracy'. (ii) State as guardian of individual freedoms
(3) Government	Ambivalent.	State-oriented.	State-oriented.
(4) Economy	Ambivalence towards social-market economy (some emphasis on role of private enterprise)	Pro-social-market economy (but emphasis on role of the state).	Pro-social-market economy (but emphasis on role of private enterprise).
(5) Welfare	(i) Expansion of state provision and increased self-help. (ii) Increased role for the market.	(i) Expansion of state provision. (ii) Limited role for the market	(i) Limited expansion of state provision. (ii) Increased role for the market.
(6) Fabric of society	(i) Radical/libertarian (ii) Emphasis on alternatives to nuclear family.	(i) Traditional/ moderate libertarian. (ii) Implicit orientation towards nuclear family	(i) Traditional/ authoritarian. (ii) Strong emphasis on nuclear family and gender roles
(7) Social groups	(i) Affirmative action (quotas). (ii) Single-issue campaigning.	(i) Affirmative action (targets). (ii) Emphasis on broad civic rights.	(i) Ambivalence. (ii) emphasis on broad civic rights.
(8) Discursive form	(i) Administrative. (ii) Some policy detail.	(i) Administrative/ technocratic. (ii) Detailed policy	(i) Administrative/ technocratic. (ii) Detailed policy.

Notes: The figure excludes the PDS and FDP (the former is excluded because of its pariah status at the
Federal level, whilst the latter is excluded for the reasons noted in this article. The figure uses
Budge's seven general 'domains' of policy, as used in his analysis of election programmes in 19
Democracies (1987: 230) + 'Discursive Form', as the two *Volksparteien* have traditionally produced
far more policy-focused documents than the Greens). Enclosed cells denote potential policy
domains for selective emphasis. Please note that all data is of a judgemental/qualitative nature,
rather than quantitative content analysis.

Sources: *Arbeit. Innovation und Gerechtigkeit: SPD- Wahlprogramme für die Bundestagswahl 1998*', SPD
1998; *'Programme zur Bundestagswahl 98*', B.90/Greens 1998; *'1998-2002 Wahl-platform'*,
CDU/CSU 1998; *'Zukunftsprogramme der Christlich Demokratischen Union Deutschlands'*, CDU
1998.

The figure demonstrates that on most of the important issues of the day the SPD could find common ground with either the Greens or the CDU. Notwithstanding a certain variance in emphasis between the parties, within the domains of 'freedom and democracy', 'economy' and 'welfare' they were either in broad agreement or the SPD's position neatly cross-cuts those of the Greens and CDU. Such a degree of relative consensus would have been unthinkable a decade before and demonstrates the extent to which Fischer in particular has succeeded in moderating the Greens' ideological stance (which, given that all the opinion polls indicated that 95 per cent of voters regarded the task of tackling Germany's chronically high unemployment as the number one priority[19] was crucial to the Greens' hopes of entering government).

Those areas of potential agreement between the SPD and Greens that excluded the CDU lay within the domains of 'fabric of society' and 'social groups', and is consistent with the strand of New Left ideology that has informed the SPD's policy stance since the period of programmatic renewal in the mid-1980s. In particular, the SPD's election programme's emphasis on the need for gender equality, a less draconian approach to illegal drug use, a higher status for the arts and, of course, an eventual phasing out of nuclear power were much closer to the position of the Greens than they were to the CDU. At the same time, the SPD was much closer to the CDU within the domains of 'foreign affairs' and 'government', with the programme reaffirming the Federal Republic's commitment to NATO and advocating 'fast-track' sentencing for convicted criminals. This contrasted with the Greens' plan to disband NATO (using the OSCE as Germany's main security forum) and rely less on custodial sentences for offenders.

The Green Party's atypical stance on these issues is consistent with its programmatic development. Moreover, as already noted, it illustrates the need to moderate its post-materialist and/or libertarian dimension as a precondition for successful coalition formation and maintenance. But this was more than just a theoretical problem and its resolution would determine whether the Greens would enter government or remain an 'outsider' party at the federal level, where the stakes are so much higher than in the Länder tier of government. If it were to share power in Bonn, any descent into the much feared 'red–green chaos' of the past would never be forgiven by Germany's electorate, elites or, indeed, its allies.

Not surprisingly, given the risks involved in co-operating with the Greens, many in the SPD preferred the CDU as their coalition partner. By all accounts, this even included Chancellor candidate Schröder. A grand coalition would have constituted a centrist 'surplus majority', which was in keeping with the politics of the *Neue Mitte*. Prior to the election, the Schröder camp calculated that such a coalition would not only involve less political risk than a red–green coalition, but it would also serve to constrain and, in time, marginalise the influence of Oskar Lafontaine. Like Schmidt in the late 1970s, Schröder would have been able to use the constraints of coalition management and the *Ressortsprinzip* of ministerial autonomy to build a cross-party alliance in order to outflank the SPD's left wing. For Schröder and the other 'modernisers' in the party, this would have been attractive as it would have facilitated the introduction of the supply-side reforms that they felt were necessary to tackle Germany's unemployment problem.

Despite the strength of these arguments, however, there were good reasons why the grand coalition option was not necessarily a *fait accompli*. First, the last period of grand coalition government in Bonn – between 1966 and 1969 – was associated with a period of crisis and instability for West German democracy. Despite its success in tackling the country's first severe economic recession of the post-war period, the coalition was always subject to mutual suspicion, especially within each party's rank-and-file.[20] Moreover, the political orthodoxy in the Federal Republic is that this cartel of the two *Volksparteien* failed to provide an effective source of parliamentary opposition and created a political vacuum that nurtured extremism on the political left (the APO) and the far right (the NPD). This view was shared by many in the CDU and goes some way to explain their reluctance to participate in such an arrangement. Second, as noted at the beginning of this article, the SPD was not a 'black box'. Internal party opinion had to be heeded and a significant proportion of the membership preferred a red–green coalition if it was a numerical possibility. For some party members, this preference was a simple ideological choice, based on an affinity with the Greens and the need to avoid being outflanked by the party's centre-right. For others, it undoubtedly arose out of a desire to avoid a grand coalition for the reasons noted above. However, in weighing up the relative merits of the SPD's two potential partners, it is reasonable to assume that many Social Democrats recognised a third (instrumental) reason for choosing the Greens: the avoidance of any coalition with an unnecessarily large 'surplus majority'.[21]

By contrast, a coalition with the Greens not only held out the possibility of a greater numerical share of the available portfolios but would also ensure that most, if not all, the important 'blue-chip' posts were held by the SPD, with the exception of the Foreign Ministry (which usually goes to the junior coalition partner). Even here, the convention that the Chancellor determines the overall parameters of foreign policy (*Richtlinienkompetenz*) meant that the SPD would still have a high degree of control over this area of policy. The SPD's potentially strong position within a red–green coalition was not only because of the Greens' numerical disadvantage *vis-à-vis* the

Social Democrats. It was also a result of its relatively narrow range of policy priorities. Because of the origins of the party (and its experience in Lower Saxony, where it failed to secure the Environment portfolio), the Environment Ministry was the main objective of its bargaining strategy. It was possible, therefore, that because of its need to secure this prize, it might be willing to discount a more generous share of the spoils in order to attain its core ideological objective.

THE COMPOSITION AND DIVISION OF PORTFOLIOS

In theory, the combination of numerical disadvantage and an ideological fixation on acquiring the Environment portfolio – as outlined above – should have resulted in a weakened bargaining position for the Greens. It follows that this weakened position would have manifested itself in a reduced share of both the office-seeking and policy-oriented payoffs. However, in practice the actual allocation of portfolios does not reflect this. The numerical evidence is set out in Table 1.

Table 1 demonstrates that the SPD's total number of ministerial portfolios (11) was nearly four times higher than the Greens' (3). However, in terms of the ratio between parliamentary seats and portfolios, the Greens actually did almost twice as well as the SPD. It took almost 28 SPD parliamentary seats to 'generate' one ministerial portfolio, whilst the Greens' ratio was only 16 to one. Thus, in numerical terms the Greens did proportionally better than the SPD despite the Social Democrats' theoretically strong bargaining position. If one accepts that the SPD was in a strong bargaining position, this is not reflected in the pure numerical distribution of portfolios, which disproportionately rewards the Green Party in relation to its parliamentary size.

However, the distribution of portfolios between the parties and the appointment of ministers demonstrates that the SPD does much better in terms of policy-related payoffs. The distribution is set out in Table 2. The pattern of appointments is in keeping with previous experience. The Greens' share of ministries conforms to the ideal type posited earlier in this article. Although failing to acquire a blue-chip portfolio other than the Foreign Ministry, it did acquire the crucial Environment Ministry and – with the creation of a separate Ministry for Health – avoid the construction of an unwieldy 'super-ministry'. At the same time, one of the requirements of the 'established' model of red–green co-operation posited earlier in this article was that the formal coalition agreement should provide the SPD with the Finance, Economics and Industry ministries, as well as reserving as many as possible of those portfolios that might be deemed 'sensitive' (such as the Ministry of Justice). On the basis of previous experience, this was desirable

TABLE 1

THE 1998 BUNDESTAG ELECTIONS (%) + RATIO OF SEATS TO PORTFOLIOS
FOR COALITION PARTNERS

Party	(Second) Vote	Seats (total: 669)	Portfolios	Ratio of Seats to Portfolios**	Surplus Majority: 10
SPD	41.0	298	11*	28: 1	—
Greens	6.7	47	3	16: 1	—

Notes: * excluding *Bundeskanzler*; ** rounded up/down to nearest whole number

Sources: Statistiches Bundesamt; 'Aufbruch und Erneuerung – Deutschlands Weg in 21. Jahr-hundert', SPD/Die Grünen, 1998

TABLE 2

COMPOSITION OF SPD–GREEN CABINET, 1998

Ministry	Minister	Party
Interior	Otto Schilly	SPD
Justice	Herta Däubler-Gmelin	SPD
Finance	Oskar Lafontaine	SPD
Economics	Werner Müller	Non-partisan
Nutrition, Agriculture and Forestry	Karl-Heinz Funke	SPD
Employment and Social Policy	Walter Riester	SPD
Defence	Rudolf Scharping	SPD
Families, Pensioners, Women and Youth	Christine Bergman	SPD
Development, Construction, Urban Development and Transport	Franz Münterfering	SPD
Education, Science, Research and Technology	Edelgard Bulmahn	SPD
Economic Co-operation and Development	Heidemarie Wieczorek-Zeul	SPD
Foreign	Joschka Fischer	Greens
Environment, Nature Protection and Reactor Safety	Jürgen Trittin	Greens
Health	Andrea Fischer	Greens

Notes: Werner Müller replaced Jost Stollmann as the coalition's choice as Economics Minister. However, given his relatively orthodox views on the economy and his closeness to the Chancellor, this article regards his appointment as a *de facto* SPD portfolio.

Sources 'Aufbruch und Erneuerung – Deutschlands Weg in 21. Jahrhundert', SPD/Die Grünen, 1998; *Der Spiegel*, 19 Oct. 1998.

because of the Greens' penchant for alarming the business community and other bourgeois interests.[22]

Taken in the round, the coalition agreement between the SPD and the Greens represents an equitable division of the spoils of office. Although the SPD's proportional share of ministerial portfolios is lower than that of the

Greens, in absolute terms it still controls the bulk of ministries and, of course, the chancellorship (which comes with what is in effect an extra cabinet post, that of Minister to the Chancellor's Office – staffed at the time by the 'moderniser' Bodo Hombach). In short, the SPD had no reason to fear the Green tail wagging the Social Democratic dog.

In policy-related terms, both parties had good reason to be satisfied with their share of the portfolios. With the exception of the Foreign Ministry, the SPD kept control of the key ministerial posts whilst the Greens' three ministries gave them a solid platform from which to launch a raft of ecological and social reforms. Given the balance struck between the two parties, it is perhaps no surprise that there was an almost seamless replacement of the outgoing Conservative-Liberal administration with the new red–green coalition. Indeed, as this was the first time that a German Chancellor had been voted out of office at an election, commentators were quick to hail this smooth transition as more evidence of the growing maturity and stability of the Federal Republic.

The appointment of Joschka Fischer as German Foreign Minister was greeted with equanimity by Germany's neighbours, whilst the presence of Jürgen Trittin at Environment provoked only a minimum of concern. With Chancellor Schröder pledging his commitment to sound economic management (against the background of a healthy trade surplus, falling unemployment and analysts forecasting growth rates of around three per cent in 1997–98), everything appeared well set for the biggest political experiment in the history of the Federal Republic.

CONCLUSION

Leaving aside the issue of the staffing and structure of the civil service (which it is too early to assess at present), there is a striking degree of correlation between the 'established' red–green model and the events leading up to the Bundestag elections and subsequent formal coalition agreement. This supports Downs' 'feedback' hypothesis. Without resorting to unnecessary repetition, at all stages of the political process under study – from the initial pre-election skirmishes, through the formulation of the parties' election platforms, during the campaign itself and the post-election bargaining process, and even with regard to the first 100 days of office – one can explain events and predict future developments in the light of past experience along the three dimensions of intra-party and inter-party conflict and co-operation, and expertise.

Thus, in terms of the parties' ideological stance and election programmes, the SPD did indeed selectively emphasise the post-materialist and/or libertarian dimension of their election programme when bargaining with the Greens. Emphasis was put on 'quality of life' issues (such as reform of the citizenship laws), whilst those areas of potential disagreement were either de-emphasised (such as Green ambivalence to consumer capitalism and the state's monopoly on legitimate force) or amended (for example, when the Green Party softened its stance on NATO). With regard to this latter issue, Joschka Fischer's role as Foreign Minister has been crucial in conditioning the Green *Basis* to accept the ditching of old shibboleths such as pacifism and hostility to NATO and reflects his own realistic assessment of the Greens' strategic options *vis-à-vis* the SPD.

Similarly, both parties could be satisfied with the composition and division of portfolios, with the SPD keeping ownership of the Finance, Economics and Industry ministries, as well as 'sensitive' portfolios such as Justice. For its part, the Green Party gained the Environment portfolio and avoided the creation of a 'super-ministry' in the process. Moreover, the SPD's overwhelming numerical weight within the coalition meant that it could easily accommodate the Greens' disproportionate share of portfolios in relation to legislative seats. During the process of coalition bargaining, the Greens' numerical weakness was – paradoxically – a source of strength as well, in that it provided the smallest surplus majority of any majority coalition outcome. In the context of such a positive-sum game, the SPD could afford to allow the Greens a greater share of portfolios to seats. As long as the Green Party kept its side of the bargain and did not encroach on the SPD's 'core' territory of economic governance.

Which, of course, did not happen. As noted earlier in this article, the question of the Greens' relative lack of expertise has been crucial to the success or failure of past sub-national red–green coalitions and no doubt this has been one of the main reasons for the collapse of Jürgen Trittin's nuclear policy so early in the life of the coalition. Even Green colleagues have criticised Trittin's policy-making style, with its emphasis on excessive secrecy, limited access beyond a trusted coterie of advisors and a lack of co-ordination with other ministries. No doubt a lack of expertise has played a part in the debacle, but the key to its ultimate failure – and the subsequent public humiliation of Trittin himself – was Chancellor Schröder distancing himself from his coalition's own nuclear policy when its impact upon the SPD's domain of business and the economy became unacceptable. Trittin's unsubtle approach to policy making could not have been more in contrast to that of Joschka Fischer or, indeed, the Chancellor himself. It is perhaps no surprise, therefore, that Schröder recently stated that what the red–green coalition needed was 'less Trittin and more Fischer'!

And Schröder is in a position to make such demands. With Lafontaine having exited the stage, Trittin cut down to size, and Fischer seemingly above the fray, the Chancellor is in a position of some strength. Either his junior coalition partners are forced to be compliant or he may choose to ditch them, perhaps in favour of a grand coalition with the CDU. With the loss of the SPD's majority in the Bundesrat, a tacit working alliance is being forged with the Christian Democrats, which leaves the door open to such a grand coalition. At the same time, recent political co-operation over a reformulation of the proposed new citizenship law has raised the renewed – but still unlikely – possibility of an alliance with the FDP. Of course, either alternative has its drawbacks as well as its attractions, and the grand coalition option holds less appeal now that Schröder's arch rival Lafontaine has resigned. But for a consummate survivor like the Federal Chancellor they both provide a means of political escape should the red–green experiment fail.

NOTES

1. <de-news@LISTSERV.GMD.DE>, 18 March 1999.
2. The CDU's effective use of the race card led to an increase in its vote (by around four per cent). Indeed, the elections saw a polarisation of the vote towards the two big *Volksparteien*, with the Greens and the FDP being squeezed. The Greens' vote halved and the FDP barely scraped through the five per cent hurdle, whilst the SPD's vote also increased (by around 1.5 per cent).
3. Abram de Swaan, *Coalition Theories And Cabinet Formation* (Elsevier, 1973).
4. R.A. Hanson, 'Majority Rule and Policy Outcomes: A Critique of the Calculus of Consent' (Ph.D. thesis, University of Minnesota, 1972); R.A. Hanson and P.M. Rice, 'Committees, Representation and Policy Outcomes', *Annals of the N.Y. Academy of Sciences* (1972).
5. Eric Browne, *Coalition Theories: A Logical and Empirical Critique* (London: Sage, 1973).
6. William H. Riker, *Theory of Political Coalitions* (Newport, RI: Yale University Press, 1962).
7. However much Schröder and his team admire the New Labour 'project' in the United Kingdom, the kind of command-and-control mechanisms used by Tony Blair to pacify the Labour Party are not available to them.
8. L.C. Dodd, *Coalitions in Parliamentary Government* (Princeton, NJ: Princeton University Press, 1976), p.217.
9. W.M. Downs, *Coalition Government Subnational Style: Multiparty Politics in Europe's Regional Parliaments* (Ohio: Ohio State University Press, 1998), pp.243–66.
10. R. Eyestone, 'Confusion, Diffusion, and Innovation', *American Political Science Review*, 71 (1977), p.441.
11. C. Lees, 'Red–Green Coalitions in the Federal Republic of Germany: Models of Formation and Maintenance' (Ph.D. thesis, University of Birmingham, 1998).
12. The first example of red–green political co-operation – although not a formal coalition – took place in Hamburg, following the June 1982 local elections. The arrangement was the shortest legislative period in the post-war history of the Hamburg (196 days). In May 1985 the Hesse SPD offered the local Greens a formal coalition arrangement, following a period of unofficial co-operation along the lines of the Hamburg experience. In return for joining the coalition, the Greens took control of the Ministry for Environment and Energy and Joschka Fischer became the Greens' first Land Minister for the Environment. Fischer's tenure in office is widely considered to have been a qualified success. As a *realo*, Fischer's pragmatism was reflected in his strategy of concentrating on the stricter implementation of existing legislation rather than a raft of new laws (*nach Gesetz und Recht*). In this he was quite successful.
    The subsequent red–green coalition of 1985–87 in Hesse is considered by many to be the template for such coalitions. It is certainly the most documented! Elsewhere in the Federal

Republic, the record of red–green coalitions has been mixed. The red–green coalition of 1989–90 in West Berlin was relatively short-lived, due to a failure of coalition management. This failure was aggravated by the circumstances in which it found itself. After the events of November 1989, the issues that had previously bound the coalition (such as the environment, nuclear and conventional disarmament and other 'quality of life' issues) were superseded by more urgent themes such as unification, nationalism and the collapse of the economy in eastern Germany. The differing responses of the Berlin Alternative Liste (as the local Greens were then called) and the SPD to these themes was to ultimately undermine the coalition and it collapsed shortly before the 1990 all-Berlin elections.

Also in 1990, a red–green coalition formed in the rural northern state of Lower Saxony. The coalition lasted a full four-year term and is widely regarded as having been successful (it would probably have been renewed – if the electoral arithmetic had demanded it – following the elections in March of 1994). The policy record of the Lower Saxony coalition is mediocre at best, but the coalition did score some notable successes in the field of environmental legislation at both the state and federal level (through the state's influence in the Bundesrat). However its significance lies in its record of successful coalition management, due to the effective working relationship forged between Gerhard Schröder as Minister President and the Greens' Jurgen Trittin (now the Federal Environment Minister). This obviously has implications for observers of the Bonn coalition.

To date, there has only been one red–green coalition in the 'new' Länder, formed after the Landtag elections of June 1994, with the tacit support of the PDS. The PDS policy of 'toleration' lasted until new elections in 1998 and produced one of the most pragmatic red–green coalitions to date. The Green Party is weak in the territory of the former German Democratic Republic and is unwilling to rock the boat, allowing SPD Minister-President Reinhard Höppner, with the PDS's approval, to push through a distinctly 'ungreen' and growth-oriented policy agenda.

More recently, there have been red–green coalitions in North Rhine-Westphalia, Hamburg and Schleswig-Holstein. Although still prone to periods of intense disagreement over policy, all of three coalitions seem to have learned from the experience of such coalitions elsewhere and appear to have found a sustainable mix of green-tinged idealism and a more hard-nosed *Machtpolitk*.

The hard-won relative stability of the 'established' red–green model is in direct contrast with its variant, the 'traffic light coalition' (with the FDP as a third partner). In the early 1990s such coalitions came to power in Brandenburg and Bremen. However, the Brandenburg coalition collapsed early in 1994, after defections from the Greens, whilst the Bremen coalition collapsed in January 1995, forcing the state elections to be brought forward from the autumn to May 1995. The evidence of these coalitions is that coalition management is almost impossible with the presence of the FDP as well as the Greens around the cabinet table.

13. As already noted, Joschka Fischer's tenure as the first Green Minister for the Environment in Hesse was characterised by a strategy of concentrating on the stricter implementation of existing legislation rather than a raft of new laws. However, his decision to do this vividly reflects both the facilitating and constraining nature of the German policy-making process. See A. Weale, *The New Politics of Pollution* (Manchester: Manchester University Press, 1992).

Because of the relatively closed and cosy policy network within the environmental sector, Fischer had a serious problem staffing his new ministry with people who enjoyed his confidence. In the end, he encountered so much institutional resistance, he was forced to appeal to the Land Administrative Court in Wiesbaden in order to be granted permission to establish a hypothecated personnel advisory board to by-pass the existing (SPD-dominated) boards. See W. Grant, W. Paterson and C. Whitson, *Government and the Chemical Industry: A Comparative Study of Britain and West Germany* (Oxford: Clarendon Press, 1988), pp.253–5.

Elsewhere, in Berlin, the established political parties staffed a high proportion of civil service posts and, given the eight-year incumbency of the previous CDU–FDP administration, it was to be assumed that a significant proportion of the *Beamten* were CDU or FDP placemen. This trend was particularly pronounced amongst the top tier of permanent officials and it was felt that there was a danger that the new red–green coalition could be hampered by what could best be described as 'implementation drag' on the part of recalcitrant officials. In the event, these worries were unfounded and the Greens encountered little institutional resistance within their 'core' City Development, Environmental Protection and Traffic ministry. See Lees, 'Red–Green Coalitions'.

    In Lower Saxony, Gerhard Schröder pre-empted any institutional resistance by replacing a tranche of senior civil servants, including the Chief of Police, all of the State Secretaries in the Ministries (regardless of party membership), a number of the state's *Regierungspräsidenten*, the *Polizeipräsidenten* of Braunschweig and Hannover, the Head of the Press Office and the head of the *Land* delegation in Bonn. In addition to this, he expanded the size and role of the *Staatskanzlei*, with the new State Secretary assuming a co-ordinating role between the Minister President and the ministries.. By contrast, Trittin's problem of finding sufficient Green supporters to fill posts within the administration put them at a considerable disadvantage during the life of the coalition. This problem was aggravated by the failure of the Greens to secure the Environment portfolio during the coalition negotiations. See ibid.

14. Cf. Raschke and Schmidt-Beck, in W. Bürklin and D. Roth (eds.), *Das Superwahljahr: Deutschland vor unkalkulierbaren Regierungsmehrheiten* (Bund Verlag, 1993).
15. Despite Lafontaine's obvious political strengths, all of the opinion poll data at the turn of the year indicated that he would fail once more to unseat Kohl (or Wolfgang Schäuble). Schröder on the other hand evidently could, at the time enjoying an opinion poll lead over Kohl of 57 per cent to 33 per cent and over Schäuble of 49 per cent to 44 per cent. *Der Spiegel*, 20 Dec. 1997.
16. <de-news@LISTSERV.GMD.DE> 14 Oct. 1997; 16 Dec. 1997; 22 Oct. 1997.
17. S. Green, 'The End of an Era: The 1998 German Bundestag Elections', *Parliamentary Affairs*, 52, 2 (1999).
18. Cf. Raschke and Schmidt-Beck, in Bürklin and Roth (eds.), *Das Superwahljahr*.
19. *Focus*, Wahl-Spezial/1998, p.44.
20. SPD activists in particular were unhappy with what they regarded as the SPD bailing out an unpopular government, whilst many in the CDU/CSU rightly worried that the SPD intended to eventually take over the government from within the coalition.
21. A 'surplus majority' coalition would disadvantage the SPD in two ways; one with regard to the numerical division of posts and other in terms of its policy priorities. First, it would lead to a 'sub-optimal' allocation of 'office-seeking' payoffs, in which the spoils of office – ministerial posts and more junior positions, patronage and privileged access to client groups – would have to be spread more thinly across the coalition as whole. Having become used to the trappings of office, the CDU would expect to receive their fair share in return for participation in the coalition. In other words, the inclusion of the CDU would imply a numerical reduction in payoffs to the SPD. For ambitious MdB's and lobbyists close to the SPD this made the prospect of a grand coalition less attractive. Second – and not unrelated this last point – the presence of such a surplus majority reduced the SPD's 'policy-related' payoffs. This was because a reduction in the numerical allocation of posts also constrained the SPD's ability to shape the overall direction of the coalition's policy making. Given its ideological position and claim to economic expertise, even if it was the 'junior' partner the CDU would probably demand at least the Economics ministry as a counter-weight to the SPD's possession of the Finance Ministry. In addition, it would almost certainly demand the Foreign Ministry and a handful of other 'blue-chip' posts.
22. The appointment of the Greens' Rupert von Plotnitz as Justice Minister in Hesse notwithstanding, the Greens' latent ambiguity towards capitalism and the state monopoly on violence would have created too many hostages to fortune.

Appendix

TABLE 1

RESULT OF THE GERMAN BUNDESTAG ELECTIONS OF 1994 AND 1998
(PARTIES WITH MORE THAN ONE PERCENT OF THE VOTE)

	Percentage of Party List Vote ('Second Votes')		Number of Seats	
	1998	1994	1998	1994
SPD	40.9	36.4	298	252
CDU	28.4	34.2	198	244
CSU	6.7	7.3	47	50
Greens	6.7	7.3	47	49
FDP	6.2	6.9	43	47
PDS	5.1	4.4	36	30
DVU	1.2	—	—	—
Republikaner	1.8	1.9	—	—
Others	3.0	3.5	—	—
Turnout	82.2	79.0	—	—
Number of Seats	—	—	669	672

Source: Presse- und Informationsamt der Bundesregierung, *Bulletin*, 69, 21 Oct. 1998, p.859.

TABLE 2

RESULTS, GAINS AND LOSSES OF THE MAJOR PARTIES IN FEDERAL STATE (LANDTAG) ELECTIONS 1994–99

Date	Federal State	CDU/CSU Share of votes	CDU/CSU Gains/losses (abs.%) compared to previous election	SPD Share of votes	SPD Gains/losses (abs.%) compared to previous election	Greens Share of votes	Greens Gains/losses (abs.%) compared to previous election	FDP Share of votes	FDP Gains/losses (abs.%) compared to previous election	PDS Share of votes	PDS Gains/losses (abs.%) compared to previous election
11/09/94	Brandenburg	18.7	-10.8	54.1	15.9	2.9	-6.3	2.2	-4.4	18.7	5.3
11/09/94	Saxony	58.1	+3.7	16.6	-2.5	4.1	-1.5	1.7	-3.6	16.5	6.3
16/10/94	Mecklenburg-West Pomerania	37.7	-0.6	29.5	2.5	3.7	-0.5	3.8	-1.7	22.7	7.0
16/10/94	Saarland	38.6	+5.2	49.4	-5.0	5.5	2.9	2.1	-3.5	—	—
16/10/94	Thuringia	42.6	-2.8	29.6	6.8	4.5	-2.0	3.2	-6.1	16.6	6.9
19/02/95	Hesse	39.2	-1.0	38.0	-2.8	11.2	2.4	7.4	0.0	—	—
14/05/95	North Rhine-Westphalia	37.7	+1.0	46.0	-4.0	10.0	5.0	4.0	-1.8	—	—
14/05/95	Bremen	32.6	+1.9	33.4	-5.4	13.1	1.7	3.4	-6.1	2.4	—
22/10/95	Berlin	37.4	-3.0	23.6	-6.8	13.2	3.9	2.5	-4.6	14.6	5.4
24/03/96	Baden-Württemberg	41.3	+1.7	25.1	-4.3	12.1	2.6	9.6	+3.7	—	—
24/03/96	Rhineland-Palatinate	38.7	0.0	39.8	-5.0	6.9	0.4	8.9	+2.0	—	—
24/03/96	Schleswig-Holstein	37.2	+3.4	39.8	-6.4	8.1	3.1	5.7	+0.1	—	—
21/09/97	Hamburg	30.7	+5.6	36.2	-4.2	13.9	0.4	3.5	-0.7	0.7	—
01/03/98	Lower Saxony	35.9	-0.5	47.9	3.6	7.0	-0.4	4.9	+0.5	—	—
26/04/98	Saxony-Anhalt	22.0	-12.4	35.9	1.9	3.2	-1.9	4.2	+0.6	19.6	-0.3
13/09/98	Bayern (CSU)	52.9	+0.1	28.7	-1.3	5.7	-0.4	1.7	-1.1	—	—
27/09/98	Mecklenburg-West Pomerania	30.2	-7.5	34.4	4.9	2.7	-1.0	1.6	-2.2	24.4	+1.7
07/02/99	Hesse	43.4	+4.2	39.4	+1.4	7.2	-4.0	5.1	-2.4	—	—
06/06/99	Bremen	38.2	+5.6	43.8	+10.4	9.2	-3.9	2.6	-0.8	3.0	+0.6

Sources: U. Andersen and W. Woyke, *Wahl '98. Zur Bundestagswahl 1998* (Opladen: Leske+Budrich, 1998), Forschungsgruppe Wahlen e.V., *Daten zur Bundestagswahl am 27. September 1998* (mimeographed, Mannheim: Forschungsgruppe Wahlen, 1998); Landeswahlleiter Mecklenburg-Vorpommern, Hessen and Bremen.

FIGURE 1

TURNOUT IN THE 1998 BUNDESTAG ELECTIONS (Broken down by Federal State)

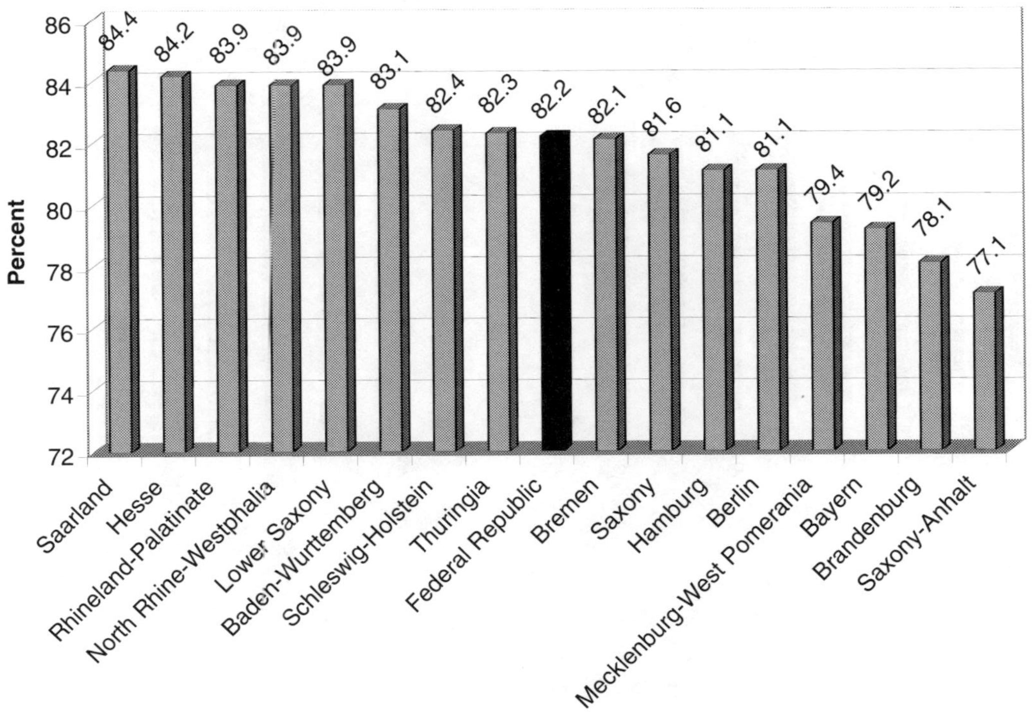

FIGURE 2

SPD RESULTS IN THE 1998 BUNDESTAG ELECTIONS (Broken down by Federal State)

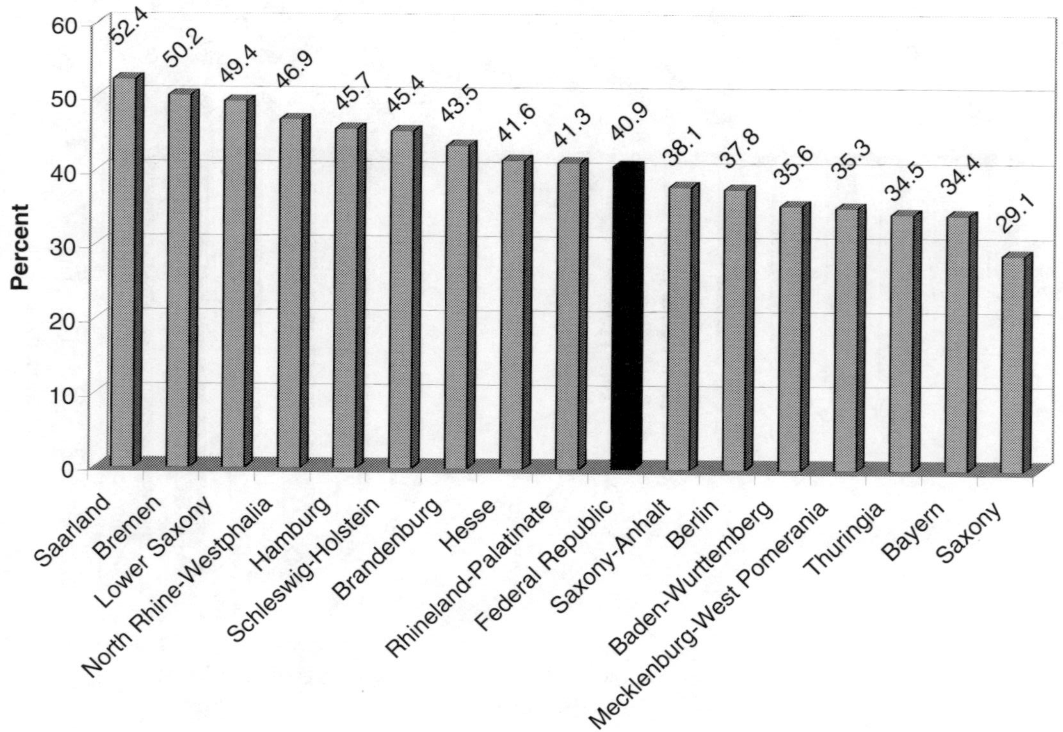

FIGURE 3

CDU/CSU RESULTS IN THE 1998 BUNDESTAG ELECTIONS (Broken down by Federal State)

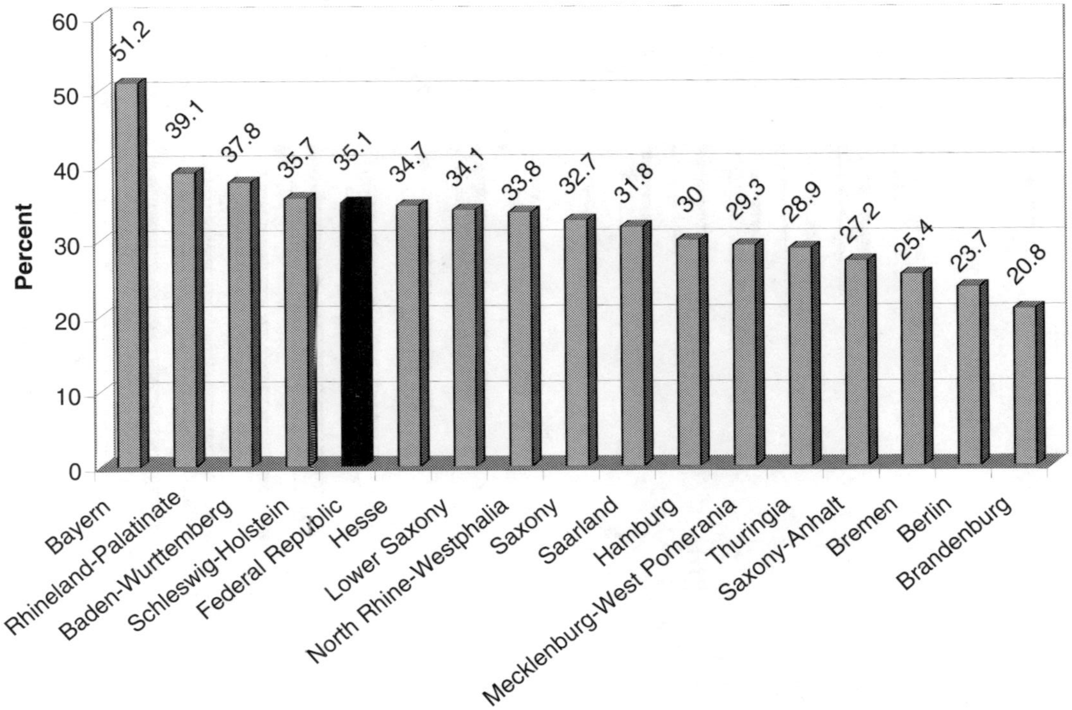

FIGURE 4

GREEN PARTY RESULTS IN THE 1998 BUNDESTAG ELECTIONS (Broken down by Federal State)

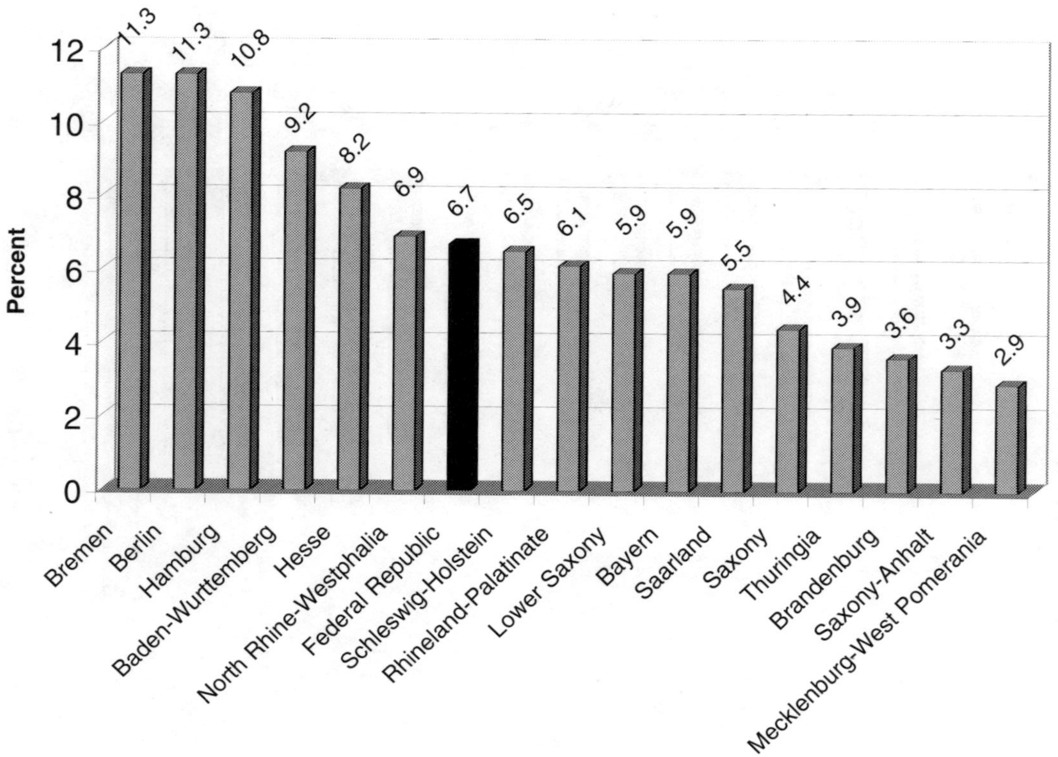

FIGURE 5

FDP RESULTS IN THE 1998 BUNDESTAG ELECTIONS (Broken down by Federal State)

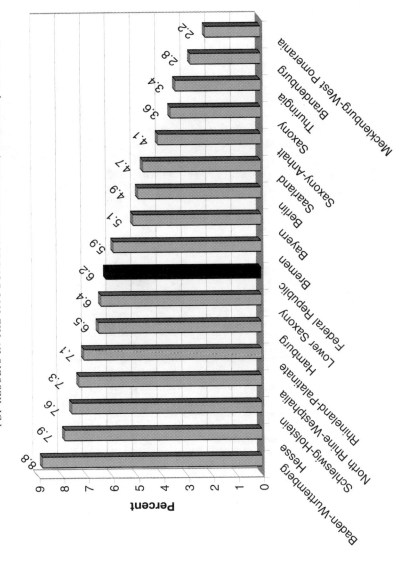

FIGURE 6

PDS RESULTS IN THE 1998 BUNDESTAG ELECTIONS (Broken down by Federal State)

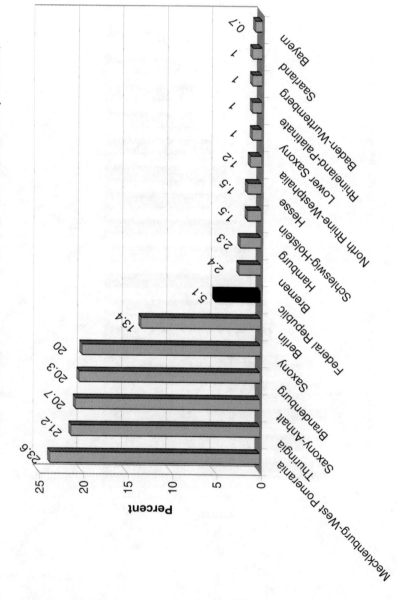

FIGURE 7

DVU AND REPUBLIKANER RESULTS AT THE 1998 BUNDESTAG ELECTIONS (Broken down by Federal State)

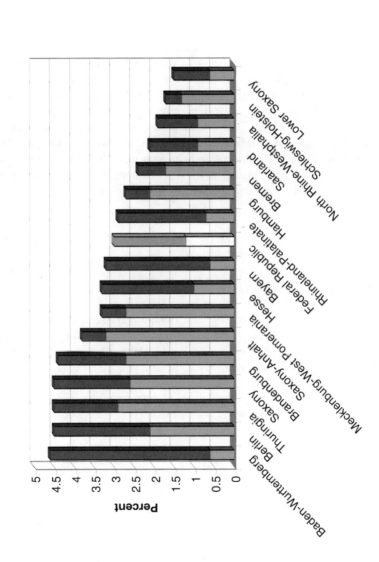

Abstracts

Social Change and the Electorate: An Analysis of the 1998 *Bundestagswahl,* by *Wolfgang Gibowski*

This article begins by identifying the causal factors behind the trend towards Social Democratic voting in the 1998 *Bundestagswahl.* The outcome of the election is explained in terms of Gerhard Schröder's ability to exploit voter dissatisfaction with the reform programme of the incumbent government in the previous legislative period. It goes on to subject electoral trends to socio-economic analysis. Voting trends in the 1998 election, it is argued, were generally uniform, varying only slightly between different social groups. Whilst socially structured partisanship continues to decline, its residual effects can still be seen in 1998. The election was won, not through any dramatic shifts in the voting behaviour of particular social groups, but through a desire for a change in the party composition of government which was particularly pronounced amongst floating voters.

Economic Conditions and the 1994 and 1998 Federal Elections, *by Jürgen Maier and Hans Rattinger*

One of the main explanations usually given for the defeat of the CDU/CSU–FDP government in the 1998 federal election is the economic situation. Using data from 1994 and 1998, this article examines whether and to what extent the voters' perceptions of economic conditions actually played a role in their decisions on election day. In 1998 perceptions of the state of the economy were noticeably more pessimistic than four years earlier. Comparisons between east and west Germany reveal only a few significant differences in the general perceptions of the state of the economy on the one hand and the voters' own economic situation before the election on the other. They reveal a stronger effect of economic adversity on east German voters. East–west differences in retrospective or prospective assessments of the economic situation have diminished. As for the perceived competence to solve important economic problems, the voters' perception of the former government parties, CDU/CSU and FDP, remained almost unchanged between 1994 and 1998, while the SPD was able to make considerable gains. Multivariate analyses show that the influence of economic variables on party choice was not very strong. Both in east and west Germany the parties' perceived economic competence had clearly the strongest impact on voting.

The East German Vote in the 1998 General Election, *by Cornelia Weins*

In 1998, a governing coalition was voted out of office for the first time in the history of the Federal Republic of Germany. The defeat of the Christian Democrats was particularly pronounced in east Germany where voting behaviour was again highly volatile. This analysis therefore focuses on the election results of the governing coalition in general and of the CDU in particular. It can be observed that the preference for Chancellor as well as the assessment of a party's competence to solve the unemployment problem had a stronger impact on voting behaviour in east Germany than in west Germany. For the first time, east German blue-collar workers predominantly voted for the SPD. Nonetheless, it cannot (yet) be concluded that the east German electorate will adapt permanently to traditional west German patterns of class-specific electoral behaviour. If short-term factors are taken into account, class and religion exercise only a minor influence on voting intention in both parts of Germany.

Parties, Leaders and Issues in the News, *by Holli A. Semetko and Klaus Schoenbach*

Based on content analysis of television news coverage and the newspaper *Bild*, this article discusses the visibility of parties, leaders and issues in the news before the 1998 Bundestag election. Although the private TV channels devoted far more attention to the campaign and the opinion polls than the public TV channels, and correspondingly less to the substantive issues over which the campaign was being fought, there was still a strong similarity between German public and private television coverage in the predominantly neutral or descriptive coverage of politicians.

The Boundaries of Stability: The Party System Before and After the 1998 *Bundestagswahl, by Stephen Padgett*

One of the outstanding characteristics of the 1998 *Bundestagswahl* was the unpredictability of the outcome, reflecting the openness and fluidity of the party system at the end of the 1990s. Employing a range of indicators derived from party system research, this article presents a structural analysis of the party landscape. In a disaggregated party system subject to electoral dealignment and ideological diversification, it is argued, inter-party relations are increasingly multifaceted and complex, intensifying the strategic dilemmas facing the parties. The result is a party system with a high potential for flux, nearing the boundaries of stability.

Changing Party Organisations in Germany: How to Deal with Uncertainty and Organised Anarchy, *by Elmar Wiesendahl*

It is particularly during election campaigns that parties are considered to have organisational capacities and strategic capabilities which, in reality, they do not have at their disposal. On the contrary, parties only function to a limited extent as rational and efficient organisations, because they encompass different sets of relatively independent actors with very different goals. The voluntaristic nature of member participation, the parties' open organisational boundaries, the fluctuation of members and the difficulties in translating the parties' aims into political decisions keep them from employing their human resources efficiently and organising well co-ordinated and goal-oriented collective action. In this article, parties are seen as 'organised anarchies' trying to cope with the contradictions of their organisational structure using vague policies, fragmented decision making, 'loose coupling' of the different organisational levels and a great deal of hypocrisy. In the past decades, German parties have undergone a planned modernisation process originating at the organisational top without ever reaching the grass-roots level. Thus they failed to complete their transformation into a new type of 'electoral-professional party' controlled by professional politicians at the top. Rather, they combine the opposing organisational structures of the pre-modern voluntaristic membership party at the grass-roots level and the modern professionalised vote-maximising party at the top by way of 'loose coupling'. It is highly probable that their uncoordinated hybrid character will be the cause of further alienation between voluntary members and professional leadership.

Luck and Good Management: Helmut Kohl as Parliamentary and Electoral Strategist, *by Peter Pulzer*

This article argues that Helmut Kohl was the first major German politician outside the Social Democratic Party to embark on a political career by consciously and systematically ascending a party hierarchy in order to achieve high office. It traces the stages of his ascent through the parliamentary and extra-parliamentary institutions of the Christian Democratic Union, first in Rhineland-Palatinate and then nationally. It argues that he showed a clearer understanding of the connection between party and executive office than most of his contemporaries, by making sure of the party leadership as a springboard to the highest office at both the Land and the federal level. His resignation of both offices after losing the 1998 election underlined his continued recognition of that link. His almost unprecedented run of election successes and ultimate defeat show that effective command of the party organisation is a necessary, but not always a sufficient condition of electoral success.

Coalition Politics and Management in the Kohl Era, 1982–98, *by Thomas Saalfeld*

The CDU/CSU–FDP coalition under Chancellor Kohl was the most durable national-level coalition government in the history of democratic German parliaments. Based on a conceptual framework derived from formal coalition theory, this article provides an analytical narrative of the main structural causes of coalition stability in the Kohl era. It demonstrates that constitutional and other structural factors such as the moderate pluralism of the Federal Republic's party system and the agreement between CDU/CSU and FDP on the most important policy dimension (economic policy) served as 'shock absorbers' reducing the impact of adverse 'external events' like severe electoral losses of the government parties at the regional level or the emergence of new, divisive issues on the policy agenda. Compared to his immediate predecessor as Chancellor, Kohl was particularly successful in establishing informal, flexible network-type institutions of coalition governance, which addressed both the inter-party and intra-party dimensions of coalition stability. Despite the emphasis on structures of coalition governance, it cannot be denied that the CDU/CSU–FDP coalition was also helped by at least one favourable external 'random' event outside the control of the actors: German unification.

The Red–Green Coalition, *by Charles Lees*

After just a few months in office the new 'red–green' coalition between the SPD and the Green Party appears to be in disarray, following significant policy reversals, defeat in the Hesse Land elections and the abrupt resignation of Finance Minister Oskar Lafontaine. However, one can explain present events and predict future developments in the light of the past experience of red–green coalitions at the Länder level. The article posits the existence of an established model of red–green co-operation, developed along the three dimensions of (i) intra-party, (ii) inter-party conflict and co-operation, and (iii) expertise. The article concludes that the key to the success or failure of all red–green coalitions lies in the selective emphasis of compatible elements within the parties' ideological profiles, the allocation of cabinet portfolios, the staffing of ministries and the 'opening up' of policy networks to the Greens' client groups.

Notes on Contributors

Wolfgang G. Gibowski is Lecturer in Political Science at the University of Stuttgart. He was formerly the deputy director of the Federal Press and Information Office of the German government and one of the directors of the Forschungsgruppe Wahlen in Mannheim. His numerous publications have been concerned with empirical analysis of electoral behaviour.

Charles Lees is Lecturer in International Relations and Politics at the University of Sussex. He took his Ph.D. at the Institute for German Studies, University of Birmingham and has written on aspects of party system change in Germany, European social democracy and coalition theory. He is currently finishing a book on red–green coalitions and undertaking new research into the 'Third Way/*Neue Mitte*' and British–German policy co-operation.

Jürgen Maier holds a doctorate in Political Science from the University of Bamberg, Germany. He is currently working at the University of Jena carrying out research on political parties in east Germany. His recent publications (with Hans Rattinger) include 'Wahlbeteiligung und Wahlnorm in der Bundesrepublik Deutschland: Eine Kausalanalyse', *Politische Vierteljahresschrift* (1995); 'The Proximity and the Directional Theories of Issue Voting: Comparative Results for the USA and Germany', *European Journal of Political Research* (1997); 'Economic Conditions and Voting Preferences in East and West Germany, 1989–94', in C.J. Anderson and C. Zelle (eds.), *Stability and Change in German Elections: How Electorates Merge, Converge, or Collide* (1998).

Stephen Padgett is Professor of Politics at the University of Liverpool, formerly Jean Monnet Reader in European Politics at the University of Essex. His publications include *Parties and Party Systems in the New Germany* (Dartmouth, 1993), amongst a wide range of books and articles on German and European parties and party systems. His book *Organizing Democracy in Eastern Germany* (Cambridge University Press, 1999) has recently appeared. He is co-editor of *Developments in German Politics* and of the journal *German Politics*.

Peter Pulzer is Gladstone Professor Emeritus of Government and Emeritus Fellow of All Souls College, Oxford. He is a Professorial Fellow of the

Institute for German Studies, University of Birmingham and Honorary Vice-President of the Association for the Study of German Politics. His most recent books are *German Politics 1945–1995* and *Germany 1870–1945: Politics, State Formation and War.*

Hans Rattinger is Professor of Political Science at the University of Bamberg. In 1987–89 and 1991–93 he held visiting appointments at the University of Toronto and at Georgetown University in Washington, DC. His recent publications with Jürgen Maier include 'Wahlbeteiligung und Wahlnorm in der Bundesrepublik Deutschland: Eine Kausalanalyse', *Politische Vierteljahresschrift* (1995); 'The Proximity and the Directional Theories of Issue Voting: Comparative Results for the USA and Germany', *European Journal of Political Research* (1997); 'Economic Conditions and Voting Preferences in East and West Germany, 1989–94', in C.J. Anderson and C. Zelle (eds.), *Stability and Change in German Elections: How Electorates Merge, Converge, or Collide* (1998).

Thomas Saalfeld is Lecturer in Politics at the University of Kent at Canterbury. His recent publications include *Großbritannien: Eine politische Landeskunde* (1998), *Members of Parliament in Western Europe: Roles and Behaviour* (1997, joint ed. with Wolfgang C. Müller) and *Parteisoldaten und Rebellen: Eine Untersuchung zur Geschlossenheit der Fraktionen im Deutschen Bundestag (1949–1990)* (1995).

Holli A. Semetko is Professor of Audience and Public Opinion Research and also the Chair of the Department of Communication Science at the University of Amsterdam, where she also teaches in the international Ph.D. programme of the Amsterdam School of Communications Research. Semetko's research interests include cross-national comparative research on media content and effects and political communication. Her recent books are: *On Message: Communicating the Campaign* (Sage, 1999) with Pippa Norris *et al.*, and *Germany's Unity Election: Voters and the Media* (Hampton, 1994), with Klaus Schönbach.

Klaus Schönbach is Professor of General Communication Science at the University of Amsterdam, where he also teaches in the international Ph.D. programme of the Amsterdam School of Communications Research. Schönbach's research interests include political communication and media audience research, and he has published dozens of articles and book chapters on these topics. His English books include *Germany's "Unity Election: Voters and the Media* (Hampton, 1994) with Holli A. Semetko, and *Audience Responses to Media Diversification: Coping with Plenty*

(Lawrence Erlbaum, 1989) with Lee B. Becker, as well as books in German on radio news, *success* factors of newspapers, and political communication in local elections.

Cornelia Weins is a member of the Department of Sociology at the University of Trier. Her recent publications include *Statistik. Grundkurs für Politologen* (1998, Uwe Gehring); 'Polizei und Fremdenfeindlichkeit', in *Monatsschrift für Kriminologie und Strafrechtsreform* (1999, with Matthias Mletzko).

Elmar Wiesendahl is Professor of Political Science at the Universität der Bundeswehr München. His recent publications include *Parteien in Perspektive. Theoretische Ansichten der Organisationswirklichkeit politischer Parteien* (1998); 'Identitätsauflösung. Anschlußsuche der Großparteien an die postindustrielle Gesellschaft', in R. Hettlage and L. Vogt (eds.), *Identitäten im Umbruch* (1999); 'Parteienkommunikation', in O. Jarren, U. Sarcinelli and U. Saxer (eds.), *Politische Kommunikation in der demokratischen Gesellschaft* (1998); and 'Die Parteien in Deutschland auf dem Weg zu Kartellparteien?', in H.H. von Arnim (ed.), *Adäquate Institutionen: Voraussetzung für 'gute' und bürgernahe Politik?* (1999).

Index

214

Books of Related Interest

Superwahljahr

The German Elections in 1994

Geoffrey K Roberts, *University of Manchester (Ed)*

The elections in 1994 in Germany gave rise to the word
"Superwahljahr" ("super-election year"). In addition to the election of a
new Bundestag in October, there was a presidential election, elections to
the European Parliament and elections for seven Länder parliaments.
This book provides a set of analyses of those elections, with emphasis
on the Bundestag election. British and German contributors examine the
effects of the elections of 1994 on the party system and consider the
ways in which party organisation in the former German Democratic
Republic affected electoral behaviour there.

166 pages 1996
0 7146 4682 2 cloth

FRANK CASS PUBLISHERS
Newbury House, 900 Eastern Avenue, Ilford, Essex, IG2 7HH
Tel: +44 (0)181 599 8866 Fax: +44 (0)181 599 0984 E-mail: info@frankcass.com
NORTH AMERICA
5804 NE Hassalo Street, Portland, OR 97213 3644, USA
Tel: 800 944 6190 Fax: 503 280 8832 E-mail: cass@isbs.com
Website: www.frankcass.com

The Kohl Chancellorship

Clay Clemens, *College of William and Mary, USA* and
William E Paterson, *University of Birmingham* (Eds)

More durable than any other contemporary democratic head of
government and all previous German chancellors since Bismarck,
Helmut Kohl has earned a place in history by helping to end his own
nation's division and shape new Europe. In this volume, six scholars
and journalists assess his leadership and legacy. They analyze the
chancellor's goals and governing style, including his part in promoting
European integration, as well as Kohl's domestic political role – vis-à-
vis his own party, its main opponents and the public – among fellow
European leaders. Written on the eve of Germany's 1998 elections, this
volume provides insight into the country's recent past and near future.

176 pages 1998
0 7146 4890 6 cloth
0 7146 4441 2 paper

FRANK CASS PUBLISHERS
Newbury House, 900 Eastern Avenue, Ilford, Essex, IG2 7HH
Tel: +44 (0)181 599 8866 Fax: +44 (0)181 599 0984 E-mail: info@frankcass.com
NORTH AMERICA
5804 NE Hassalo Street, Portland, OR 97213 3644, USA
Tel: 800 944 6190 Fax: 503 280 8832 E-mail: cass@isbs.com

Constitutional Policy in Unified Germany

Klaus H Goetz, *London School of Economics* and
Peter J Cullen, *University of Edinburgh* (Ed)

Prompted by unification, the German constitution has in recent years
undergone the most fundamental re-examination since the foundation of
the Federal Republic. The high hopes of many that the achievement of
unification would be crowned by a new constitution for the unified
Germany have been dashed; but although continuity may seem to
prevail, unification and, even more so, the process of European
integration have provided powerful forces of constitutional change. This
volume seeks to identify some of the central challenges which
constitutional policy faces and analyses how, and with what degree of
success, they are being met.

184 pages 1995
0 7146 4631 8 cloth
0 7146 4160 X paper

FRANK CASS PUBLISHERS
Newbury House, 900 Eastern Avenue, Ilford, Essex, IG2 7HH
Tel: +44 (0)181 599 8866 Fax: +44 (0)181 599 0984 E-mail: info@frankcass.com
NORTH AMERICA
5804 NE Hassalo Street, Portland, OR 97213 3644, USA
Tel: 800 944 6190 Fax: 503 280 8832 E-mail: cass@isbs.com
Website: www.frankcass.com